高等学校试用教材

建筑类专业英语
建筑学与城市规划

第一册

王庆昌　余曼筠　　　　主编
谢工曲　赵凤霞　刘雁鹏　编
霍维国　　　　　　　　主审

中国建筑工业出版社

《建筑类专业英语》编审委员会

总 主 编　徐铁城
总 主 审　杨匡汉
副总主编　（以姓氏笔划为序）
　　　　　王庆昌　乔梦铎　陆铁镛
　　　　　周保强　蔡英俊
编　　委　（以姓氏笔划为序）
　　　　　王久愉　王学玲　王翰邦　卢世伟
　　　　　孙　玮　李明章　朱满才　向小林
　　　　　向　阳　刘文瑛　余曼筠　孟祥杰
　　　　　张少凡　张文洁　张新建　赵三元
　　　　　阎岫峰　傅兴海　褚羞花　蔡慧俭
　　　　　濮宏魁
责任编辑　庞大中

前　言

经过几十年的探索，外语教学界许多人认为，工科院校外语教学的主要目的，应该是："使学生能够利用外语这个工具，通过阅读去获取国外的与本专业有关的科技信息。"这既是我们建设有中国特色的社会主义的客观需要，也是在当前条件下工科院校外语教学可能完成的最高目标。事实上，教学大纲规定要使学生具有"较强"的阅读能力，而对其他方面的能力只有"一般"要求，就是这个意思。

大学本科的一、二年级，为外语教学的基础阶段。就英语来说，这个阶段要求掌握的词汇量为2 400个（去掉遗忘，平均每个课时10个单词）。加上中学阶段已经学会的1 600个单词，基础阶段结束时应掌握的词汇量为4 000个。仅仅掌握4 000个单词，能否看懂专业英文书刊呢？还不能。据统计，掌握4 000个单词，阅读一般的英文科技文献，生词量仍将有6%左右，即平均每百词有六个生词，还不能自由阅读。国外的外语教学专家认为，生词量在3%以下，才能不借助词典，自由阅读。此时可以通过上下文的联系，把不认识的生词猜出来。那么，怎么样才能把6%的生词量降低到3%以下呢？自然，需要让学生增加一部分词汇积累。问题是，要增加多少单词？要增加哪一些单词？统计资料表明，在每一个专业的科技文献中，本专业最常用的科技术语大约只有几百个，而且它们在文献中重复出现的频率很高。因此，在已经掌握4 000单词的基础上，在专业阅读阶段中，有针对性地通过大量阅读，扩充大约1 000个与本专业密切有关的科技词汇，便可以逐步达到自由阅读本专业科技文献的目的。

早在八十年代中期，建设部系统院校外语教学研究会就组织编写了一套《土木建筑系列英语》，分八个专业，共12册。每个专业可选读其中的三、四册。那套教材在有关院校相应的专业使用多年，学生和任课教师反映良好。但是，根据当时的情况，那套教材定的起点较低（1 000词起点），已不适合今天学生的情况。为此，在得到建设部人事教育劳动司的大力支持，并征得五个相关专业教学指导委员会同意之后，由建设部系统十几所院校一百余名外语教师和专业课教师按照统一的编写规划和要求，编写了这一套《建筑类专业英语》教材。

《建筑类专业英语》是根据国家教委颁发的《大学英语专业阅读阶段教学基本要求》编写的专业阅读教材，按照建筑类院校共同设置的五个较大的专业类别对口编写。五个专业类别为：建筑学与城市规划；建筑工程（即工业与民用建筑）；给水排水与环境保护；暖通、空调与燃气；建筑管理与财务会计。每个专业类别分别编写三册专业英语阅读教材，供该专业类别的学生在修完基础阶段英语后，在第五至第七学期专业阅读阶段使用，每学期一册。

上述五种专业英语教材语言规范，题材广泛，覆盖相关专业各自的主要内容：包括专业基础课，专业主干课及主要专业选修课，语言材料的难易度切合学生的实际水平；词汇以大学英语"通用词汇表"的4 000个单词为起点，每个专业类别的三册书将增加1 000～1 200个阅读本专业必需掌握的词汇。本教材重视语言技能训练，突出对阅读、翻译和写作能力的培养，以求达到《大学英语专业阅读阶段教学基本要求》所提出的教学目标："通过指导学生阅读有关专业的英语书刊和文献，使他们进一步提高阅读和翻译科技资料的能力，并能以英语为工具获取专业所需的信息。"

《建筑类专业英语》每册16个单元，每个单元一篇正课文(TEXT)，两篇副课文(Reading Material A & B)，每个单元平均2 000个词，三册48个单元，总共约有十万个词，相当于原版书三百多页。要培养较强的阅读能力，读十万个词的文献，是起码的要求。如果专业课教师在第六和第七学期，在学生通过学习本教材已经掌握了数百个专业科技词汇的基础上，配合专业课程的学习，再指定学生看一部分相应的专业英语科技文献，那将会既促进专业课的学习，又提高英语阅读能力，实为两得之举。

本教材不仅适用于在校学生，对于有志提高专业英语阅读能力的建筑行业广大在职工程技术人员，也是一套适用的自学教材。

建设部人事教育劳动司高教处和中国建设教育协会对这套教材的编写自始至终给予关注和支持；中国建筑工业出版社第五编辑室密切配合，参与从制定编写方案到审稿各个阶段的重要会议，给了我们很多帮助；在编写过程中，各参编学校相关专业的许多专家、教授对材料的选取、译文的审定都提出了许多宝贵意见。

本书为《建筑类专业英语》建筑学与城市规划专业第一册。由王庆昌和余曼筠主编，霍维国主审，谢工曲、赵凤霞、刘雁鹏参加编写。承艾贵三协助收集资料，李中英和陈海龙为书稿录入，王晓为本书插图付出了辛勤的劳动，谨此致谢。

《建筑类专业英语》是我们编写对口专业阅读教材的又一次尝试，由于编写者水平及经验有限，教材中不妥之处在所难免，敬请广大读者批评指正。

《建筑类专业英语》

编审委员会

Contents

UNIT ONE
 Text　　Architecture ·· 1
 Reading Material A　The Study of Architecture ·· 6
 Reading Material B　Modern Education of the Architecture ································· 8

UNIT TWO
 Text　　Housing ··· 10
 Reading Material A　Early Housing ·· 15
 Reading Material B　Recent Trends of Housing ·· 17

UNIT THREE
 Text　　The Language of Architecture (Ⅰ) ··· 20
 Reading Material A　The Language of Architecture (Ⅱ) ································· 25
 Reading Material B　The Language of Architecture (Ⅲ) ································· 27

UNIT FOUR
 Text　The Financial Setup (Ⅰ) ··· 30
 Reading Material A　The Financial Setup (Ⅱ) ·· 35
 Reading Material B　The Financial Setup (Ⅲ) ·· 36

UNIT FIVE
 Text　　The Domain of Urban Design ·· 39
 Reading Material A　City Country Fingers ··· 45
 Reading Material B　City Planning ··· 47

UNIT SIX
 Text　　Shopping Center ··· 50
 Reading Material A　Web of Shopping ·· 56
 Reading Material B　Green Streets ·· 58

UNIT SEVEN
 Text　　Roof Layout ·· 61
 Reading Material A　Cascade of Roofs ··· 67
 Reading Material B　Roof Garden ··· 68

UNIT EIGHT
 Text　　Lighting ··· 71
 Reading Material A　Pools of Light ·· 77
 Reading Material B　Acoustics ·· 79

UNIT NINE
 Text　　The Evolution of Cluster Housing ·· 83
 Reading Material A　House Cluster ··· 90

  Reading Material B Low-rise, Medium-density Cluster Housing ················ 92
UNIT TEN
  Text Where do We Go from Here—Architecturally ················ 95
  Reading Material A Structural Systems for Multi-use High-rise Buildings ············ 100
  Reading Material B Four-story Limit ················ 102
UNIT ELEVEN
  Text Tall Building ················ 105
  Reading Material A Design Criteria of Tall Building ················ 110
  Reading Material B Stiffness and Drift Limitation ················ 112
UNIT TWELVE
  Text Parking ················ 115
  Reading Material A Nine Percent Parking ················ 121
  Reading Material B Shielded Parking ················ 124
UNIT THIRTEEN
  Text Ornament ················ 126
  Reading Material A Architecture is the Ornament of Human Environment ············ 132
  Reading Material B The Function of Ornament ················ 135
UNIT FOURTEEN
  Text The Development of a Low-rise Urban Housing Alternative ················ 138
  Reading Material A Magic of the City ················ 145
  Reading Material B Activity Nodes ················ 146
UNIT FIFTEEN
  Text The Architecture of Hospital——Breaking the Paradigm ················ 149
  Reading Material A Theater ················ 155
  Reading Material B Holy Ground ················ 157
UNIT SIXTEEN
  Text The Practice of Architecture (Ⅰ) ················ 159
  Reading Material A The Practice of Architecture (Ⅱ) ················ 164
  Reading Material B The Futural Practice of Architecture ················ 166
Appendix Ⅰ Glossary ················ 168
Appendix Ⅱ Translation for Reference ················ 176
Appendix Ⅲ Key to Exercises ················ 198

UNIT ONE

Text　　　　　　　　Architecture

[1]　　Architecture is the art of building. Virtually all architecture is concerned with the enclosure of space for human use. The precise activities to be housed in any specific building, ranging from an assembly line in a factory to a living room in a home, should dictate the size and shape of the several areas within. ① These spaces also must be arranged in some logical relation to each other. Furthermore, the movement of human beings within the building requires halls stairs or elevators whose size is governed by the expected load of traffic. ② The plan of a structure, always the first consideration of an architect, is the resolution of these different purposes into an organization of spaces that will fulfill the intent of the building. ③ Good planning guides the visitor to his destination in the structure and impresses him, perhaps subconsciously, by visibly relating the several units of the edifice. Conversely, a bad plan results in inconvenience, waste and visual confusion.

[2]　　Furthermore, a structure must be well built, it could have such permanence as the purpose for which it is intended demands and as the materials chosen may allow. The raw materials of architecture-stone, brick, wood, steel, or glass-in part govern the forms of the building and are expressed by them. Stone can resist compression almost indefinitely. While it is possible to crush stone in a laboratory, for practical purposes its compressive strength is unlimited. ④ On the other hand, stone is weak in withstanding tension. Any beam spanning a void tends to bend downward between the supports, putting the lower half of the beam under tension. It follows from the tensile weakness of stone that beams of this material must be comparatively short and supported at frequent intervals. ⑤ Moreover, stone columns must be sturdy, rarely more than 10 times as high as they are wide. In stone buildings, windows, doors, and the spaces between columns are almost compelled to be taller than they are wide-the vertical rectangle of the stone aesthetic.

[3]　　Wood, a fibrous material, withstands tension as readily as it does compression. ⑥ Wooden beams may be relatively longer than stone beams, and wooden posts slender and widely spaced. ⑦ A horizontal rectangle, wider than it is high, results from the natural properties of wood, as may be seen in Japanese architecture. ⑧ Steel also has tensile strength that is equal to or greater than its compressive strength. Anyone who has observed a steel building under construction must have noticed the gridiron of horizontal rectangles produced by the slender, widely spaced columns and the long beams of each floor. The nature of wood and of steel suggests frame construction-a skeleton to support floors and roof-with whatever surfacing material may be necessary. Wood and steel also permit cantilever construction in which beams project beyond the last point of support.

[4]　　Finally, architecture must do more than meet the physical requirements of strength and

space; it must also content the spirit of man. The building should form an aesthetic unity to which the several parts contribute. Thus, the sides and rear of a structure should bear sufficient correspondence to the front to make them all related parts of a single whole. ⑨The major internal divisions, too, require some expression in the external design. The nave, aisles, transepts, apse, and radiating chapels of Gothic cathedrals, for example, are all visible on the exterior, so that the visitor is subconsciously prepared for what he will find inside.

[5]   Architecture calls for good proportions-a pleasing relationship of voids to solids, of height to width, of length to breadth. Many attempts have been made to explain good proportions by mathematical formulas, such as the golden section. These efforts have not found general acceptance, however, although good results have been achieved through the repetition of some dimension (for example, a module that is half the diameter of a column) throughout a design. Such repetitions help to produce the visible order that the human mind seems to crave.

[6]   A building also should have what architects call "scale": that is, it should visually convey its true size. Such elements as benches, steps, or balustrades, though slightly variable in size, are, by their very purpose, related to the normal dimensions of human beings. ⑩ They therefore become, almost imperceptibly, units of measurement for gauging the size of the whole edifice. Because these units are so small in comparison to the whole building, other elements of intermediate size are needed. Stairs and a balustrade may give a clue to the size of a doorway; that, in turn, to the height of a colonnade; and finally, the colonnade to the whole structure. The Petit Trianon at Versailles is perfect in scale. The absence of small elements in St. Peter's in Rome makes it difficult to perceive its vastness.

[7]   Although all decoration is rejected in some modern architecture, it was employed in the past either for its inherent beauty or to emphasize some point of importance in the building. Decoration or ornament may be used to contribute to character, the visible expression of the purpose of the building. Thus a bank should look like a bank, and a church should be immediately identifiable as such. Ideally, too, any building should seem to belong on its site, with some relationship to its architectural neighbors and to the local geography.

Words and Expressions

enclosure * [inˈkləuʒə]	n.	围墙（栏）；封围
dictate [dikˈteit]	v.	规定；限定
subconsciously [ˈsʌbˈkɔnʃəsli]	ad.	下（潜）意识地
edifice [ˈedifice]	n.	大厦，大建筑物；体系
compression * [kɔmˈpreʃən]	n.	压力；压缩
withstand * [wiðˈstænd]	v.	经受得住；抵抗
span * [spæn]	v.	跨过；架设
	n.	跨度；开度
void * [vɔid]	n.	空间（位），虚（空）体

		a.	空的，无人使用的；虚的
tensile *	['tensail]	a.	张力的，拉力的
sturdy	['stə:di]	a.	结实的，坚固的
rectangle *	['rektæŋgl]	n.	长方形，矩形
aesthetic	[i:s'θetik]	a.	美学的，审美的
fibrous *	['faibrəs]	a.	含纤维的，纤维状的
readily	['redili]	ad.	容易地，不费力
gridiron	['gridaiən]	n.	梁格结构，格状结构
skeleton	['skelitn]	n.	构架；草图；轮廓
cantilever	['kæntili:və]	v.	悬臂梁，突梁
project *	[prə'dʒekt]	v.	伸（突）出；设计
correspondence	[kəris'pɔndəns]	n.	符合，一致；相应
nave	[neiv]	n.	（教堂的）正厅；（火车站等建筑的）中间广场
aisle	[ail]	n.	走廊，侧廊
transept	['trænsept]	n.	（教堂的）袖廊，翼部
chapel	['tʃæpl]	n.	小礼拜堂
apse	[æps]	n.	多边形（或半圆形）凹室；耳（室）房
Gothic	['gɔθik]	n.	哥特式建筑的
cathedral	[kə'θi:drəl]	n.	大教堂，主教堂
module *	['mɔdju:l]	n.	模度（数，量）；模件
crave	[kreiv]	v.	渴望，需要
imperceptibly	[impə'septəbli]	ad.	觉察不到地
balustrade	[bæləs,treid]	n.	栏杆，扶手
colonnade	[kɔlə'neid]	n.	柱廊，柱列
inherent *	[in'hiərənt]	a.	内在的，固有的
ornament	['ɔ:nəmənt]	n.	装饰（物）
identifiable	[ai'dentifaiəbl]	a.	可识别的，可区别的

Notes

①被动式动词不定式短语作名词定语时，不仅含有被动的意思，而且也具有将来的概念。因此，to be housed in any specific building 可译作"将要容纳在具体建筑物里的"。house 作动词用，意为"收容；供宿；遮蔽"等。

②load of traffic 直译为交通负荷，也可译为交通量。

③…the resolution of these different purposes into an organization of spaces that will fulfill the intent of the building. 直译为：解决了把这些不同的目的安排成满足建筑意图的空间组合。（正文见参考译文）。

④while 作为并列连接词使用时，连接的是一个事物两个相反的方面，一般置于第二个并列分句之首，译作"而"。但有时也置于第一个分句前面，或译作"虽然……但……"，或

仍译作"而"与第二个分句的译文连在一起。

⑤其中词组 follow from 意为"根据（是从）……得出的"。

⑥…withstands tension as readily as it does compression.

其中 does 代替 withstands.

⑦…and wood posts slender and widely spaced.

句中 wood posts 与 slender 之间省去了 may be 二词。

⑧…as may be seen in Japanese architecture.

as 引导的句子系特种定语从句（special attributive clause），修饰前边整个句子。

⑨…should bear sufficient correspondence to…

意为"应当与……保持充分一致"。

⑩该句的主要结构是 Such elements…are…related to the normal dimensions of human beings. 其中 by their very purpose 是谓语的状语。

Exercises

Reading Comprehension

I. Say whether the following statements are true (T) or false (F) according to the text, making use of the given paragraph reference numbers.

1. The very purpose of a building is to provide indoor spaces for human beings to have activities inside. (Para. 1) ( )

2. Building materials, such as stone, brick, wood, steel or glass, require permanence from an architectural structure. (Para. 2) ( )

3. Wood has tensile strength that is equal to or greater than its compressive strength. (Para. 3) ( )

4. It is essential that architecture must meet the need of human spirit. (Para. 4) ( )

5. Efforts of using mathematical formulas in a design may help achieve good proportions between structures, though they have been not widely accepted. (Para. 5) ( )

6. While small elements are related to the average size of human beings and therefore used as units to measure buildings, elements of intermediate size are still needed for the same purpose. (Para. 6) ( )

7. According to the last paragraph, the author prefers not to use decoration or ornament in modern architecture. (Para. 7) ( )

II. Fill in the missing words or expressions for the following sentences from the text.

1. These spaces also must be arranged in some _____ each other.

2. Any beam spanning a void tends to bend downward between the _____, putting the lower half of the beam _____.

3. The natures of wood and steel suggest _____, with whatever _____ may be necessary.

4. The building should form an aesthetic _____ to which several parts contribute.
5. Thus, the sides and rear of a structure should _____ to the front to make them all related parts of a single whole.
6. Although all decoration is rejected in some modern architecture, it was employed in the past either _____ or _____ in the building.
7. Stairs and a balustrade may give a clue to the _____ of a doorway; that, in turn, to the _____ of a colonnade; and finally, the colonnade to the _____.

Vocabulary

I. Complete the following sentences with some of the words listed below, changing the form where necessary.

withstand	project	enclosure
identifiable	inherent	void
fibrous	correspondence	

1. The _____ within the fence is large enough for the community to have a public park.
2. The old arch stone bridge was so well structured that it can still _____ heavy traffic.
3. It is better for a new building to bear _____ to its neighboring buildings in height.
4. Human beings, especially women, have an _____ love of beauty.
5. The house is easily _____ as Chinese traditional structure because of its typical classic mode.

II. Complete each of the following statements with one of the four choices given below.

1. Usually an _____ consists of several units, which have some relation-ship between each other.
   A. space   B. edifice   C. room   D. office
2. The _____ between the supports is a little bit long, so steel beams should be used.
   A. column   B. frame   C. span   D. skeleton
3. _____ unity in building style is one of the purposes that architects always try to achieve in their designing plan.
   A. Aesthetic   B. Spacious   C. Economic   D. Content
4. A roof cap functions as not a mere _____, but also a finishing mark of the roof and a touch with the sky.
   A. cover   B. separation   C. ornament   D. structure
5. Wood can withstand greater _____ strength than stone.
   A. compressive B. deformable   C. vertical   D. tensile
6. Being a _____ material, wood has a fine property to withstand tension and compression in structure.
   A. stiff   B. fibrous   C. flexible   D. soft

7. The majorities of the interior spaces of residential houses as well as office buildings are in shape of _____.
   A. rectangle   B. round   C. square   D. triangle
8. As the first step in the process of designing, an architect usually draws a (an) _____ for the project.
   A. outline   B. weather map C. working chart D. skeleton
9. The long passage through a series of gates makes the worshippers who enter the great cathedral _____ arouse a feeling of holiness.
   A. consciously   B. pleasantly   C. specially   D. subconsciously

Reading Material A

The Study of Architecture

What courses do the students of architecture follow at their schools? The following illustrations are the common components of the subject of architecture at most schools.

In a five-year Bachelor of Architecture program, the primary concentration is design. In some schools "design" may be a required course every semester. It is almost always a studio course, and certain aspects of an actual or hypothetical architectural problem are emphasized.① The student finishes the project with a preliminary design solution for the problem, with a graph presented.② For centuries, "juries" of faculty and professionals have been used to discuss and evaluate the student solutions.③

Usually some non-architectural courses also play key roles in determining architectural solutions—the behavioral sciences, engineering (structural and mechanical), and economics are among the more obvious ones. While some schools have made concerned efforts to teach these and other disciplines in an integrated studio situation, in most programs the actual instruction is provided in separate, different courses.

A typical architecture program will recognize the importance of graphic skills, and early instruction will be given in freehand drawing and graphic delineation. Various media will be made use of, including pencil, ink, and color.

Many programs will require at least one course in basic design or composition before architectural design to develop a fundamental understanding of both two-and three-dimensional forms. This course (or courses) may conclude with direct application to a specific architectural problem, thus begin the transition to more complex design problems.④

Common to many schools is an introductory course in architecture, which may range from a sampling of various aspects of the profession to an overview of the historical development of man's building activities. In a sense it is a preview of future courses.

The problem of designing a structure to withstand the forces of gravity, wind, and earthquakes is usually taught through another series of courses. Most schools require at least one course in calculus and descriptive geometry before the introduction of engineering statics.⑤ There may be an additional course on structural materials, particularly in engineering-oriented programs. The actual structures courses may be organized according to various sequences, such as the type of structural element (beam, column, etc.), or the structural material itself (timber, steel, reinforced concrete). Each material has different characteristics and requires separate considerations, but the ultimate objective in the engineering sense is to determine the most efficient (economical) system for the design solution. (Obviously, the design affects the structural system and vice versa.) Today most final structural calculations are done by specialists. It is not necessary for an architect to master it, however, an understanding is essential. Again, the emphasis in this area will vary widely from program to program.

Specialists exist for nearly every aspect of professional practice: programming, specifications, contracts, cost estimating, construction supervision, site planning, interiors, acoustics, lighting, heating and air conditioning, and electrical and structural design, to name a few of the most common.⑥ And if you look through the catalogs of several programs you will probably find courses covering each of these and other subjects. They may be either required or optional, or may be integrated into a broader course such as "architectural technology", "professional practice", "contract documents", or "building systems". Fundamental to most programs is sequence of courses in architectural history, sometimes including "theory". In a few cases these courses are taught in art departments, but nearly always include discussion of not only what mankind has constructed since the pyramids but how and why.⑦ A thorough understanding of the differences in style and technology of our predecessors provides the foundation for understanding our present culture relative to its building needs.

Notes

①设计课几乎始终是设计作业课,它对一个实际的或假定的建筑课题的某些方面加以强调。
studio course 此处按意思译为"设计作业课"。
②(要求)学生完成该工程的初步设计方案,并绘制成图。本句中的 solution 一词在本文中多次出现,均指设计方案。
③长期以来,都是由教师和专业人员组成的"评审组"来审查和评定学生的设计方案。juries 是 jury 的复数,意为"评审组"、"陪审团"。
④这门课(或几门课)可以直接用于解决建筑方面的某一具体问题,从而开始过渡到解决更复杂的问题。
句中词组 conclude with 本意是"以……结束",此处引伸为"导致某一结果"。
⑤Calculus 微积分;descriptive geometry 画法几何;engineering statics 工程静力学。
⑥建筑工程的各个方面几乎都有各自的专家。最常见的有:任务规划、施工细则、合同签订、造价预算、施工管理、基址规划、室内设计、音响、照明、供热与空调、电气与结构设计等。

句中 to name a few of the most common 系动词不定式短语作独立成份，意为"提一下最普遍的几个例子吧"。

⑦……但是这些课程几乎总是包括了研讨自金字塔以来人类建造了些什么建筑物，而且是怎样建造的、为什么要建造。

Reading Material B

Modern Education of the Architecture

In the final decades of the twentieth century the course of study at a typical school of architecture consists largely of: four years at university level, combining history and theory of architecture with technical courses and design projects, leading to a professional degree. Next, three years of practical experience under a registered architect or engineer, followed by the state or national examination. This last may be taken several times if the applicant fails, or he may retake a part of it if that is all he has failed.① There is no disgrace connected with taking the exam several times. Some of our most glorious "name" architects have gone through the fire more than once. For those who, for one reason or another (no money, early marriage, etc.), cannot attend a full time course of study, it is possible to work for an architect during the day as a draftsman and take two or three evening courses.② This generally takes up to twelve years and can play hell with one's family life and health. If at the end of this time one passes the state exam, one deserves the shingle if anyone does.③

The schools themselves vary, of course, in the emphasis they put on the various aspects of architectural study. Roughly speaking, they fall into three categories:

1. **Traditional** The largest number of schools are still more or less traditional, in that they stress the design project method of study, using the technical and theoretical courses as auxiliaries to the central purpose, architectural design.④ The hazard here is that these auxiliary courses, by the very fact of being placed in a secondary position, do not always get the attention they deserve, nor do the teaching posts tend to attract the best professors. Design, on the contrary, may often be overstressed, leading to a crop of architects whose work looks great on paper, but does not always turn out so well when built.⑤ Nevertheless, it is hard to argue against the central point, which is that design is what architecture is all about.

2. **Bauhaus** A smaller number of schools take what is sometimes called the Bauhaus approach——named for the German school which early in the century revolutionized both the teaching and practice of architecture, giving us the new concepts of functionalism and honesty of structural expression, as well as a score of major architectural talents.⑥ By this system students do not design until they have become tangibly familiar with materials of construction. They mix cement, build brick walls, and chisel away at stone-and when they design they use these materials in the clear and direct way their experience has taught them. The hazard here

is that the theoretical base of the system tends to become almost religious in its purity, and the leaders, or teachers, become minor (or major) gods. Actually, this particular phenomenon was often seen in the old days of the Beaux Arts, when students came to school for their lectures, but did their real work, their designing, in separate ateliers under separate masters. ⑦ In this case the adulation of the master was compounded by the pressure of competition with other ateliers and other masters. ⑧

3. **Community** The third type of school, still fairly rare, is the one which feels architecture to be part of the general sociological process of mankind, along with economics, environment, and city planning. The design of an individual building, in this view, may only be considered in relation to the community as a whole, because that is the way it does, in fact, function. Hence, this school will stress urban studies, and the collection of data concerning race, income levels, employment, transport, and so on, as a background to design. In this case the hazard-there seems to be a hazard in any system—is that the background tends to become the foreground. The students learn to put together magnificent statistical reports but produce rather meager architectural designs.

Some schools have attempted to merge the three general approaches in an effort to achieve a balanced architectural education. It is too early, at this point, to judge their success or failure. At present, let us say, all methods have their virtues and shortcomings. The young architect will take his choice, and, if he is lucky, make up whatever his school has failed to give him during the early years of his own practice.

Notes

① 如果申请人考试不及格，他可以多次攻克这最后一关，或者重考只是不及格的那一部分。
② draftsman：描图员。
③ …, one deserves the shingle if anyone does.
　……如果他挂招牌的话他是有资格的。
④ 大多数学校差不多仍是学院式（传统性）的，它们强调学习设计方案的方法。技能课和理论课是主课、即建筑设计的辅助课。
⑤ …leading to a crop of architects
　……导致了一大群建筑师……
⑥ 有一小部分学校采用包豪斯教学——因在本世纪初大幅度改革了建筑教学和实践的一所德国学校而得名。包豪斯教学法给我们提供了功能主义和真实的结构表现主义的新概念，同时它也造就了一批有影响的建筑学天才。
⑦ Beaux Arts——花花公子艺术（又译：情人艺术），beaux 原系法语词。
⑧ 在这种情况下，对导师的奉承由于受到其它设计室里的导师的竟争压力而冲淡了。
⑨ 第三种学校更少。这类学校认为建筑学和经济学、环境学、城市规化学一起都是人类总的社会过程的构成部分。

UNIT TWO

Text   Housing

[1]   Housing is living quarters for human beings. The basic function of housing is to provide shelter from the elements, but people today require much more than this of their housing.① A family moving into a new neighborhood will want to know if the available housing meets its standards of safety, health and comfort. A family may also ask how near the housing is to churches, schools, stores, the library, a movie theater, and the community center.

[2]   In the mid-1960's a most important value in housing was sufficient space both inside and out. A majority of families preferred singlefamily homes on about half an acre of land, which would provide space for spare-time activities. ②Many families preferred to live as far out as possible from the center of a metropolitan area, even if the wage earners had to travel some distance to their work. About four out of ten families preferred country housing to suburban housing because their chief aim was to get far away from noise, crowding, and confusion. ③ The accessibility of public transportation had ceased to be a decisive factor in housing because most workers drove their cars to work. People were chiefly interested in the arrangement and size of rooms and the number of bedrooms.

[3]   The majority of residents in rural and suburban areas live in single-family dwellings. Housing developments containing many single-family units have been built by professional land developers. Levittown, N. Y. is a mass-produced development that contains homes for more than 60,000 people. Since they are mass-produced, development houses tend to be identical or very similar. For the same reason they are usually less expensive than houses that are individually built.

[4]   In crowded areas where land is fairly expensive, the semidetached, or two-family, house is frequently found. In a semidetached house two dwellings share a central wall. Construction and heating are cheaper than in one-family houses, but residents have less privacy. Row houses, in which a number of single-family houses are connected by common walls on both sides, are still less expensive to build.

[5]   City land is too expensive to be used for small housing units, except in the upper price brackets. A more efficient type of building, which houses many family on a plot of ground that would hold only a few single-family units, is the multistory multiple dwelling, or apartment houses. Apartment houses may range from houses of only a few stories, without elevators, to structures of 20 or more stories, with several elevators. ④ Some apartment houses offer city dwellers a terrace or a backyard, where they can grow a few plants or eat. Many apartment houses provide laundromats, garage space, and gardened foyers. Huge apartment developments may cover several square blocks and include parks, playgrounds, shops, and community centers.⑤

[6]   Two modern ideas in apartment housing are cooperative and condominium apartments. In cooperative housing all tenants together form a corporation. Each tenant owns the right to occupy his apartment by virtue of having bought shares in the corporation and by paying his share of charges for building maintenance, service, and repair. In case a tenant defaults on taxes or mortgage payments, the corporation as a whole is responsible. Condominium housing differs in that each individual actually owns and holds title to his apartment and accepts sole financial responsibility for it. The individual tenant also pays a share of the maintenance of such public facilities in the buildings as elevators, hallways, and incinerators.

[7]   Housing is considered standard in quality if it meets the customary conditions or regulations of the locality. Local zoning laws set up standards for the acceptable size of a building lot and determine whether it may be put to residential, commercial, or industrial use. Building codes require that plans for new housing be submitted in advance to the local authority for approval in the form of a building permit. Housing codes, such as the tenement-house laws in cities, require that dwellings be safe, sanitary, and in good repair.

[8]   Good housing means a satisfactory community, as well as proper shelter. ⑥Residential neighborhoods should have a maximum of quiet, privacy, cleanliness, and safety. They should be served by hospitals, schools, and police, fire, sanitation, and street departments. Parks and social centers weld a group of individual homes into a community. These conditions create good standard housing. However, the housing of more than a half of the people in the world is considered below standard.

Words and Expressions

housing ['hausiŋ]	n.	住房；住房建筑
quarters ['kwɔːtəz]	n. (pl.)	住处，住宅
element ['elimənt]	n. (pl.)	风雨
shelter ['ʃeltə]	n.	掩蔽所；屏蔽
neighborhood ['neibəˌhud]	n.	住宅小区；街坊
single-family ['siŋgl'fæmili]	a.	独户的
	n.	独户
metropolitan [metrə'pɔlitən]	a.	都市的，大城市的
wage earners [weidʒ'əːnəz]	n.	工薪者（层）
confusion [kən'fjuːʒən]	n.	混乱
accessibility * [æksesi'biliti]	n.	可达性，可接近性
dwelling ['dweliŋ]	n.	住处，寓所
mass-produced [mæsprə'djuːsd]	a.	批量生产的
semidetached ['semidi'tætʃid]	a.	（房屋）一侧与邻屋相连的，半独立的
row houses ['rəu'hausiz]	n.	排式平房
bracket ['brækit]	n.	等级；托架（建）

upper price brackets		高级（等）
plot [plɔt]	n.	小块地皮；基址
terrace ['terəs]	n.	台地，露台
foyer ['fɔiei]	n.	（法）(剧场、旅馆等处的）门厅，休息处
condominium [ˌkɔndə'miniəm]	n.	共管式；(公寓中）个人拥有的一套房间
tenant ['tenənt]	n.	房客，住户
by virtue of		凭借，依靠；由于
default [di'fɔːlt]	vi.	拖欠，不履行
mortgage ['mɔːgidʒ]	n.	抵押借款
laundromat ['lɔːndrəmæt]	n.	自动洗衣店（间）
sole [səul]	a.	单独的
hallway ['hɔːlˌwei]	n.	门厅，过道
incinerator [in'sinəreitə]	n.	垃圾焚烧炉
tenement ['tenimənt]	n.	住房；一套房间
tenement-house		经济公寓；租用房屋
to hold title to		拥有……的权利
to accept responsibility for		对……承受（担）责任
customary ['kʌstəməri]	a.	（合乎）习惯的，惯例的
locality [ləu'kæliti]	n.	地方；所在地
zoning ['zəuniŋ]	n.	分区制
building codes		建筑（施工）规范
sanitary ['sænitəri]	a.	卫生的
sanitation [ˌsæni'teiʃən]	n.	卫生设备

Notes

① …to provide shelter from elements…

element 的复数形式可表示"风雨"、"自然力"

shelter from elements 意为"遮蔽风雨"的栖身之处。

② …which would provide space for sparetime activities.

这是一个修饰词组 single-family house on about half an acre of land 的特种定语从句（special attributive clause）；关系代词 which 在句中做主语，谓语用单数。

which 可译为"这"。

③ "数词＋out of ＋数词"有两种意义：

1) 表示后面的数减去前面的数。如：

Two out of five is three. 5 减去 2 等于 3。

2) 表示分数，这种情况一般是作为定语修饰后面的名词，如：four out of ten families。

④ 句中介词短语 without elevators 修饰 houses，而 with several elevators 则修饰 structures。二者均系非限定性定语，有补充说明的作用。

⑤大型公寓开发区可占数个街区……

在美国 block 指街区，街段。但在口语中也指具体的某栋楼房。

⑥本句实质上在讲良好的住房要具备良好的室内外环境。本段下几句都是在描述室外环境的必不可少的要素。

Exercises

Reading Comprehension

Ⅰ. Say whether the following statements are true (T) or false (F) according to the text.

1. The very purpose of housing is to offer human beings some place to protect them from the natural force. (Para. 1) ( )
2. In the mid-1960's, people preferred to live in the center of metropolitan area because of the accessibility of public transportation. (Para. 2) ( )
3. Mass-produced houses tend to be identical and more expensive than that individually built. (Para. 3) ( )
4. In the semi-detached house, residents have much more privacy than that in a single-family house. (Para. 4) ( )
5. City land is always not used for small housing units because of its high price and it is so even in the upper price brackets. (Para. 5) ( )
6. In the city center, the high-rising dwelling is a more efficient type of house because it may house many families on a small piece of land. (Para. 5) ( )
7. In the cooperative housing, all tenants have the right to occupy their apartments because of having bought the shares in the cooperations and paying their shares of charges for building maintenance etc. (Para. 6) ( )
8. If a housing satisfies the customary conditions or the local regulations, it may be said as standard housing in quality. (Para. 7) ( )
9. Housing developers may get the building permits from the local authority at any time they want. (Para. 7) ( )
10. A standard housing is that it not only meets people's needs for a maximum of quiet, privacy etc., but serves residents with public facilities such as hospitals, schools etc. (Para8) ( )

Ⅱ. Complete the following statements with the correct words or phrases from the four suggested answers according to your understanding of the text.

1. Housing is living quarters for human being. Here "living quarters" means _____.
  A. public square   B. rural area
  C. dwelling place   D. suburban area

2. When a family moves into a new house, they would always want to know whether it can satisfy their demand for _____.

        A. safety   B. health
        C. comfort   D. all of above
3. In order to have space for spare-time activities, _____ families preferred single-family home on about half an acre of land.
        A. a half of   B. many of
        C. a quarter of   D. some of
4. The mass-produced development, Levittown, New York, contains more than 60,000 _____.
        A. people   B. families
        C. houses   D. dwelling units
5. A semidetached house is _____.
        A. an unfinished house   B. a room shared by two families
        C. a two-family house   D. a single-family house.
6. Apartment houses usually _____.
        A. have no elevators
        B. have an elevator
        C. have several elevators
        D. have no elevators when they are only of a few stories
7. The size of building lot and the use of the land is determined by _____.
        A. customary conditions   B. building codes
        C. housing codes   D. local zoning laws
8. Housing codes is included in _____.
        A. regulations of the locality B. local zoning laws
        C. tenement-house laws   D. building codes
9. _____ is not mentioned about good housing.
        A. Public service   B. Community centers
        C. Sports grounds   D. Healthy environments

Vocabulary

I. Fill in the blanks with the words or expressions listed below, changing the form where necessary.

house (V.)	elements	mass-produce	single-family
accessibility	by virtue of	hold the title to	
semidetached	range from…to	quarters	

1. The rooms here can not _____ so many people at one time.
2. In order to survive, the primitive people invented many things to fight against _____.
3. This type of machine will be _____ exactly after its model.

4. We found excellent _____ at a small inn when we were traveling in Huangshan mountain.
5. If a house is connected to another by a common wall, we call it _____ house.
6. Usually, people in rural and suburban areas prefer to live in a _____ house as this has more privacy and space.
7. The _____ of public services such as transportation、schools etc. has been the decisive factor of people's choosing houses.
8. Each house owner has the right to his apartment _____ paying all the fees or expenses to the housing developers.
9. Nowadays, more and more high-rise office buildings appear, which _____ 20 stories _____ thirty stories.
10. Each tenant who has bought the shares of the corporation and paid the shares of charges for building maintenance service and repair _____ his apartment.

II. Fill in each blank in the short passage with a proper word form the four choices labeled with a, b, c, and d, after each corresponding number.

In the less developed parts (1) the vast areas of Africa, Asia, and Latin America, housing (2) falls far short of the needs of the public. High population growth and increased urbanization intensify the need (3) new housing. (4) greatest single lack is in the production of low-cost housing. (5) the result of a study of housing, the United Nations Economic and Social Council has (6) doubt that the mass of African people can ever (7) satisfactorily housed, because a majority of the population cannot afford (8) pay even ¥10 a month (9) rent.

1. a. for	b. of	c. in	d. on
2. a. production	b. result	c. question	d. usage
3. a. with	b. at	c. for	d. about
4. a. An	b. A	c. Some	d. The
5. a. For	b. As	c. In	d. With
6. a. expressed	b. been expressed	c. expressing	d. express
7. a. will be	b. were	c. are	d. be
8. a. for	b. with	c. to	d. on
9. a. about	b. under	c. at	d. for

Reading Material A

Early Housing

In ancient times, housing developed largely without any central planning or control. Many towns and cities were encircled by fortified walls for military protection. Urban dwellings, even including the houses of the rich, tended to be closely crowded together within the walls. In the countryside the typical community was the village, often a long row of small huts or cottages in which peasant farmers lived. Landowning nobles often held country estates. In the Middle Ages some of the greater nobility lived in large fortified castles with courtyards in which the peasants could find protection in case of attack. As the countryside became more orderly, the wealthy built handsome unfortified houses surrounded by extensive parks. ①

With the coming of the Industrial Revolution the cities expanded rapidly to accommodate the influx of many factory workers. ②Much new housing was built by speculators who saw a chance for a quick profit. In the absence of zoning or building restrictions, they often built poorly planned cheap housing that quickly deteriorated into slums. In the United States vast slum areas developed in the larger cities, especially in Chicago and New York. Somewhat more substantial housing was built by industrial companies for their employees. Textile towns and mining towns were company housing communities. As a rule, row houses made up the streets of the company towns. ④The houses were drearily identical, ill lighted and often unsanitary.

In Great Britain some steps to improve housing conditions were taken by humanitarian and charitable groups, such as the Society for Improving the Dwellings of the Labouring Classes, which was formed in 1845. Government entered the field in 1851 with the passage in Britain of the Shaftesbury Act, legislation that set minimum standards for lower-class housing. ⑤

In the United States the dangerous and unsanitary conditions of slum living gave rise to the first tenement-house regulations which were passed in New York City in 1867 and revised and strengthened in 1879 and again in 1901. ⑥ These laws set minimum standards in such matter as light, ventilation, fire protection, and sanitation. Laws patterned on the New York City code sprang up in many other parts of the country, ⑦ With the Great Depression of the 1930's came a shift in emphasis in housing laws from merely regulating the conditions of housing to providing government aid for the building of low-cost homes. The Federal Housing Administration (FHA) was established in 1934 to administer a program of government insurance of loans for building houses, was empowered to lend up 90 percent of the cost of approved projects to clear slums and build low-income family housing. In 1947 the functions of a number of housing agencies were absorbed by the Housing and home Finance Agency (HHFA), which was replaced in 1965 by the Department of Housing and Urban Development.

Notes

①随着农村治安状况变得越来越好，有钱人就修建了不设防的、四周尽是名贵花园的漂亮房子。
②随着工业革命的到来，城市迅速扩展，以便容纳涌入工厂当工人的人们。
③…that quickly deteriorated into slums.

……很快沦为贫民窟。

④通常，排式平房构成排列着公司商号的城镇街道。

⑤1851年英国通过了沙佛拉伯法，该法令确定了下层社会的最低住房标准，这样使得政府也介入了这一领域。

  passage 在此表示（法案的）通过

  with the passage in Britain of the Shaftesbury Act＝with the passage of the Shaftesbury Act in Britain

  Shaftesbury（1620——1683）英国政治家

⑥give rise to：引起，发生

⑦以纽约城市法规为模式的法律在全国其它地方也兴起来了。

Reading Material B

Recent Trends of Housing

All over the world urban concentration and the growth of suburbs have affected housing requirements.① Much city planning has been broadened into regional planning to make for balanced growth in a nation.②

United States After World War II an acute shortage of housing resulted from sharp increases in marriage and birthrates, general prosperity, and veteran's benefits in home buying.③ Rent controls protected rental tenants. The National Housing Act of 1949 continued the financial aid offered to home builders through the FHA and the Veterans Administration (VA).④ In addition, it supported urban renewal, or the demolishing of slums and building of public housing.

In the 1950's many giant industrial companies moved form the cities into outlying districts, bringing thousands of workers to areas with no housing for them. Local planning and zoning boards quickly mobilized to set standards and impose restrictions on land use in order to prevent speculative building and the growth of slums.⑤ Thus there developed many government aidedurban renewal projects in areas fringing great cities, as well as in the cities themselves.⑥

The National Housing ACT of 1961 provided for low-rent public housing, low interest mortgages, and direct loans for urban renewal, slum clearance, university housing, and housing for the elderly. The Housing and Urban Development Act of 1965 greatly expanded federal aid for housing. The act provided for grants-in-aid for slum clearance and housing rehabilitation, improvement of sewage and water facilities, supplementary rent payments to low-income families, health and recreation facilities, urban renewal, and suburban community development.⑦ In 1967 the Department of Housing and Urban Development began its Model Cities Program. Among the aims of the program were the improvement of housing and other conditions in slum areas. Finally, the Housing and Urban Development Act of 1968 established a long-term-program for the construction or rehabilitation of 26 million housing units by 1978.

Canada A rapidly growing population since World War Ⅱ, from 11,500 000 in 1941 to more than 20 000 000 in 1970, has strained Canadian housing facilities, particularly in cities. The Canadian National Housing Act, which is administered by the Central Mortgage and Housing Corporation, helps solve housing problems. Under the act the corporation insures privately financed mortgages up to 95 percent of the value of the property, and in some cases it makes direct loans for building houses. ⑧ Low interest rates and low down payments are other advantages offered by the corporation. The act further provides government aid for building low-rent public housing projects, for housing for the elderly, and for redevelopment of slum areas.

Europe In tremendous spurt of building during the decade after 1950, European areas that had suffered intensive bombing in World War Ⅱ were cleared, and new housing was erected. Building costs have increased owing to higher wages in the building trades, higher costs of materials and land, and higher housing standards. In the more developed of the countries of Europe, however, wages tend to rise more rapidly than housing costs. This brings better housing within the reach of more people both in free-enterprise countries and in countries with centrally planned economies. ⑨ In centrally planned economies the government stimulates housing by giving free or at cost the land, plans, materials, equipment, and technical assistance that are needed for home building, as well as by granting tax exemptions and loans. ⑩

Africa Asia, and Latin America. In the less developed parts of these vast areas, housing production falls far short of the needs of the public. High population growth and increased urbanization intensify the need for new housing. The greatest single lack is in the production of low-cost housing. ⑪As the result of study of housing the United Nations Economic and Social Council has expressed doubt that the mass of African people can ever be satisfactorily housed, because a majority of the population cannot afford to pay even ￥10 a month for rent. Most of the available dwellings in these areas are substandard. Except in large cities most houses are built by the families who will occupy them or by local craftsmen, and standards of water supply, waste disposal, light, air, and safety are primitive. In urban areas the lack of suitable low-cost housing results in shantytowns.

Notes

①urban concentration：意指城市人口的稠密化
②许多城市规划已经被扩展成区域规化，以使整个国家的发展趋于平衡。
其中 make for 意为"促使"，"走向"
③二战以后，急剧上升的结婚率和出生率，国家的大繁荣及在房屋购买中一些富有经验的获利者的猛增，使得住房短缺问题非常尖锐。

④FHA＝Federal Housing Act：联邦住房条例
　Veterans Administration（住房）开发商管理局
⑤地方规划部门迅速动员起来确立标准，并对土地的使用加以限制以防止一些投机建筑和贫民窟的发展。
⑥government-aid urban renewal project：政府补贴的城市改建工程
⑦该条例提供拨款清除贫民窟、更新住房、改善给排水设施、给低收入家庭补贴房租；改善医疗、娱乐设施，支持城市改建和社区发展。
⑧按照该法令，这家公司从资金上独自担保了财产价值高达95％抵押贷款，并且在某些情况下它直接为建房贷款。
⑨free-enterprise economies：自由经济
　centrally planned economies：中央计划经济
⑩在中央计划经济中，政府既通过免税和贷款，也通过免费或交费提供住宅建设所需要的土地、规划、建材和技术帮助住房建设。
⑪唯一巨大的不足在于建设低造价的住房。

UNIT THREE

Text   The language of Architecture (Ⅰ)

[1]   When we speak of a building as expressing this or that we are clearly assuming that architecture, in addition to its functional tasks, is also a medium of communication. It conveys meaning, just as these words printed on this paper, convey-it is hoped—meanings. Of course, those who have the meanings to convey, in this case the architects, and those who "read" the messages must possess some common knowledge of the language being used. For people who have been brought up in the same society this is a simple matter; they acquire their knowledge without effort, just as they learn to speak. A person from another culture, say an aboriginal tribesman from the South Pacific, might have the same difficulty understanding our architecture that he has with our language, customs, and moral standards. ①He probably would not be able to tell a church from a post office. In fact, he would not know what a church is, let alone a post office. But if it is your own culture, one you have been raised in and perhaps have had a hand in shaping, you not only understand the basic statements made by buildings, such as "I am a church" or "I am a gas station, " you also can read modifying comments and nuances, such as "am a refined home. Welcome, but do wipe your feet. "② Or, "I am a palace. Take off you hat and prepare to be frisked. "

[2]   It follows, then, that the architect, the man who speaks through his building, must 1) be quite clear as to what he wants to say, lest he reveal himself to be a blithering fool, and 2) have a good command of the language so that those who try to understand him—his readers, if you like—will not put him down as a confused illiterate. ③

[3]   Language, as we know it, consists of symbols—words, sentences, gestures, forms—anything that may be put together to communicate. In architecture the symbols are walls, roofs, doors, windows, steps, spires, and so on—the elements of which buildings are made. Each can be designed in an infinite number of ways and then put together in innumerable variations. Thus the final meaning is an indeterminate intangible which depends, just as does poetry or music, on the creative and expressive power of the creator and the interpretive or receptive capacity of those who respond. ④ Since both ends of this act of communication can be so extremely different, according to the individuals involved—their experiences, prejudices, convictions, and sensitivities—it is small wonder that the same piece of architecture can mean so many different things to different people, and be the occasion for so much fierce debate. ⑤

[4]   Let us consider that humblest and apparently simplest of architectural "word" the door. What is a door? Essentially, it is an opening that violates a wall. That is to say that before you can have a door you have a wall. The wall has been built to separate things. It keeps certain people in. It keeps others out, as well as wind, rain, cold, and wolves. On some occasions, though, special people or things have to pass through the wall. Hence an opening is cut, an

opening which can be closed off when not in use. That is a door. And its size and shape will depend upon what has to go through it.

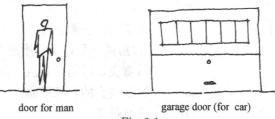
door for man   garage door (for car)
Fig. 3-1

[5] From the size and shape of the door you can "read" what it is meant for. The door for a man is, say, six foot six high (very few men are taller) and it might be a bathroom door, a closet door, a tool shed door, or even the entrance to a modest cottage. If there is a small door cut into the bottom it is for Rover or Pussy, while a slot with a hinged cover is for mail. Put all three together and you might as well paint a sign on the wall: Modest home with pet, probably suburban or rural. The door that is wider than it is high, we know, is for a vehicle. At small scale it is for a private car. At a larger size it could be for an a bus or airplane.

[6] When an important man entered the courtyard of a ducal mansi on he might be on the horseback. Therefore the doorway would have to be taller and wider.

[7] Or if a troop of warriors rode out to battle—or even more important, if they returned victorious—the doorway would have to be still wider and high enough to allow for their lances and banners. Eventually this gateway, through long association with glorious events, began to take on a glory of its own , so that sooner or later it became separated from its func-

man on horseback
Fig. 3-2

tion as a passage through a wall and took on a role of its own. Thus we find triumphal arches standing in the centers of squares or plazas and used almost exclusively for the celebration of festivals, memorials and the like.

men on horseback

Fig. 3-3

a triumphal arch

Fig. 3-4

New Words and Expressions

aboriginal [ˌæbəˈridʒənl]	a.	土著的，土著居民
tribesman [ˈtraibzmən]	n.	部落的一员；同宗族的人
nuance [nju(:)ˈɑːns]	n.	（意义、感情、颜色、音调等）细微差别
refined [riˈfaind]	a.	过于讲究的，精细的
frisk [frisk]	vt.	遍身搜查
blithering [ˈbliðəriŋ]	a.	啰苏的，胡说八道的
put down		认为，估计
illiterate [iˈlitərit]	a.	文盲的，无知的
spire [ˈspaiə]	n.	塔尖；尖顶
innumerable [iˈnjuːmərəbl]	a.	无数的
indeterminate * [ˌindiˈtəːminit]	a.	模糊的；不确定的
intangible [inˈtændʒəbl]	a.	触摸不到的；无形的
interpretive [inˈtəːpritiv]	a.	解释的；阐明的
receptive [riˈseptiv]	a.	有接受能力的；感受的
conviction [kənˈvikʃən]	n.	深信；确信
humble [ˈhʌmble]	a.	地位低下的；谦卑的
violate [ˈvaiəleit]	vt.	侵犯；扰乱
closet [ˈklɔzit]	n.	壁橱；衣橱
slot [slɔt]	n.	狭孔；缝
hinge [hindʒ]	n.	折叶
ducal [ˈdjuːkəl]	a.	公爵的
mansion [ˈmænʃən]	n.	宅第；大厦
doorway [ˈdɔːwei]	n.	入口；门口
warrior [ˈwɔriə]	n.	武士；勇士
allow for		考虑到；估计
lance [lɑːns]	n.	长矛；旗杆矛
banner [ˈbænə]	n.	旗帜
gateway [ˈgeitwei]	n.	入口；门口
take on		呈现（新面貌）；具有（特性）；承担
triumphal arch		凯旋门
plaza [ˈplɑːzə]	n.	（城市中的）广场
exclusively * [iksˈkluːsivli]	ad.	专有地；独占地

Notes

①句中 have the same difficulty understanding our architecture = have the same difficulty in understanding our…

关系代词 that 引导的定语从句修饰的是 difficulty。

②本句主要结构是 you not only understand the basic statements made by building，…you also can read modifying comments and nuances…

代词 one 是 culture 的同位语；词组 have a hand in shaping 意为"参与形成"，"参与塑造"。

③It follows that 这是英语的一种固定表达法，意为"由此可见（得出）"，"因此"。if you like 作插入语，意为"如果你愿意这样说（称呼）的话"。

④just as does poetry or music，系主谓倒装结构，作插入语，由于它的插入造成了固定搭配 depends on 的分隔。

⑤（1）it is small wonder = it is no wonder，意为"难怪"。that 后引导的是主语从句。

（2）be the occasion 前省略了情态动词 can，这部分与前边的 can mean so many… 是并列关系。

Exercises

Reading Comprehension

Ⅰ. Say whether the following statements are true (T) or false (F) according to the text, making use of the given paragraph reference numbers.

1. Just like the words printed on paper must convey meaning, we hope the buildings we have designed will convey something. (Para. 1)　　　　　　　　　　　　　　　(　　)

2. In a same culture, it is usually easy for people to understand the basic ideas made by buildings. (Para. 1)　　　　　　　　　　　　　　　　　　　　　　　　(　　)

3. Those who want to express themselves through architecture and those who want to understand architecture should understand the language of architecture. (Para. 1)　(　　)

4. An architect should know what to say and how to express it, otherwise he will prove himself to be illiterate. (Para. 2)　　　　　　　　　　　　　　　　　　　(　　)

5. In spite of departure of the receptive capacity of the responders from the creative and expressive power of the creators, the final meaning of a building is always clear. (Para. 3)
　　　　　　　　　　　　　　　　　　　　　　　　　　　　　　　　　　　(　　)

6. The main function of a wall is to separate things while that of a door is to serve as a passage through the wall. (Para. 4)　　　　　　　　　　　　　　　　　　(　　)

7. According to the author, we should build doors of different size for people of different

size. (Para. 5) ( )
8. Gateway has long been associated with the celebration of victory, and therefore serves more as a symbol of glory than as a passage through a wall. (Para. 7) ( )

II. Fill in the blanks with the expressions from the text.
1. From the _____ of the door you can "read" what it is meant for.
2. If there is a small door cut into the _____ it is for Rover or Pussy, while a _____ with a hinged cover is for _____.
3. The door that is _____ it is high is for a vehicle. At _____ it is for a private car.
4. If it is your own culture, one you _____ in and perhaps have _____, you not only understand the basic statements made by buildings,...
5. Eventually this gateway, through long association with _____, began to _____ a glory of its own.

Vocabulary

I. Complete the following sentences with some of the words listed below, changing the form where necessary.

defined	slot	infinite	put down	lance
interpretive	take on	allow for	exclusively	innumerable
violate	indeterminate	small wonder		

1. The development of high building is _____ as destroying townscape by some architects.
2. Buildings, as a medium of communication, can be designed in an _____ number of ways and then put together in _____ variations.
3. The final meaning of a building is _____, depending on the creative and expressive power of the creator and the interpretive capacity of the people who try to understand it.
4. You can often understand what a person means right away from the expression in his or her eyes, so it is _____ that people say "the eyes are the windows of the soul."
5. The tiny show windows is _____ used for displaying a single piece of jewelry to make the jewelry seem more valuable.
6. This is a _____ apartment and every detail is carefully designed.
7. the door of apartment buildings should be designed tall and wide enough to _____ furniture.
8. After renovation, the ancient mansion has _____ a new look.

II. Complete each of the following statements with one of the four choices given below.
1. The _____ sculpture on the cathedral express the extreme holiness of the building.
   A. nuance   B. refined   C. modifying   D. spire
2. The architecture uses great arches forming the _____ to direct the eye and the atten-

tion of the viewer where he wishes.

   A. balcony   B. space   C. structure   D. doorways

3. In order to save space, a _____ is usually built in the wall of a small apartment.

   A. closet   B. door   C. window   D. mirror

4. In each residential community, there should be a _____ for social interaction.

   A. plaza   B. resting place   C. public building   D. shopping center

5. Although the ancient _____ bridge has a long history of centuries, it's still as solid and firm as before.

   A. round   B. arch   C. curved   D. bending

6. Building are made by such _____ as walls, roofs, doors, windows, steps and so on, which are the symbols of architecture.

   A. things   B. matters   C. substance   D. elements

Reading Material A

The Language of Architecture (Ⅱ)

The great arches forming the doorways of cathedrals express the extreme holiness of the building and the act of worship that goes on inside.① The scale is so large that the doors themselves became quite immovable except by battalions of men. Smaller, workable doors are therefore cut into the large ones, much as Ruver's or Pussy's doors are cut into the large ones of their masters. We get the message. "God is great," say the doors. "and his worship is all important. But the worshippers themselves are insignificant. May they realize this and be humble."②

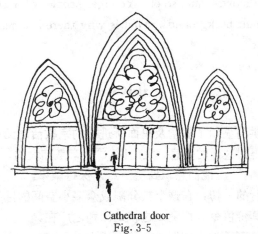

Cathedral door
Fig. 3-5

In a sense, the human-sized door of a typical office building say the same things. There is usually a long row of doors—six, ten, twelve. The people flow in and out anonymously. They are as insignificant, individually, as the worshippers in the cathedral. What is more important, though—and this is where the difference lies—is what goes on in the building above, the great hive of tiny cubicles in which people toil away their lives at (mostly) routine tasks of doubtful value or interest. ③ What is important is the abstraction business—a vague deity with no particular attitude towards us as living beings. ④ It is perhaps for this reason that we find so much commercial architecture cold and impersonal. It is architecture that is not saying much, and what it does say is pretty dispiriting.

The architect further uses doors to direct the eye and the attention of the viewer where he wishes. For a door suggests movement. It says, "Pass through here," so that even if you do not use the door, the thought is subconsciously in you mind and you respond to it. ⑤ A Freudian would have no trouble associating this response with the emotional significance attached to entrance to and exit from Mother's womb. ⑥ Be that as it may, the fact is the door is the point at which you enter a building or room or leave it. ⑦ In either case it means a change of state, from inside to out, or the other way around. And since very little affects you as profoundly as matters concerning you own skin, when the architect uses a door as device to communicate with you, he is speaking your language. ⑧ As proof, if proof is needed, just recall how annoyed you were when you could not see the entrance to a building, or the nightmares all of us have had in which we were trapped somewhere and could not find an exit. ⑨

And as long as we are speaking of language, consider how much emotional symbolism the word door has in our spoken language. ⑩ "Never darken my door." ⑪ "The wolf is at the door." "My door is always open," "Here's your hat, there's the door." The bride is carried through the door. The stable door is locked too late. In a mystery thriller the door creaks. "Open Sesame!" ⑫ cries the hero and the rock moves. A thousand associations, a thousand thoughts—as many different responses as there are different people. Of course, in any given period people of the same generation will have many similar responses, having heard the same fairy tales, seen the same movies, and so on. Younger people will react differently than older people, having had different backgrounds. That is why there is a generation gap in architecture, as in everything else.

Notes

①构成教堂入口的巨形拱门显示了教堂及里面所进行的宗教活动无比神圣。
②上面三句译为：我们得到这样的信息，大门说："上帝是伟大的，作礼拜是最重要的，而上帝的臣民则是渺小的。"愿他们意识到这一点，保持谦卑。
③更重要的是楼上所进行的一切，在这个被分割成众多小空间的巨型蜂箱里，人们把时间耗在了例行公事上，其价值令人怀疑，这就是区别之所在。
  句中 toil at 意为"辛辛苦苦地工作"。

  本句主要结构是 what is more important…is what goes on in the building above, … 后边的 the great hive of … 是上述表语从句的同位语。
④重要的是商业这个抽象的词汇是个无形的上帝，对我们人类毫无情感。

⑤…the thought is subconsciously in your mind and you respond to it………门这个概念已潜意识地存在于你的脑海中,你自动作出反应。
⑥弗洛伊德学派的人会很自然地把这种反应与母体出入口的情感意义联系在一起。
⑦Be that as it may …尽管如此。
⑧And since…concerning your own skin, …
因为几乎没有什么东西能像触及你的皮肤一样对你影响深刻……
⑨作为论证的依据,如果需要证明这一点的话,你只要想一想:如果你找不到建筑物的入口或是在我们都作过的恶梦中,我们被困在什么地方,又找不到出口,会是什么样的感觉和心情。
⑩就语言而言,想一想"门"这个词在我们的口语中有着多么深刻的情感上的象征意义。
⑪ "Never darken my door." "别进我的门。"
⑫ "Open Sesame!" 本意是开门咒,出自《一千零一夜》中的一故事,这里译为"开门!"。

Reading Material B

The Language of Architecture (Ⅲ)

Window is another word in the architect's vocabulary. Much of what has been said about doors applies also to windows; both are affective elements in architectural design—strongly affective, since they evoke associations with human acts.① Looking at a door, however, makes you think of going through it, while looking at a window does not (unless you are a burglar or a desperate stockbroker); rather it suggests the act of seeing, which in many respects has a more profound emotional connotation than walking. Apparently we think more of our eyes than of our feet. Note, for example, the reflection of this feeling in our verbal language. "The eyes are the windows of the soul." (pretty poetic, what? But wait.) "Her eyes met mine." (this could be rather uncomfortable if taken literally.) "The windows looked out over a broad valley." "My bedroom windows faced courtyard." The use of the word faced in this connection is significant in that windows are considered to be so much like eyes that their position gives a face to the building—a facade, to use the architectural term.②

The supposed existence of a face or facade implies also its opposite, rear and sides.③ All of this is imaginary, it goes without saying, since a building is a neutral whole, having no face,, rear, or sides except in our concepts.④ To a dog seeking a corner appropriate to his purposes these concepts do not exist; he makes his choices on entirely different grounds. Still, since architect designs for humans he can make use of the anthropo morphism which we inevitably apply to everything in our environment, and by the skillful placing of doors and windows give us images of structures "facing" this way or that, welcoming us or rejecting us, impressing us or making us feel important, and so on.⑤

Incidentally, speaking of importance, it should not be overlooked that a large window does much the same thing as does a large door: It lends importance to user.⑥ A large window means a large room, with a grand view; hence the occupant must be a person of greater stature and dignity than, say, the one who has just a humble casement to peer through. To give an extreme example, consider the dictator, president, general, or rock-and-roll star who appears on a balcony, framed by a great arched or pedimented window. Even at the outermost fringes of the cheering crowed he presents an image of mystical greatness. It is the window that does it of course. The architects who work for celebrities know what they are doing. So do the celebrities who engage them.

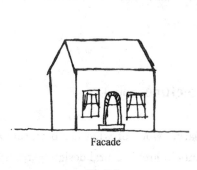
Facade
Fig3-6

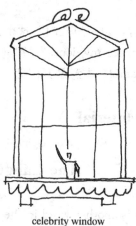
celebrity window
Fig3-7

What about a strip of equally large windows 40 yards long and repeated upward for 110 stories?⑦ Here again, as with the strip of doors at the entrance to an office building, neither the view nor the individual person is of any importance whatsoever, so that once more we have the same feeling of impersonality about the architecture; it cares nothing about us, and we return the sentiment.⑧

On occasion unexpected smallness can be used instead of large size to express importance. Thus, for example, a tiny show window in which a single piece of jewelry is exhibited may make the jewelry seen more valuable than if it were displayed in a large window, in which its uniqueness would be diminished. Or a small, diamond-paned window in a country inn, which might give an impression of snugness and warmth within, may be very much preferable to a large window behind which one feels oneself too easily seen eating or scratching. In short, the architect who designs large plate glass windows for Miss Katherine's Cozy Kitchen is just as wrong as the one puts cute little bottle-glass ones on the facade of a Bickford's Cafeteria.

Much the same sort of expressive functions are performed by the other architectural elements—columns, roofs, steps, railings, and so on. To explain each would be both redundant and self-indulgent; suffice it to say that, no matter how skillfully the architect uses his "words," it is the quality of the total thought he expresses that matters.⑨ If what he has to say is worth saying, the language will be adequate.

Notes

①Much of what has been said about doors applies also to windows…上述许多对门的论述对窗户也适用……

②在这一点上,"面对"这个词的使用是很有意思的,因为人们把窗户比作眼睛,用建筑术语来说,窗户的位置就决定了建筑物的"正面"。

③设想中的正立面的存在意味着还有与其相应的背立面和侧立面的存在。

④无须说,所有这些都是想象而已,因为建筑物是个中性整体,在我们的意念之外不分前、后、左、右。

⑤此外,由于建筑设计是以人为本的,建筑师可以用我们在环境中随处不可避免地会用到的拟人化手法,并通过巧妙地安排门窗位置,给我们创造出建筑物"面对"这边或那边,欢迎我们或拒绝我们,给我们留下深刻的印象或是抬高我们的身份,如此等等的形象。

⑥它给使用者带来身份和地位。

⑦…so that once more we have the same feeling of impersonality about the architecture; it cares nothing about us, and we return the sentiment.

……因此,我们又一次感到建筑物缺乏人情味,它根本不考虑我们,同样,我们也不关注这些建筑。

⑧…it is the quality of the total thought he expresses that matters.

……他所表达的整体思想的质量(效果)才是重要的。

UNIT FOUR

Text　　　　The Financial Setup（Ⅰ）

[1]　　Certain building—museums, libraries, schools, churches, etc. —are built without monetary profit in mind. But the obvious majority—hotels, office buildings, apartment houses, theaters, and so on—have one main purpose: to produce income for their owners. An architect, therefore, will often find himself expected to prepare for his client, before anything else is done, an analysis of the project in investment term—cost of land and construction, mortgages, interest and maintenance, income and profit—which together are known by the phrase financial setup. ① For the client, aside from wanting to build a monument to himself or his firm, has the curious quirk of preferring his books to read in the black at the end of the year—a quirk which has no doubt had something to do with his becoming a corporate head in the first place. ②

[2]　　The architect whose financial setups usually work out more or less accurately gets quite a good name in the client fraternity, while one whose analyses are off the mark a bit too often will soon find himself joining the ranks of the unemployed. Thus, to the architect's basic obligations—to express the nature of his society and to help create a fertile environment for the development of human aspiration—one must add necessity of treating the financial setup as a high priority item. ③

[3]　　The financial setup is made up of three main parts followed by a conclusion, familiarly known as the button, or clincher, for it is the item which most often decides whether or not the project will go ahead. ④

[4]　　Part one consists of a statement of estimated costs—land, construction, architect's and engineer's fees, legal fees, permits, and so forth. The total is then divided into two sections, one being the actual cash which the investor must put up, the other being the money to be borrowed, in other words, the mortgage or mortgages. ⑤

[5]　　Part two is the cost of maintaining, or running, the project, after it has been built. The largest item, probably, will be the mortgage interest and amortization (the paying off of the mortgage principal); next, the building employee's salaries, taxes, fuel, repairs, insurance, and so on; note that amortization, or paying off mortgage, reduces the principal, and thus the annual interest, from year to year, if the mortgage has been so written. Some of the other items slide up or down as the years pass, so part two must be given a variable value against a time scale. ⑥

[6]　　Part three, sometimes called the rent roll, is an estimate of the gross income the building is expected to produce. The method generally used to arrive at this is to assume the building to be fully rented at current rentals for the area and type of building (say an apartment house or office building) and subtract 10 percent for "vacancies." The word vacancies is put in

quotes because it is largely fictional. In times of building shortages, of course, there will be no vacancies to speak of. But in periods of excess space available the project will probably not be undertaken in the first place. Still, it is argued that the item is justified in that it presumably compensates management for costs incurred and rental lost during turnover—that is, when one tenant moves out and another moves in.⑦

[7]　　The button, or clincher, is arrived at by subtracting part two, the maintenance costs, from part three, the gross income; the remainder is net income, the magic figure which is then set against the actual cash investment in part one to get a percentage. This is the profit rate, and determines whether or not the building goes ahead. Ordinarily, the investor will want at least 15 percent return on his money or he will put it into something else. Or, he may ask the architect to revise the whole scheme to make the figures come out better.

[8]　　All this is less complex than it may seem on first reading, and perhaps the easiest way to make it clear is to invent an imaginary case and devise a financial setup for it.

[9]　　let us assume that the project under consideration is to be an apartment house whose total cost, it is proposed, will be $2 million—a not unusual figure for a modern high-rise. By a rule of thumb, one fifth of this sum, or $400 000, will go for the land.⑧

[10]　　The balance of the money, $1.6 million, will go for the cost of construction, fees of all sorts, permits, and so on (which we will lump together for the purpose of simplification). 90 percent of the total $2 million, or $1.8 million, will be provided by a lending institution-bank, savings and loan society, insurance company, whatever—in the form of a mortgage at, say, 10 percent annual interest plus an amortization of 2 percent per year. That leaves $200 000 to put up by the promoter, your client. It may be his own money, his father-in-law's, or his winnings in Las Vegas. It doesn't matter. It's cash, and he puts it up. And that is part one.

New Words and Expressions

setup ['setʌp]	n.	预算；预备
monetary ['mʌnitəri]	a.	钱的；金融的
client ['klaiənt]	n.	委托人；客户
quirk [kwəːk]	n.	（奇怪的）行为；妙语
corporate ['kɔːpərit]	a.	法人的；社团的；共同的
fraternity ['frætəːniti]	n.	一群同职业的人（同行）
off the mark		不合格；达不到要求
join the ranks of		加入……的行列
obligation [ˌɔbli'geiʃən]	n.	职责；义务
fertile [fəːtail]	a.	丰富的
aspiration [æspi'reiʃən]	n.	愿望，志向
clincher ['klintʃə]	n.	定论；定性的人（物）

mortgage ['mɔːgidʒ]		n.	抵押，保证
amortization [əmɔːtiˈzeiʃən]		n.	分期偿还（债务）
principal ['prinsipl]		n.	本金；资本
time scale			时间表
rent roll			租金滚动
gross [grɔs]		a.	总的，全部的
gross income			毛收入
rental ['rentəl]		n.	租金；租赁
		a.	出租的，租用的
fictional ['fikʃənəl]		a.	虚构的
vacancy ['veikənsi]		n.	空房间；空处
compensate ['kɔmpenseit]		v.	补偿；赔偿
presumably [priˈzjuːməbli]		ad.	大概；估计可能
incur [inˈkəː]		v.	蒙受；招致
turnover ['təːnəuvə]		n.	更换率；周转
remainder [riˈmeində]		n.	剩余部分
investor [inˈvestə]		n.	投资者（人）
lump [lʌmp]		v.	把……归并
simplification [ˌsimplifiˈkeiʃn]		n.	简化
promoter [prəˈməutə]		n.	发起人；创办者

Notes

① "terms" 这里意指 "费用"。

②(1) his books to read in the black

"books" 这里指帐本；"read in the black" 意为 "盈利，赚钱" 与 "read in the red" "赤字" 相反。

(2) a quirk which has no … in the first place. 系 the curious quirk 的同位语。

③thus, to the architect's … one must add the necessary of…

(1) 理解此句时应注意词组 add…to… 结构的倒装，即实际上是 add the necessity of …to the architect's basic obligation。

(2) 句中不定式短语 to express the nature... 和 to help create a ... 是 basic obligations 的同位语。

④(1) "button" 是西方音乐家们表示 "合弦，定音" 时用的一个俚语，此处等于 clincher。

(2) go ahead 本意 "前进"，此处意为 "施工；进行"。

⑤投资的第一部分指由投资者提供的现金部分，虽然在总投资中所占比例不大，但往往却是最后 "定音" 的关键款项。

⑥ "against a time scale" 按照时间表。

⑦(1) 本句中自 that the item is justified 至句末 another moves in 为主语从句，第一个 it 为

形式主语，第二个 it 指代 the item。

（2）句中短语 is justified in 后跟 that 引导的名词性从句意为"在……方面证明是正确的"；若后跟动名词则意为"有理由（或应当）做……"。

⑧ "By a rule of thumb, …" 根据约略的估计。

Exercises

Reading Comprehension:

I. Say whether the following statements are true (T) or false (F) according to the text, making use of the paragraph numbers.

1. All the buildings are built for the purpose of making money. (Para. 1) （ ）
2. Financial setup is an analysis of the project in investment terms before the project actually starts. (Para. 1) （ ）
3. For the client, he wants not only to set a good name for himself or his firm, but also to make much more money from his investment. (Para. 1) （ ）
4. As an architect, no matter how well the financial setup he has made, he will never lose his job. (Para. 2) （ ）
5. To think of the financial setup as a high priority item is the only basic duty of an architect. (Para. 2) （ ）
6. The clincher is a conclusion which most often decides whether or not the project should get started. (Para. 5) （ ）
7. Part one is an estimate of costs which can be divided into two sections, one being the actual cash the investor must provide and the other thing being the money provided by the lending institutions. (Para. 6) （ ）
8. Part two is the cost of maintaining, or running, the project, after it has been rebuilt, so this part must be given a changeable value according to a time table. (Para. 7) （ ）
9. Part three is an estimate of the gross income that the client hopes to produce by the building. (Para. 8) （ ）
10. If the investor can get 10 percent return on his money, he will accept the setup worked out by his architect and not want any change in the whole scheme. (Para. 9) （ ）

II. Fill in the blanks in the short passage according to what you have learned from the text.

Financial setup consists of _____ parts followed by a _____, which most often decides whether or not the project will go ahead. The _____ is arrived at by subtracting part two, the maintenance costs, from _____, the _____ income; the remainder is _____ income. The figure which is then set against the actual cash investment in part one to get a percentage. This is the _____ and determines whether or not the building goes ahead.

Vocabulary

Ⅰ. Match the definitions in column B with the corresponding words or expressions in column A.

A	B
1. turnover	a. not occupied or taken up
2. gross income	b. the rate of renewal
3. net income	c. all the money received without suotracting the costs
4. vacancy	d. the neat profit
5. mortgage	e. people who are joined together by common interest
6. fraternity	f. taking the property as the security of paying for a debt or loan

Ⅱ. Complete the following sentences with words or expressions listed below, changing the forms where necessary.

setup	investor	clincher	in the black
off the mark	join the rank of	compensate…for	
by rules of thumb	be justified in	put up	

1. Before starting a project, the architect must first do the financial _____ for the client.
2. According to the architect's analysis of the project, the _____ will see how much profit he gets and decides whether or not the project is worth investing.
3. As the end of the year, the investor prefers to read his books _____ not in the red.
4. It is from the _____ that the promoter decides whether it is worth putting money on the project.
5. The gross income of the factory will be up to $28 000 000 _____.
6. By raising the rent, the promoters often _____ them _____ the loss resulted from tenant's turnover.
7. One part in the total investment is the actual cash which the inventor must _____.
8. If the analysis of the project in investment terms worked out by architect is _____, he will certainly get a bad name in his fraternity.
9. During 1930s' Depression, most people _____ the unemployed.
10. The client _____ firing the architect if he does a bad analysis of financial setup for the project.

Reading Material A

The Financial setup (Ⅱ)

Part two is basically just as simple, although it contains more items. The biggest one is the annual interest on the mortgage, 10 percent of $1.8 million, or $180 000. Next is amortization, or paying off the mortgage principal. At 2 percent this will be $36 000. Taxes, insurance, inspection fees, and so forth, may, again by rule of thumb, be set at 3 percent (of the entire project cost) or $60 000. Salaries, repairs, fuel, and so on, may also be estimated at 3 percent, or another $60 000. A somewhat airy item is the interest the promoter would have earned on his $200 000 if he had not put it into the project; this is also put down as a cost.① Assuming a possible interest rate of 6 percent, the promoter's "loss" is set down as $12 000.② And that is part two. So far, then, our financial setup looks like this:

Part One Cost.
  1. land ··· $400 000
  2. Building
   (including all fees) ································ 1 600 000
   Total ··· $2 000 000
(provided by a mortgage of $1.8 million and private funds of $200 000.)

Part Two Running Expenses (annual)
  1. Interest on mortgage ···························· $180 000
  2. Amortization   36 000
  3. Taxes etc ·· 60 000
  4. Maintenance ······································ 60 000
  5. Lost interest on cash ··························· 12 000
   Total ·· $348 000

Note again that as amortization proceeds from year to year, the mortgage principal is reduced, bringing the interest down.③ However, other items, such as taxes and maintenance may well rise—in fact, they usually do—so that at least for the first few years the total shown in part two may be considered more or less constant.

Now we compute part three, which, as has already been explained, consists basically of gross and net income. Knowing current building costs the architect can guess very closely how many square feet of rentable space he can put up for $1.6 million; and knowing as well how much space of this type is renting for, he can readily state the total potential income, or rent roll.④ Deducting the ritualistic 10 percent for vacancies he arrives at an adjusted rent roll, which in our imaginary case comes out to $384 000, on a full rent roll of $427 000.⑤

The next step is to subtract part two from part three, to get a net annual income. Thus:

Net rent roll (part three) ·················· $384 000
Annual cost (part two) ···················· 348 000

Net income ································ $36 000

Now, at last, we are ready for the button, or clincher. $36 000 does not seem like much money to be earned by a $2 million project, but remember that the client, or promoter, did not put up the $2 millionth. He put up $200 000. And on $200 000, $36 000 is 18 percent, which is enough to make him smile in his sleep. "My architect," he tells his friends over his second martini, "is a humdinger. His fees will make you turn pale, but he's worth every penny."⑥ The friends make a note of the architect's name.

Notes

①如果创办人没有把这笔钱投入这项工程, 那么这一部分就是空想的他投资 $2 000 000 所得的利息。
②be set down as 被看作是……
③请再注意, 随着一年又一年的分期偿还债务抵押本金也减少了, 继而也降低了利息。bring …down: 降低 (减少) ……
④Knowing current building costs…; and knowing…
两个分词短语分别作两个并列分句的原因状语。
⑤扣除形式上的10%的空余房间, 他得出一个经过调整的比较合适的租金滚动。这样在我们所想象的例子当中, 他就可在全部租金滚动的 $427 000 当中获取 $384 000。
⑥喝完第二杯马丁尼酒后, 他告诉他的朋友: "我的建筑师是一位了不起的人, 他的费用可吓得你脸变色, 但却值了。"
humdinger: 非正式用法, 等于 a wonderful person

Reading Material B

The Financial Setup (Ⅲ)

As the years go by, the promoter gradually pays himself back his original investment.① (In our imaginary case, this was $200 000.) He may earn less than $36 000 per year as the building gets older and less desirable, but whatever he earns, set above a diminishing investment, still shows a most attractive profit in terms of percentage. If he lives long enough to pay off all of his investment, his profit leaves the realm of percentage altogether and becomes that mystical and magic element—pure profit.②

It is for this reason that institutions such as universities, banks, churches—and private heirs of several generations—find old properties (slums, if you like) to be so valuable. Since the properties outlive the original investor many times over, their income from such property is unequaled in its classic style. But if anyone should buy this kind of property, he would at once find himself with an investment figure over which it is most unlikely that his profit, if any, will look very good.③ Conclusion: old building—slums—are splendid to own, if you have owned them long enough. They are disasters to buy or sell, since the buyer will most often lost his shirt, while the seller will get very little on the market.

Returning to the financial setup, let us consider what happens when the button comes out to less than 15 percent, that being the lowest profit a promoter will find satisfactory. The simplest solution, of course, is to drop the project then and there. The architect is paid form his services to date, and that is that.④

Another approach is to try to reduce the bottom half of the profit fraction—the costs. This can be done in several ways. The most familiar is to cut construction costs by cheapening the quality, and we are all well acquainted with the kinds of buildings in which this has been done: low ceilings, cracking plaster, and walls so thin that one becomes all too familiar with the neighbor's television tastes and domestic problems. Or, the promoter might try a better mortgage, one which, say, called for a smaller annual interest over a longer period, or a larger mortgage, thus reducing the personal cash item and proportionately boosting the profit fraction.⑤ The most popular device is a combination of the steps that increase the rent roll: first, lower the ceilings (see above) to get an extra story or two into the same overall height; second, use smaller rooms to get more rentable units into the same area.⑥ Regrettably, one must report that these devices are all too often used, resulting in cities full of new "luxury" apartments, which, in every respect, might well be described as per—slums.⑦

Very often, part of the rentability of a new building is in its design—aesthetically speaking, of course.⑧ The "in" look, the "today" look, has much to do with the daily rates charged by the most popular resort hotels, which the "traditional" look may add a thousand or two to the prices of houses in certain suburban developments.⑨

What about the architect who participates in this process? Is he merely the skilled servant of the clients whose purposes it is not his province to judge, but to whom he rents out his taste, his knowledge, his experience, his ingenuity?⑩ Or must he share responsibility for the huge volume of architecture built according to the dictates of the financial setup, not all of which is bad, but which is more often than not rather inhuman? Not that either the promoters or the architects are inhuman. It is merely that their concern has been with profit rather than humanity.

The architect must ask himself this question, and only he can answer it.

Notes

①Pay back 收回来

②如果他能活到把所有的投资都付清的话，那么他的利润只留下总的百分数这个范围。他的利润就会变得神秘且有魔力，因为这是一个纯利润。

③但如果有人买了这种财产，他立刻就会发现自己有了一个投资数目，这项投资不大可能给他带来好的利润（如果有利润的话）。

④that is that＝that is the end of the matter

⑤proportionately boosting the profit fraction：成比例的提高利润部分

⑥The most popular device is a combination of the steps that increase the rent roll...

最普遍的方法是把增加租金的步骤综合起来……

⑦…resulting in cities…well be described as per-slums.

……结果，在城市中充满了所谓豪华的新公寓，但无论从那方面看它们实在都是些贫民窟的前身。

⑧rentability 出租率，可出租性

⑨"时髦"的外观，"现代"的外观与那些人们常去的旅游胜地的饭店每天的进帐有极大关系；而在某些郊区的开发区中"传统"的外观则可使房价增加一、两千美元。

⑩这两句可译为：但是参加这个过程的建筑师的情况如何？他仅仅是客户们所希望的技术熟练的仆人吗？这不是建筑师决定的范围。但是他对客户们出租的是他的感受、知识、经验和独创性。

第二个问句是一个结构不规范的句子。其中 whose 和 whom 均指 clients 而 his、he 则均指 architect。

UNIT FIVE

Text   The Domain of Urban Design

[1]　　We can start identifying the elements of urban design by defining the domain of urban design. Urban design is that part of the planning process that deals with the physical quality of the environment. That is to say, it is the physical and spatial design of the environment. However, it should be quite clear to us that in designing the environment, planners and designers cannot design all elements and components; they cannot in every instance design entire buildings. It might be possible to do this in new towns or planned residential communities, but in an existing community, such complete design is quite difficult.

[2]　　In addition, the domain of urban design extends from the exterior of individual buildings outward, with consideration of positive and negative effects of individual buildings on each other's interiors. ① "Designing cities without designing buildings" we may, therefore, say that the spaces between the buildings are the domain of urban design. But how do we design these spaces?

[3]　　Using the nomenclature of the Urban Design Plan of San Francisco, we can distinguish among the purposes of four interrelated groups of spaces: (1) internal pattern and image, (2) external form and image, (3) circulation and parking, and (4) quality of environment. Internal pattern and image describe the purpose of spaces between urban structures at the microlevel, that is, key physical features of the city's organization—focal points, viewpoints, landmarks and movement patterns. External form and image focus on the city's skyline and its overall image and identity. Circulation and parking look at street and road characteristics—quality of maintenance, spaciousness, order, monotony, clarity of route, orientation to destination, safety and ease of movement, and parking requirements and locations. ② Finally, quality of environment includes nine factors: compatibility of uses, presence of natural elements, distance to open space, visual interest of the street facade, quality of view, and quality of maintenance, noise, and microclimate.

[4]　　The domain of urban design as just set forth does not pinpoint very specific physical elements (plaza, mall, seating areas, trees, lamp posts), but it is a reasonable way of grouping them and gives direction to study and identification of the more specific elements that are unique or important to a community. ③ Since every community has different physical characteristics, the range of specific elements may vary extensively from one community to another, from one downtown to another, from one city to another.

[5]　　In the past, most planners and designers have emphasized the first two groups of elements—internal pattern and image and external form and image—probably because these two groups are strongly oriented toward the form-making aspects of urban design. Yet when we also consider these elements from the standpoint of function and environmental quality, the

spaces created for people (both those who are walking in the streets and those who are living inside the buildings) are potentially more pleasant.

[6] For example, we might observe a beautifully designed plaza that very few people use, simply because it does not have any direct sunlight or it is windswept. On the other hand, there are plazas that have been designed only tolerably well, and crowds of people use them. It is undoubtedly true that there might be a number of factors involved (location, support for activity, and so on), but such environmental considerations as wind, noise, sun, view, and natural elements always contribute significantly to successful urban design.

[7] Having thus identified the framework for analysis of urban design—that is, the domain of urban design—we now shall attempt to identify a method of presenting this information in the form of policies, plans, guidelines, and programs. Variations in analysis of the elements of urban design (or lack of any analysis at all) has created variety in the form and range of policies, plan, guidelines, and programs in different cities. Even close examination of the urban design of various cities does not make one certain that planners have used a framework of analysis or have identified a specific element as the most important one to zero in on.④ Perhaps a lack of comprehensiveness in their framework has caused concentration on a few physical items.

[8] However, we can now move from the four groups of analysis just outlined to a third categorization of the elements of urban design:

  1. Land use
  2. Building form and massing
  3. Circulation and parking
  4. Open space
  5. Pedestrian ways
  6. Activity support
  7. Signage
  8. Preservation

[9] The categories we are using are of course interrelated. Urban design strategies for specific urban areas or cities will necessarily have to group, or distinguish among, the physical elements identified here according to the problems and opportunities of the area under study.

New Words and Expressions

domain *	[dəˈmein]	n.	范围，领域
spatial *	[ˈspeiʃəl]	a.	空间的
planner	[ˈplænə]	n.	设计者，规划者
existing	[igˈzistiŋ]	a.	现存的，存在的
nomenclature	[nəuˈmenklətʃə]	n.	名称，术语
circulation *	[ˌsəːkjuˈleiʃən]	n.	交通线路

interrelate *	[ˌintə(ː)riˈleit]	v.	相互联系
image	[ˈimidʒ]	n.	意象
microlevel	[ˈmaikrəuˈlevəl]	n.	微级
landmark	[ˈlændmɑːk]	n.	地标，界标，地物
skyline	[ˈskailain]	n.	（大厦等）空中轮廓
identity	[aiˈdentiti]	n.	个性，特性
spaciousness	[ˈspeiʃəsnis]	n.	宽敞，广阔
monotony	[məˈnɔtəni]	n.	单调，千篇一律
orientation *	[ˌɔːrienˈteiʃən]	n.	方向，方位
compatibility *	[kəmˌpætəˈbiliti]	n.	互换性，一致性
facade	[fəˈsɑːd]	n.	（房屋的）正面，立面
microclimate	[ˈmaikrəuˌklaimit]	n.	小气候
pinpoint	[ˈpinpɔint]	vt.	提出，确认
mall	[mɔːl]	n.	林荫道，购物中心
lamp-post	[ˈlæmpəust]	n.	路灯柱（杆）
identification *	[aiˌdentifiˈkeiʃən]	n.	确定，识别
orient *	[ˈɔːriənt]	vt.	调整，定…的位
standpoint	[ˈstændˌpɔint]	n.	观点，立场
windswept	[ˈwindˌswept]	a.	挡风的
tolerably	[ˈtɔlərəbli]	ad.	过得去地，还算不错地
guideline *	[ˈgaidlain]	n.	指导路线，方针
categorization	[ˈkætigəraiˈzeiʃən]	n.	分类，分列入目录中
mass	[mæs]	vt.	集中，聚集，遍布
signage	[ˈsainidʒ]	n.	识标，位标
preservation	[ˌprezəːˈveiʃən]	n.	保存，维护

Notes

①在介词短语 with consideration of positive and negative effects of individual buildings on each other's interiors 中还包含了三个介词及其短语。其中第一个 of 前后表示的是动宾关系，第二个 of 前后表示的是所属关系，至于 on 则是前面名词 effects 的固定搭配 effect on（对……的影响或作用）所要求的。

②Circulation and parking look at…
  （1）circulation 在建筑学和城市规划方面的文章中常常指的是室内、室外环境中的整个道路系统，有时译为"交通流线"。
  （2）look at 此处意为"着眼于"、"考虑"。

③句中 as just set forth 系修饰 the domain of urban design 的定语从句，省略了助动词 has been。括号中 plaza 一词指的是城市中的小型广场，或建筑物之间可以公用的空地，square 一般指较大较正式的广场。

④…or have identified a specific element as the most important one to zero in on. 其中代词 one=an element；词组 to zero in on 本意是开枪射击时的"瞄准"，但在俚语中常表示"集中精力"、"全神贯注"。

Exercises

Reading comprehension

Ⅰ. Say whether the following statements are true (T) or false (F) according to the text, making use of the paragraph numbers.
1. The most important thing in urban design is to identify the domain of urban design. (Para. 1) ( )
2. Environment design involves all the elements including the design of an entire building. (Para. 1) ( )
3. The domain of urban design virtually deals with the relation between the exteriors and interiors of individual buildings. (Para. 2) ( )
4. The domain of urban design refers to the four interrelated groups of spaces, but not the specific physical elements such as plaza, mall and so on. (Para. 3. 4) ( )
5. Specific elements are not important and not worth studying. (Para. 4) ( )
6. Most planners and designers pay more attention to the first two groups of elements, for these two groups can define the rest groups of elements. (Para. 5) ( )
7. A beautifully designed plaza may not be certainly enjoyed by people while an ordinary one sometimes meets people's need because of its favorite location. (Para. 6) ( )
8. Not only the location and support for activity but also such environmental considerations as wind, noise, sun and so on are associated with the success of urban design. (Para. 6) ( )
9. When planning cities, planners do not certainly use framework of analysis because they strongly neglect it. (Para. 7) ( )

Ⅱ. Supply the missing information according to the text.
1. Urban design is the part of _____ that deals with _____. That is to say, it is _____ design _____.
2. The domain of urban design extends from _____, and it is spaces between _____.

3.

```
                              ┌ (1) _____
                              │     describing _____
                              │ (2) _____
          ┌ expressed in four │     focusing on _____
          │ groups of spaces  │ (3) _____
          │                   │     dealing with _____
          │                   │ (4) _____
          │                   └     including _____
          │                   ┌ (1) _____
domain of │ presented in      │ (2) _____
urban    ─┤ the form of       │ (3) _____
design    │                   └ (4) _____
          │                   ┌ (1) _____
          │                   │ (2) _____
          │                   │ (3) _____
          │ the third         │ (4) _____
          │ categorization    │ (5) _____
          │                   │ (6) _____
          │                   │ (7) _____
          └                   └ (8) _____
```

Vocabulary

I. Complete the following sentences with some of the words listed below, changing the form where necessary.

nomenclature	distinguish	maintenance
guideline	define	range
zero in on	orient	interior
circulation	identity	microlevel
skyline		

1. Using the _____ of architecture, we can divide the domain of urban design into four interrelated groups of spaces.
2. In urban design, planners generally follow a process that includes development of long _____ goals.
3. Designers should identify the more specific elements that are unique or important to a community to _____.

43

4. Internal pattern and image can be _____ as the spaces between urban structures at the microlevel.
5. The condition of a building is decided by the original workmanship, building materials and the _____.
6. In a design process, the exterior and _____ of a building should be given equal consideration.
7. The _____ of the city is visible far away.
8. These residential buildings look identical, but each apartment has its own _____.

II. Complete each of the following statements with one of the four choices given below.

1. Early in the century, planners focused on the major _____ of cities such as street facade, park, civic centers and so on.
   A. sights   B. views   C. visual elements   D. standpoints
2. City dwellers feel comfortable when they have _____ living rooms.
   A. spatial   B. spacious   C. wide   D. broad
3. _____ and parking lots are important elements in city planning considered by planners.
   A. Circles   B. Corridors   C. Circulation   D. Communication
4. City planners today are concerned with the total fabric of cities, not only the _____ seen in three dimensions, but the economic, social, legal and human aspects.
   A. physical aspects   B. visual interest
   C. negative effects   D. positive effects
5. Such complete design is possible for _____ to be constructed, but not for an existing one.
   A. neighboring area   B. residential communities
   C. living area   D. constructing projects
6. The _____ of urban design is in fact the physical and spatial design of the environment.
   A. space   B. domain   C. field   D. area
7. Since the bedrooms, living room, bathroom and kitchen are four _____ spaces, so they should be considered together in interior decoration.
   A. interrelated   B. closed   C. connected   D. associated
8. The street _____ reflects to some extend the development of the city.
   A. spaciousness   B. facade   C. communication   D. monotony
9. At the meeting someone suggested housing development should be _____ wage earners.
   A. oriented to   B. focused on   C. concentrated on   D. reached toward
10. The high-rise buildings in the city are in the form of _____, which adds no beauty to the city.
    A. identical   B. the same   C. monotony   D. identity

Reading Material A

City Country Fingers

People feel comfortable when they have access to the countryside, experience of open fields, and agriculture; access to wild plants and birds and animals. ① For this access, cities must have boundaries with the countryside near every point. ② At the same time, a city becomes good for life only when it contains a great density of interactions among people and work, and different ways of life. ③ For the sake if this interaction, the city must be continuous—not broken up. ④ In this pattern we shall try to bring these two facts to balance.

Let us begin with the fact that people living in cities need contact with true rural land to maintain their roots with the land that supports them. ⑤ A 1972 Gallop poll gives very strong evidence for this fact. ⑥ The poll asked the question: "If you could live anywhere, would you prefer a city, suburban area, small town, or farm?" and received the following answers from 1465 Americans:

City	13%
Suburb	13
Small town	32
Farm	23

And this dissatisfaction with cities is getting worse. In 1966, 22 percent said they preferred the city—in 1972, only six years later, this figure dropped to 13 percent.

It is easy to understand why city people long for contact with the countryside. Only 100 years ago 85 percent of the Americans lived on rural land; today 70 percent live in cities. Apparently we cannot live entirely within cities—at least the kinds of cities we have built so far—our need for contact with the countryside runs too deep, it is a biological necessity.

But it is becoming increasingly difficult for city dwellers to come into contact with rural life. In the San Francisco Bay Region 21 square miles of open space is lost each year. As cities get bigger the rural land is farther and farther away.

With the breakdown of contact between city dwellers and the countryside, the cities become prisons. Farm vacations, a year on the farm for city children, and retirement to the country for old people are replaced by expensive resorts, summer camps, and retirement villages. And for most, the only contact remaining is the weekend exodus from the city, choking the highways and the few organized recreation centers. ⑦ Many weekenders return to the city on Sunday night with their nerves more shattered than when they left.

If we wish to reestablish and maintain the proper connection between city and country, and yet maintain the density of urban interactions, it will be necessary to stretch out the urbanized area into the diagram below. Not only will the city be in the form of narrow fingers, but so will the farmlands adjacent to it.

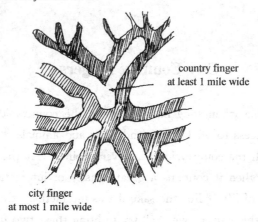

Fig. 5-1

The maximum width of the city fingers is determined by the maximum acceptable distance from the heart of the city to the countryside. We reckon that everyone should be within 10 minutes' walk of the countryside. This would set a maximum width of 1 mile for the city fingers.

The minimum for any farmland finger is determined by the minimum acceptable dimensions for typical working farms.③ Since 90 percent of all farms are still 500 acres or less and there is no respectable evidence that the giant farm is more efficient, these fingers of farmland need be no more than 1 mile wide.

The implementation of this pattern requires new policies of three different kinds. With respect to the farmland, there must be policies encouraging the reconstruction of small farms, farms that fit the one-mile bands of country land. Second, there must be policies which contain the cities' tendency to scatter in every direction. And third, the countryside must be truly public, so that people can establish contact with even those parts of the land that are under private cultivation.

Imagine how this one pattern would transform life in cities. Every city dweller would have access to the countryside; the open country would be a half-hour bicycle ride from downtown.

Keep interlocking fingers of farmland and urban land, even at the center of the metropolis. The urban fingers should never be more than 1 mile wide, while the farmland fingers should never be less than 1 mile wide.

Notes

①…when they have access to…open fields…
……当他们走进乡间，亲临旷野……
②为了接近乡村，城市的四周应与乡村接壤。
③…only when it contains a great…ways of life.

……只有当城市包容了人与人之间不同工作及生活方式之间频繁的相互联系和影响时……

④…not broke up. 为了达到这种相互联系和影响的目的，城市必需保持连续性而不被分割。

⑤…to maintain their roots with the land that supports them.

……使他们的根扎在养育他们的土地上。

⑥Gallop poll，Gallop 民意测验中心

⑦…the only contact…recreation centers.

……唯一剩下可接触到的是大批外出渡周末的人流，拥挤的高速公路和少数娱乐中心。

⑧农场指形条块面积的最小数值取决于具有代表性的、正在经营着的农场所能接受的最小面积。

Reading Material B

City Planning

City planning also called "town" or "urban" planning, is the art and science of the design, planning, and construction of cities and parts of cities. City planning principles can also be extended to include areas larger than cities, as in regional planning.① Persons who practice city planning are often called city planners or urban or town planning, though some prefer to be called simply planners.

City planning is an ancient calling, but as practiced today, it is a product of the 20th century.② Early in the century, planners were mostly privately sponsored, but this changed rapidly to sponsorship by local, municipal, or country governments.③ Early in the century, planners were mostly concerned with the major visual elements of cities, parks, boulevards, civic centers, and parkways.④ Today planners are concerned with the total fabric of cities, not only the physical aspects, now seen in three dimensions rather than two as before, but the economic, social, legal, and human aspects.⑤ Previously, planners devoted much attention to streets and squares, public buildings, docks and harbors, and railroads. Today they are still concerned with these factors but also with transportation of all kinds; buildings of all kinds, including housing; utility distribution; and all other aspects of urban life.⑥

In the past, most planning was performed by architects, engineers, and landscape architects. Today many planners come from those professions, but there are also planners trained as economists, sociologists, geographers, and so on, reflecting the attention given to factors other than the physical planning of urban areas.⑦

The work of planners may be divided into five major areas: preparing master plans, ordinances and regulations, and improvement programs for urban areas; preparing regional master plans for larger areas; planning of portions of urban areas, such as shopping centers, neighborhoods, and so on; planning for urban renewal, slum clearance and redeveloping older areas;

and planning new towns.⑧

To accomplish this work, planners generally follow a process that includes development of long-range goals and objectives; study and analysis of existing conditions, physical, economic, and social; study and analysis of the problems; preparation of master plans covering aspects such as land use, transportation, buildings, and other facilities; and pitting the master plans into effect, with the aid of zoning and subdivision regulations, codes, ordinances, and other means.

Planners make studies of many kinds, including projections of future employment patterns; population growth; movement of people, industries, and businesses into and out of areas; needs for transportation and utilities; and so on. They then translate these studies into reports and master plans that define the future needs and character of cities and demonstrate how the needs can be met and the character fulfilled in the best manner. They also make studies of portions of cities or specific problems and translate these into reports and plans to meet the needs or problems. Planners also are concerned with zoning and building codes, and with development and redevelopment that take place in cities.⑨ Regional planners are concerned with the same subjects as city planners, but perform their work for whole regions rather than single cities.

Planning offers careers to many types of people, since it involves social and economic planning, and the physical planning of cities, in a manner similar to the work of architects, landscape architects, and engineers. A great variety of functions are performed by planners, some by people who are essentially creative, others by those who are primarily studious, and still others by those who are active by nature. All must be interested in urban life and in the process of improving urban life and its setting, the cities.

Notes

①城市规划的原理也可以扩大到比城市更大的范围，类似于区域规划。
②城市规划是个古老的行业，但我们今天所从事的城市规划是20世纪的产物。
③本世纪初，规划师主要是从私人那里获得赞助，但这种赞助形式很快发生了变化，变成了由当地政府、市政府及国家机构向规划师提供赞助。
④civic centre 市政中心。
⑤今天，规划师考虑的是城市的整体结构，不仅仅是形体方面，即考虑的是立体空间而不是从前的平面，还要考虑经济、社会、法律和人性方面的问题。
⑥utility distribution 公共设施的分布。
⑦…reflect the attention…urban area.
　……表明人们已经注意到了城市环境规划以外的因素。

⑧规划师的工作可以分成五个主要方面：制定总图、条例和章程、城区改善方案；制定大面积的区域总图；规划市区的分段，如购物中心、住宅小区等；规划市区更新、贫民窟清除以及旧城改造；规划新城镇。
⑨zoning and building codes 区划规范和建筑规范。

UNIT SIX

Text   Shopping Center

[1]   A shopping center is a building, or group of buildings, in which a number of stores and service establishments are located, with provisions for automobile parking nearby. It is often in a suburban location but may be in a city or town.

[2]   **Big Stores**   Shopping centers are just like big stores which contain a collection of smaller stores. They therefore resemble the downtown shopping areas cities and towns have had for many years and which the developers of shopping centers have tried hard to replace.① Shopping centers are different from their downtown counterparts in some ways. First, there probably never would have been any shopping centers if there had not been a mass movement of people out of cities and towns to suburbia. And there might not have been any real suburbia if it had not been for the proliferation of automobiles. In a sense then, shopping centers had their genesis in the widespread use of automobiles and have been automobile-oriented ever since. In fact, the earliest centers had large parking areas which almost dominated the stores that face them. Later centers have turned inward, the stores facing spaces for people and turning their backs on automobiles. In many suburban areas, new "edge cities" have been formed as office space and hotels are built in close proximity to existing and enlarged shopping centers, often convenient to airports.② Thus the shopping mall has become the new pedestrian minicity and is at the center of major employment areas. Almost all urban growth now takes place in these peripheral cities. As population grows, shopping mall are built in conjunction with stations of subway systems and near major highways.

[3]   **Merchandising Principles**   Since shopping centers are essentially stores, they must be designed to sell goods effectively if they are to be successful. Like any store, a shopping center must arouse the interest of potential customers and lure them inside. Then customers must be attracted into the individual stores whose interests are served by selling products. Merchandising principles apply to both stores and shopping centers, but the latter must draw potential customers who arrive in automobiles as a rule rather than on foot as is often the case in downtown stores.

[4]   A shopping center contains individual stores, any of which may offer any combination of staples or demand goods, convenience products, and impulse or luxury items.③ In addition, the whole shopping center functions much like a large department store, with the individual stores acting like departments. Thus the merchandising of the entire shopping center is important, but once inside, the individual stores must also be merchandised. Customers must be able to move easily through the entire shopping center, must be attracted into various individual stores and then be lured through their interiors.

[5]   **Types**   The two major types of shopping centers are the neighborhood or community

center and the regional center. Neighborhood or community centers often contain only a few stores, usually including a supermarket and a drugstore and sometimes one or more branches of department stores. These centers serve limited marketing areas in cities, towns, or suburbia. Regional centers serve large marketing areas, sometimes drawing customers from many miles away. The keystones of these centers are department stores, of which there may be one to four or more in a single center.

[6] A regional center may contain stores of almost every possible kind, from small specialty shops, such as florists, candy stores, or bakeries, to service establishments, such as barber and beauty shops or banks, to large, complete department stores. Supermarkets are not usually found in regional shopping malls. In addition, regional centers may also have entertainment facilities, such as disco houses or bowling alleys. Many have dining facilities, such as restaurants, cafeterias, or food courts. Some have professional offices for doctors, dentists, and others; branch libraries; post offices; gasoline service stations; and almost every type of commercial operation imaginable.

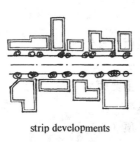

strip developments

Fig. 6-1

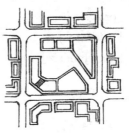

cluster development

Fig. 6-2

[7] **Master Plans** The major types of master plans for shopping centers include row or strip developments, in which stores are lined up along sidewalks with automobile parking often facing a street or highway, and cluster developments, in which the various elements containing stores are arranged around a pedestrian area in the middle, with parking around the perimeter of the cluster. ④ Cluster developments, usually called "shopping malls", have open spaces or enclosed malls in the middle between the stores. ⑤ Shopping centers may be one-story or two-story affairs, the most usual today and some have more than two stories. ⑥ Sometimes existing malls are enlarged with additional floors and new stores.

[8] One of the most important principles in the design of a shopping center with a mall is the design of the mall itself. It must be made into an attractive pedestrian area with appealing shops on the sides, their fronts facing inward toward the mall. Many malls have comfortable seating areas, shrubbery, flowers and trees, sculpture, fountains, and even elaborate recreational facilities.

[9] Another important aspect of shopping center design is provision for efficient automobile parking facilities and easy access into the center. Parking may be provided at ground level outside, on the roof, or in parking garages. For shopping centers, a great deal of space is required for parking, ranging from about 2.5 car spaces per 1 000 ft of leasable store area in a down-

town center to 6 or more car spaces per 1 000 ft in suburban centers.

[10]　　Because of the many types of stores and other establishments that may be included, the complexities of providing for buildings, for automobile traffic and parking, and for pedestrian traffic, shopping centers have become a sort of universal building type. They test the design abilities of architects who must somehow put all the pieces of the puzzle together so that the whole functions properly as well as all the various parts. Not all shopping malls succeed, often due to the difficulty of access and limited parking.

Words and Expressions

counterpart ['kauntəpɑːt]	n.	相对物；一对中之一
suburbia [sə'bəːbiə]	n.	（总称）都市的郊区，郊区居民
proliferation [prəulifə'reiʃn]	n.	激增，扩散
genesis ['dʒenisiːz]	n.	起源，发生
proximity * [prɔk'simiti]	n.	接（临）近
peripheral * [pə'rifərəl]	a.	周边的
merchandise ['məːtʃəndaiz]	v.	（美）经商，推销
lure [ljuə]	vt. & n.	诱惑，吸引
staple ['steipl]	n.	常用品，主要商品
impulse * ['impʌls]	n.	刺激；脉冲
keystone ['kiːstəun]	n.	关键；拱顶（心）石
florist ['flɔrist]	n.	花商
candy ['kændi]	n.	（美）糖果
bakery ['beikəri]	n.	面包烘房，面包店
establishment [is'tæbliʃmənt]	n.	企业，机关
beauty shop	n.	美容店
disco ['diskəu]	n.	迪士科舞厅
bowling alley	n.	保龄球场
cafeteria [kæfi'tiəriə]	n.	自助食堂
sidewalk ['saidwɔːk]	n.	人行道
perimeter [pə'rimitə]	n.	周边（长、围）
appealing [ə'piːliŋ]	a.	引人入胜的，动人的
shrubbery ['ʃrʌbəri]	n.	灌木丛（林）
sculpture ['skʌlptʃə]	n.	雕塑
fountain ['fauntin]	n.	喷泉，喷水池
recreational [rikri'eiʃənəl]	a.	休养的，娱乐的
leasable ['liːzəbl]	a.	可租借的

Notes

①在本句中，the downtown shopping areas 有两个限定性定语从句，一个是 cities and towns have had many years，另一个是由 which 引导的从句。

②形容词短语 often convenient to airports 在这里是作全句主语 new "edge cities" 的非限制性后置定语，被 as 引导的状语从句分隔。

③句中 demand goods, convenience products 作 staples 的同位语；而 luxury items 则是 impulse 的同位语。or 在此不表示选择。

④这个句子虽然较长，但结构排列很对称，全句的主要结构是 The major types of master plans for shopping centers include row or strip developments,... and cluster developments...

⑤mall 一词最初的含义是指"步行街"和专供散步的"林荫道"，但近年来在美国也常用来表示"购物中心"。在本句中，shopping mall ＝shopping center，而 enclosed mall 则意为"封闭的林荫道"。

⑥(1) affairs 在此表示购物中心的商业活动。

(2) the most usual today 修饰本句主语 shopping center，由于是补充性的说明，故而放在了较后的位置并用逗号隔开。

Exercises

Reading Comprehension

Ⅰ. Say whether the following statements are true (T) or false (F) according to the text, making use of the paragraph numbers.

1. The location of shopping centers may be in either urban areas or suburban areas, with the fact of being more often in urban ones. (Para. 1)　　　　　　　　　　　　　　( )

2. For many years, there has been a strong tendency for shopping centers to replace the downtown shopping areas though they bear close resembles. (Para. 2)　　( )

3. The emergence of shopping centers has something close to do with the widespread use of automobiles. (Para. 2)　　　　　　　　　　　　　　　　　　　　　　　( )

4. The most essential function of shopping centers is to draw as more automobiles as possible. (Para. 3)　　　　　　　　　　　　　　　　　　　　　　　　　　　( )

5. Community center and regional center are two major types of shopping centers. (Para. 5)　　　　　　　　　　　　　　　　　　　　　　　　　　　　　　　　　　( )

6. In a regional center, you can see several department stores, including at lest one supermarket. (Para. 5, Para. 6)　　　　　　　　　　　　　　　　　　　　　( )

7. Regional shopping centers may provide so wide a range of services that they include al-

most every type of commercial items you could imagine. (Para. 6)   ( )
8. Row or strip developments and cluster developments are the two major types of master plans for shopping centers. (Para. 7)   ( )
9. Efficient parking space and convenient passages into the center are one of the important principles to design shopping centers. (Para. 9)   ( )
10. It is usually not a difficult task for architects to design a shopping center, because they have the ability to put all the pieces of puzzle together. (Para. 10)   ( )

II. Organize the information concerning shopping centers and fill in the table with the concepts about the items. (Some have been done for you)

Items	Concepts
types of shopping center	1. community center 2.
location	1. 2. urbau arcas
types of master plan	1. 2.
principles in designing a center with a mall	1. 2. 3. easy access

III. Complete the following statements according to your understanding of the text.
1. The essential purpose of designing shopping centers is _____.
   A. to give automobiles an easy access into the center
   B. to supply citizens with entertainment facilities
   C. to sell goods
   D. to park cars
2. Shopping centers may be one-story or two-story affairs. Here "affairs" is referred to _____.
   A. business   B. floors   C. events   D. duties
3. _____ helped form new "edge cities".
   A. Mass movement of people out of cities to suburbia
   B. Office space and hotels close to shopping centers
   C. Airports
   D. New pedestrian minicity
4. Thus the merchandising of the entire shopping center is important, but once inside, the individual stores must also be merchandised. From this sentence we may learn _____.

A. the sales-volume（营业额）by the entire center is more important

B. the sales-volume by the individual stores is in fact more important

C. all the clerks are merchants whether they work for the entire center or for the individual stores

D. merchandising is the No. One affairs for both the entire center and for the individual stores.

5. Enclosed malls usually exist in _____.

   A. supermarket   B. department stores
   C. row developments   D. cluster developments

Vocabulary

I. Match the words in Column A with their corresponding definitions or descriptions in Column B

A	B
1. peripheral	a. demand goods
2. mall	b. suburbs in general
3. impulse	c. surrounding or of periphery
4. staple	d. shopping center; green street
5. suburbia	e. origin; beginning
6. cafeteria	f. provocative; impetus
7. genesis	g. a restaurant where diners serve themselves

II. Complete the following sentences with the words given below, changing the forms where necessary.

proximity	beauty shop	sidewalk
fountain	proliferation	keystone
perimeter	establishment	sculpture

1. The _____ in front of the hotel attracted many people on the street not only because they were appealing landscapes, but also it was too hot on that day.

2. Currently young people are in favor of having their hair cut in _____ while the aged prefer to go to barbers.

3. In order to avoid traffic accidents, grids between _____ and the main streets are often seen in big cities.

4. An overhead bridge was newly built in close _____ to the subway station in convenience for the pedestrian traffic.

5. Local zoning laws often serve as the _____ in urban planning.

6. _____ here and there in urban areas not only beautify the environment, but provide

the chance for people to enjoy the national culture.

7. As a showcase of a nation's civilization, service _____ should not only seek economic effects, but strive for spiritual civilization.

Reading Material A

Wed of Shopping①

Large parts of towns have insufficient services. New shops which could provide these services often locate near the other shops and major centers, instead of locating themselves where they are needed. In an ideal town, where the shops are seen as part of the society's necessities and not merely as a way of making profit for the shopping chains, the shops would be much more widely and more homogeneously distributed than they are today.②

It is also true that many small shops are unstable. Two-thirds of the small shops that people open go out of business within a year. Obviously, the community is not well served by unstable businesses, and once again, their economic instability is largely linked to mistakes of location.

To guarantee that shops are stable, as well as distributed to meet community needs, each new shop must be placed where it will fill a gap among the other shops offering a roughly similar service and also be assured that it will get the threshold of customers which it needs in order to survive.③ We shall now try to express this principle in precise terms.

The characteristics of a stable system of shops is rather well known. It relies, essentially, on the idea that each unit of shopping has a certain catch basin—the population which it needs in order to survive.④ The units of any given type and size will therefore be stable if they are evenly distributed, each one at the center of a catch basin large enough to support it.

The reason that shops and shopping centers do not always, automatically, distribute themselves according to their appropriate catch basin is easily explained by the situation known as Hotelling's problem.⑤ Imagine a beach in summer time—and, somewhere along the beach, an ice-cream seller. Suppose now, that you are also an ice—cream seller. You arrive on the beach. Where should you place yourself in relation to the first ice-cream seller? There are two possible solutions.

In the first case, you essentially decide to split the beach with the other ice-cream seller. You take half the beach, and leave him half the beach. In this case, you place yourself as far away from him as you can, in a position where half the people on the beach are nearer to you than to him.

In the second case, you place yourself right next to him. You decide, in short, to try and compete with him—and place yourself in such a way as to command the whole beach, not half of it.

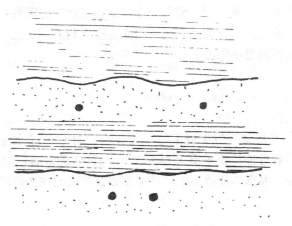

Two approaches to the ice-cream problems

Fig. 6-3

Every time a shop, or shopping center opens, it faces a similar choice. It can either locate in a new area where there are no other competing businesses, or it can place itself exactly where all the other businesses are already in the hope of attracting customers away from each other.

The trouble is, very simple, that people tend to choose the second of these two alternatives, because it seem, on the surface, to be safer. In fact, however, the first of the two choices is both better and safer. It is better for the customers, who then have stores to serve them closer to their homes and work places than they do now. And it is safer for the shopkeepers themselves since—in spite of appearance—their stores are much more likely to survive when they stand, without competition, in the middle of a catch basin which needs their services.

It is necessary that each new shop follow the following three-step procedure when it chooses a location:

1. Identify all other shops which offer the service you are interested in, locate them on the map.
2. Identify and map the location of potential consumers. Wherever possible indicate the density or total number of potential consumers in any given area.
3. Look for the biggest gap in the existing web of shops in those areas where there are potential consumers.

Thus, new shops can choose best locations for themselves and form a reasonable shopping web.

Notes

①Web of Shopping——商业网
②在一个理想的城市中，商店被看作是社会需要的一部分，而不仅仅是作为给连锁商店获取利润的一种方式，因而商店会比现在的分布更加广泛和均匀。

③为了保证商店的稳定性，同时为了使其分布能够满足社会的需要，每个新商店应当开设在能够填补服务性质大同小异的其它商店之间的空白地方。而且，为了生存，应当保证它所需要的顾客人数的最小限度。

④catch basin：范围，领域。

⑤…the situation known as Hotelling's problem.

……叫做"投宿问题"的情况。

Hotelling's problem 是经济领域中使用的一个术语，它指人们在投宿饭店时，不考虑实际工作需要与方便而盲目选择繁华市区（downtown area）的饭店，造成那里的饭店拥挤，从而带来了房价昂贵、办事不便等弊端。这里用来说明人们在选择商店地址时同样的错误心理。

Reading Material B

Green Streets

In a typical low density American suburb, more than 50 percent of the land is covered with concrete or asphalt paving. In some areas, it is more than 65 per cent.

This concrete and asphalt have a terrible effect on the local environment. They destroy the microclimate; they do nothing useful with the solar energy that falls on them; they are unpleasant to walk on; there is nowhere to sit; nowhere for children to play; the natural drainage of the ground is devastated; animals and plants can hardly survive.

The fact is that asphalt and concrete are only suitable for use on high speed roads. They are unsuitable, and quite unnecessary, on local roads, where a few cars are moving in and out. When local roads are paved, wide and smooth, like major roads, drivers are encouraged to travel past our houses at 35 or 40 miles per hour. What is needed, instead, on local roads is a grassy surface that is adapted to the primary uses of the common land between the buildings, with just enough hard paving to cope with the few cars that do go on it.

The best solution is a field of grass, with paving stones set into it. This arrangement provides for animals and children and makes the street a focal point for the neighborhood. On hot summer days the air over the grass surface is 10 to 14 degrees cooler than the air over an asphalt road. And the cars are woven into this scheme, but they do not dominate it.①

Of course, such a scheme raises immediately the question of parking. How shall it be organized? It is possible to arrange for parking on green streets, so long as it is parking for residents and their guests, only. When overflow parking from shopping streets and work communities sprawls onto streets that were intended to be quiet neighborhoods, the character of the neighborhood is drastically altered.② The residents generally resent this situation. Often it means they cannot park in front of their own homes. The neighborhood becomes a parking lot for strangers who care nothing about it, who simply store their cars there.

The green street will only work if it is based on the principle that the street need not, and should not, provide for more parking than its people need. Parking for visitors can be in small parking lots at the ends of the street; parking for people in the individual houses and workshops can either be in the same parking lots or in the driveways of the buildings.

This does not imply that commercial activities, shops, and businesses should be excluded from residential areas. In fact, it is extremely important to build such functions into neighborhoods. The point is, however, that businesses cannot assume when they move into a neighborhood that they have the right to a huge amount of free parking.③ They must pay for their parking; and they must pay for it in a way which is consistent with the environmental needs of the neighborhood.

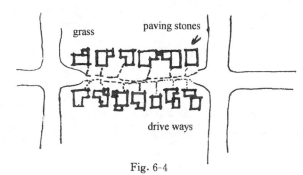

Fig. 6-4

Fruit trees and flowers will make the street more beautiful and the paving stones which form the beds for cars to drive on, can themselves be laid with cracks between them and with grass and moss and flowers in the cracks between the stones.④ When a road is a green street, it is so pleasant that it naturally tends to attract activity to it. In this case, the paths and the green street are a common land. However, even when the street is green, it may be pleasant to put in occasional very small lanes, a few feet wide, at right angles to the green streets.

Therefore we suggest:

On local roads, closed to through traffic, plant grass all over the road and set occasional paving stones into the grass to form a surface for the wheels of those cars that need access to the street. Make no distinction between street and sidewalk. Where houses open off the street, put in more paving stones or gravel to let cars turn onto their own land.⑤

Notes

①车辆在这种布局里蜿蜒而行，但决不会处于支配地位。
②但是，当商业街和工作区所停放的车辆由于过多而延伸到人们希望成为宁静的街区的绿色道路上时，街区的特征就会发生根本的变化。
③然而，关键在于当它们迁入街区后，不能呈现出有权大量自由驻车的现象。
④果树和花卉会使得街道更加美观；那些用作车辆行驶路基的铺石本身在铺砌时就留有缝隙，可生长青草、苔藓和鲜花。

⑤在房门临街的地方，多铺些石头或鹅卵石，以便车辆拐向自己的房前。

严格讲，open off 是指"垂直通向……"；their own land 是指住户在自家门口用较多的铺石铺筑成的场地，以作自己调车或停车之用。

UNIT SEVEN

Text   Roof Layout

[1]   What kind of roof plan is organically related to the nature of your building?

[2]   We know that the majority of spaces in an organic building will have roughly—not necessarily perfectly—straight walls because it is only then that the space on both sides of the walls can be positive, or convex in shape.①

[3]   And we know that the majority of the angles in the building will be roughly—again not exactly—right angles, that is, in the general range of 80 to 100 degrees.

[4]   We know, therefore, that the class of natural plans may contain a variety of shapes like half circles, octagons, and so on—but that for the most part, it will be made of very rough, sloppy rectangles.②

[5]   We also know that entire wings should be under one roof whenever possible and that the building is to be roofed with a mixture of flat roofs and sloping or domical roofs, with the accent on those which are not flat.

[6]   The problem of defining a roof layout is that given an arbitrary plan of the type described above, how can we fit to it an arrangement of roofs which conforms to the cascade of roofs and sheltering roof and roof gardens③?

[7]   Before explaining the procedure for laying out roofs in detail, we underline five assumptions which provide the basis for the procedure.

[8]   1. The "pitched" roofs may actually be pitched, or they may be vaults with a curved pitch, or barrel vaults. The general procedure, in all three cases, is the same. (For curved vaults, define slope as height-to-width ratio.)

[9]   2. Assume that all roofs in the building, which are not flat, have roughly the same slope. For a given climate and roof construction, one slope is usually best; and this greatly simplifies construction.

[10]   3. Since all roofs have the same slope, the roofs which cover the widest wings and/or rooms will have the highest peaks; those covering smaller wings and rooms will be relatively lower. This is consistent with main building, cascade of roofs, and ceiling height variety.

[11]   4. Any place where the building helps to enclose an outdoor room or courtyard needs an even eaves line so that it has the space of a "room".④ An irregular roof line, with gable ends, will usually destroy the space of a small courtyard. It is necessary, therefore, that roofs be hipped in these positions to make the roof edge horizontal.

[12]   5. In all other positions, leave the ends of buildings and wings as gable ends.

[13]   We shall now discuss the rules for roofing a building by using an example of a house designed by a layman. This building plan is shown below. It is a single-story house and it contains no roof gardens or balconies.

a version of roof layout

Fig. 7-1

[14]　We first identify the largest rectangular cluster of rooms and roof it with a peaked roof, the ridge line of which runs the long direction:

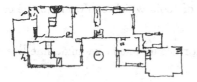

Fig. 7-2　　　　　　　　　　　　Fig. 7-3

[15]　Then we do the same with smaller clusters, until all the major spaces are roofed.

[16]　Then we roof remaining small rooms, alcoves, and thick walls with shed roofs sloping outward. These roofs should spring from the base of the main roofs to help relieve them of outward thrusts; their outside walls should be as low as possible.

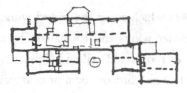 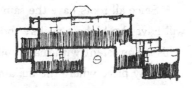

Fig. 7-4　　　　　　　　　　　　Fig. 7-5

[17]　Finally, we identify the outdoor spaces (shown as A, B, and C), and hip the roofs around them to preserve a more continuous eaves line around the spaces.

[18]　We shall now discuss a slightly more complicated example, a two-story building. We begin with the top story, roofing the entire master bedroom and bath under one peaked roof with the ridge running lengthwise.

[19]　Next we move to the lower story, roofing the children's wing under a flat roof to form a roof garden for the master bedroom, and the larger living room under a pitched roof, again with the ridge running lengthwise.⑤ Then we bring the roof over the master bedroom down over the interior loft.

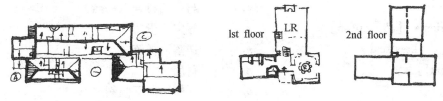

Fig. 7-6　　　　　　　　　　　　　　Fig. 7-7

[20]　Finally, we smooth the living room roof ridge line into the side of the roof over the loft. This completes the roof layout.

[21]　It is very helpful, when you are laying out roofs, to remember the structural principle outlined in Cascade of Roofs. When you have finished, the overall arrangement of the roofs should form a self-buttressing cascade in which each lower roof helps to take up the horizontal thrust generated by the higher roofs—and the overall section of the roofs tends toward a rough upside down catenary.

[22]　We may, therefore, conclude the procedure for laying out roofs as four points:

1. Arrange the roofs so that each distinct roof corresponds to an identifiable social entity in the building or building complex. 2. Place the largest roof—those which are highest and have the largest span—over the largest and most important and most communal spaces; 3. build the lesser roofs off these largest and highest roofs; 4. and build the smallest roofs of all off these lesser roofs, in the form of half—vaults and sheds over alcoves and thick walls.

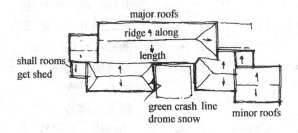

Fig. 7-8

New Words and Expressions

organically [ˌɔːˈgænikəli]	ad.	有机地，有组织地
positive [ˈpɔsətiv]	a.	实际（在）的；肯定的
convex * [ˌkɔnˈveks]	a.	凸的，凸面的
octagon [ˈɔktəgən]	n.	八边形

sloppy ['slɔpi]		a.	不整齐的，不系统的
wing [wiŋ]		n.	厢房，侧厅，配楼
domical ['dəumikəl]		a.	圆屋顶的，穹顶的
accent ['æksənt]		n.	重点，强调
conform to		v.	与…相符合（一致）
assumption * [ə'sʌmpʃən]		n.	假定，设想
cascade * [kæs'keid]		n.	迭落，梯流
pitch [pitʃ]		n.	斜度
		v.	（使）向下倾斜
vault [vɔ:lt]		n.	穹顶，拱顶
consistent [kən'sistənt]		a.	(with)（和…）…一致（协调）
eaves [i:vs]		n. (pl)	屋檐
gable ['geibəl]		n.	山（形）墙，三角墙
irregular [i'regjulə]		a.	不整齐的，不规则的
hip [hip]		n.	屋脊，斜（屋）脊
		v.	给屋顶造屋脊
layman ['leimən]		n.	门外汉，外行
balcony ['bælkəni]		n.	阳台
rectangular * [rek'tæŋgjulə]		a.	长方形的
ridge [ridʒ]		n.	屋脊
		v.	装屋脊
alcove ['ælkəuv]		n.	耳房，凹室
shed roof			单坡屋顶
spring from			升起；由……产生
lengthwise ['leŋθwaiz]		ad.	沿长的方向，纵长地
loft [lɔft]		n.	阁楼，顶楼
self-buttress [self'bʌtris]			自扶墙；拱墙
take up			消除；吸收
upside down			颠倒，倒转
catenary [kə'tinəri]		n.	悬垂线，悬曲线
building complex			群体建筑
entity ['entiti]		n.	实体；统一体
communal ['kɔmjunəl]		a.	公共（用）的；社区的

Notes

①破折号间的 not necessarily perfectly 是插入成分。
②the class of natural plans 此处 natural 意为"通常的，普遍的"，与 usual，ordinary 等意。
③cascade of roofs（迭落式屋顶）和 roof garden（屋顶花园）的含义及其要求详见本单元

Reading Material A 和 B；而 sheltering roofs（遮蔽型屋顶）的主要含义是指屋顶不仅遮盖房体，而且较多地延伸房体之外，对部分室外空间也形成遮蔽，一般要求该屋顶坡度较大。

④…to enclose an outdoor room or courtyard…room. 这里指空间，而句中引号里的 room 则仍指房间。

⑤分词短语 roofing the children's wing…and the larger living room… lengthwise，在这里对先行词 lower story 起了非限定性的修饰作用，表明与低层屋顶有关的情况。其中 again with the ridge running lengthwise. 是带有复合宾语的介词短语，作分词补语的状语，起着补充说明的作用。

Exercises

Reading Comprehension

Ⅰ. Say whether the following statements are true (T) or false (F) according to the text, making use of the paragraph numbers.

1. The majority of spaces in an organic building must have perfectly straight wall, and most of their angles must be exact right angles. (Para. 2) ( )
2. Although roofs may be of various shapes, the more part of them should be roughly rectangular. (Para. 3) ( )
3. As for the entire building, we prefer to adopt a combination of flat roofs with sloping roofs and domical roofs. (Para. 4) ( )
4. Vaults with a curved pitch is one of the forms of pitches roofs. (Para. 8) ( )
5. To be convenient to construction, all roofs in a building had better have roughly the same slope. (Para. 9) ( )
6. An irregular roof line, with gable ends helps to form a good room-like outdoor enclosure. (Para. 11) ( )
7. The house designed by laymen usually have no roof gardens and balconies. (Para. 13) ( )
8. In order to help relieve the main roofs of outward thrusts, the roofs of the remaining small rooms should go up from the base of the main roofs and their outside wall should be as low as possible. (Para. 16) ( )

Ⅱ. Fill in the following table with the information given in the text, with each item having one done for you.

　　Shapes, Types and Arrangement of Roofs.

Shapes	rectangles		
Types			domical roofs
Arrangements		sheltering roofs	

Vocabulary

I. Complete the following sentences with words or expressions given below, changing the forms where necessary.

sloppy	catenary	communal	hip
lengthwise	simplify	ridge	pitch
relieve…of		conform to	

1. The arrangement of roofs of this building _____ cascade of roofs.
2. The rain water would not stop on the roof of this house, because the roof _____ sharply.
3. The government is landing in a financial trouble, in order to cut down the governmental expenses it is going to _____ its administrative structure.
4. Speaking of roof layout, Professor Smith emphasized that sloping roofs should _____ in a horizontal direction.
5. You'd better _____ your wife _____ the heavy burden of the house work.
6. The students' apartment building on campus all run _____, hence the paths around them all look straight.
7. The span of a suspension bridge hangs from _____ cables instead of resting on posts.
8. It is essential to leave a _____ open space for every residential neighborhood.

II. Match the words or expressions in Column A with their corresponding definitions or description in Column B.

            A   B

1. thrust
2. building complex
3. wing
4. eaves line
5. vault

a. part of a building which stretches out from the main part to one side
b. arched roof
c. over hanging edges of a sloping foof
d. forceful pressure from one object onto another
e. something that has real existence

6. entity   f. a building consisting of a number of closely attached parts or a group of building built separately but closely related

Reading Material A

Cascade of Roofs

  Few building will be structurally and socially intact, unless the floors step down toward the ends of wings, and unless the roof, accordingly, forms a cascade. ①

  This is a strange pattern. Several problems, from entirely different spheres, point in the same direction. But there is no obvious common bond which binds these different problems to one another. It shows we have not succeeded in seizing the single kernel which forms the pivot of the pattern. ②

  Let us observe, first, that many beautiful buildings have the form of a cascade: a tumbling arrangement of wings and lower wings and smaller rooms and sheds, often with a single highest center. Hagia Sophia, the Norwegian stave churches, and Palladio's villas are imposing and magnificent examples. ③ Simple houses, small informal building complexes, and even clusters of mud huts are more modest ones.

  What is it that makes the cascading character of these buildings so sound and so appropriate?

  First of all, there is a social meaning in this form. The largest gathering places with the highest ceilings are in the middle because they are the social centers of activities; smaller groups of people, individual rooms, and alcoves fall naturally around the edges. ④

  Second, there is a structural meaning in the form. Buildings tend to be of materials that are strong in compression. Compressive strength is cheaper then tensile strength or strength in bending. Any building which stands in pure compression will tend toward the overall outline of an inverted catenary. ⑤ When a building does take this form, each outlying space acts to buttress the higher spaces. The building is stable in just the same way that a pile of earth, which has assumed the line of least resistance, is also stable. ⑥

  And third, there is a practical consideration. Wherever roof gardens occur, they should not be over the top floor, but always on the same level as the rooms they serve. This means, naturally, that the building tends to get lower toward the edges since the roof gardens step down from the top toward the outer edge of the ground floor.

  Why do these three apparently different problems lead to the same pattern? We don't know. But we suspect that there is some deeper essence behind the apparent coincidence. We leave the pattern intact in the hope that someone else will understand its meaning.

  Finally, a note on the application of the pattern. One must take care, in laying out large

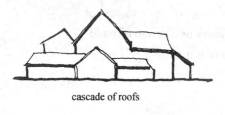

cascade of roofs

Fig. 7-9

buildings, to make the cascade compatible with wings of light. If you conceive of the cascade as pyramidal and the building is large, the middle section of the building will be cut off from daylight. Instead, the proper synthesis of cascade and wings of light will generate a building that tumbles down along relatively narrow wings, the wings turning corners and becoming lower where they will.⑦

Therefore, we should visualize the whole building, or building complex, as a system of roofs. Place the largest, highest, and widest roofs over those parts of the building which are most significant: when you come to lay the roofs out in detail, you will be able to make all lesser roofs cascade off these large roofs and form a stable self-buttressing system, which is congruent with the hierarchy of social spaces underneath the roofs.⑧

Notes

①除非建筑物的楼层向其两翼逐步降低,而它们的屋顶也相应地形成高低不一的迭落层次,否则它们很少能在其结构和社会功能上是完善的。

②这表明我们尚未把握住形成这种布局的关键要领。

③挪威的圣索菲亚阶式教堂和帕拉弟奥别墅是宏伟的迭落式布局的范例。

④... smaller groups of people, individual rooms...

由有于本句讲的是建筑的一些室内空间,所以 smaller groups of people 在此应理解为"活动人数较少的厅室"。

⑤任何一个处于单纯受压状态的建筑物都会趋于呈现出倒弦曲线形的总剖面。

⑥一堆土,由于呈现出最小抗力外形因而是稳固的。上述建筑物因为其轮廓像一堆土,因而也是稳固的。

本句 line 一词作"外形"解。

⑦相反,屋顶的迭落与侧部的采光之间合理地结合将形成一个沿着相对窄的侧立面逐层下降的建筑物,而侧立部分则可在适当的地方作转角和降低处理。

⑧... you will be able to make all lesser roofs off these large roofs and form a stable self-buttressing system...

……你就能使所有次要的屋顶与大型屋顶区分开,并形成一个稳固的自撑系统。

Reading Material B

Roof Garden

A vast part of the earth's surface, in a town, consists of roofs. Couple this with the fact that the total area of a town which can be exposed to the sun is finite, and you will realize that it is natural, and indeed essential, to make roofs which take advantage of the sun and air. ①

However, we know that the flat shape is quite unnatural for roofs from psychological, structural, and climatic point of view. It is therefore sensible to use a flat roof only where the roof will actually become a garden or an outdoor room; to make as many of these "useful" roofs as possible; but to make all other roofs, which cannot be used, the sloping, vaulted, shell-like structures specified by sheltering roof and roof vault. ②

Here is a rule of thumb: if possible, make at least one small roof garden in every building, more if you are sure people will actually use them. ③ Make the remaining roofs steep roofs. The roof gardens which work are almost always at the same level as some indoor rooms. This means that at least some part of the building's roofs will always be steep. We shall expect, then, that this pattern will generate a roof landscape in which roof gardens and steep roofs are mixed in almost every building.

We now consider the flat roof, briefly, on its own terms. ④ Flat roof gardens have always been prevalent in dry, warm climates, where they can be made into livable environments. In the dense parts of towns in Mediterranean climates, nearly every roof is habitable: they are full of green, private screens, with lovely views, places to cook out and eat and sleep. And even in temperate climates they are beautiful. They can be designed as rooms without ceilings, places that are protected from the wind, but open to the sky.

However, the flat roofs that have become architectural fads during the last 40 years are quite another matter. ⑤ Gray gravel covered asphalt structures, these flat roofs are very rarely useful places; they are not gardens. And taken as a whole, they do not meet the psychological requirements. To make the flat parts of roofs truly useful, and compatible with the need for sloping roofs, it seems necessary to build flat roof gardens off the indoor parts of the buildings. ⑥ In other words, do not make them the highest part of the roof; let the highest parts of the roof slope; and make it possible to walk out to the roof garden from an interior room, without climbing special stairs. We have found that roof gardens that have this relationship are used far more intensely than those rooftops which must be reached by climbing stairs. The explanation is obvious: it is far more comfortable to walk straight out onto a roof and feel the comfort of part of the building behind and to one side of you, than it is to climb up to a place you cannot see. ⑦

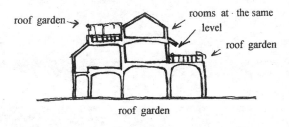

Fig. 7-10

It is, therefore, suggested to try to make parts of almost every roof system usable as roof gardens. Make these parts flat, perhaps terraced for planting, with places to sit and sleep, private places. Place the roof gardens at various stories, and always make it possible to walk directly out onto the roof garden from some lived-in part of the building.

Notes

① 城市中能暴露在阳光中的总面积非常有限,把这个事实与上述现象联想起来,你就会认识到修建可以充分利用阳光、空气的屋顶是十分自然而又重要的了。

② …but to make all other roofs, which cannot be used, the sloping, vaulted, shell-like structures specified by sheltering roof and roof vault.

……但是,将所有其它不能利用的屋顶,修筑成符合遮蔽形屋顶、穹顶规格的坡式、拱式和壳式结构。

③ more if = make more roof gardens if

④ 根据平屋顶自身的条件,我们来简单地研究一下这种屋顶。

⑤ 但是,以往40年间形成建筑风尚的那种平屋顶则是另外一码事。

⑥ …to build flat roof gardens off the indoor parts of the buildings.

……在室外修建平屋顶花园。

off the indoor parts = in the outdoor places.

⑦ 原因很清楚:直接从室内走到屋顶平台上,领受建筑在你身后和身旁所提供的逸乐总比爬上一处在下边看不着的地方舒服得多。

UNIT EIGHT

Text Lighting

One needs light to see by, but sometimes there is more truth to be found in the dark.

[1]　　Lighting is directly affective to architecture, since it makes the forms visible to the viewer. It allows one to perceive mass, height, volume, texture, color, and ornament. In short, it is the mechanical medium by which architecture communicates. What it communicates is another story, which has already been dealt with in some depth. At the moment we are concerned with the process.

[2]　　**Illumination**　Too much, and you squint and reach for your sunglasses. Too little and you feel a headache coming on as you strain to see.① Naturally, the right degree of illumination for any occasion will vary according to what the seeing task is to be. If you are searching for a particular brand of anchovies in a supermarket you will want a very high level indeed, so that you can see the labels. But if you are planning a romantic dinner, to be followed perhaps by a marriage proposal, it would seem more likely that you want some persuasive dimness, relieved by the gentle glow of a candle.② In the theater you will want a combination: only enough light in the auditorium to find your seat, plenty of light on stage to see the performance—except for the "mood" scenes, in which the director wants to show you only a very tiny and carefully measured bit of action.

[3]　　Illumination is measured in foot-candles, a foot-candle being the light thrown by one candle on a surface everywhere one foot away.③ More colloquially, it is often the source of light that is measured, rather than the amount. So the power to be used is specified as, for instance, 600 watts over the meat counter, 200 watts over the vegetables, and 40 watts over the cosmetics display.

[4]　　**Distribution**　The light level of an entire room, hall, gallery, terminal, or what you have is called the general lighting. It needs to be high enough to allow you to move about comfortably—find your table in the restaurant, your counter in the shop, your ticket booth at the terminal, and so on. For specific tasks, such as reading the menu, filling out a deposit slip, or fixing your mascara, you need a higher level in a more concentrated area. This, then, is called local lighting.

[5]　　Exactly as with sound, the reflective surfaces play a major role.④ A white, smooth, shiny ceiling will greatly increase the effectiveness of general lighting, while a darker shade, or a rough texture—which casts many tiny shadows—will keep local light from spreading too far, even when the immediate intensity is high.

[6]　　**Glare**　Generally, glare is excessively bright light, such as sunlight on snow, or the like. In addition, the retina of the eye contains two kinds of light-sensitive nerve ends—one

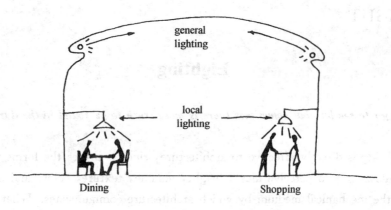

Fig. 8-1

kind for bright light and color, the other for dimness. When one group is working the other is turned off, not functioning. That is why, coming into a movie theater from the bright outside, you are temporarily unable to see the aisles, seats, or people. There is not enough light for your "brights," while your "dims" take a while to get to work. Similarly, when you come out of the theater, assuming it is still daytime, the street seems excessively bright, and you squint against the light.

[7] The critical point in all this, worth repeating, is that only one set of light receptors works at a time. When you try to make them work together you experience an acute sense of discomfort which you may legitimately name glare. A single bare bulb in a dim room glares. A candle in a black box glares. The headlights of an approaching car when you are driving at night glare. In short, any lighting contrast severe enough to stimulate both sets of receptors at once will be felt as glare.⑤

[8] **Ambiance** Again we find a parallel with acoustics. Some settings seem to cry out for the proper lighting and to suffer acutely without it.⑥ Imagine, if you can, a cathedral interior ablaze with motion picture floodlights. Or a museum in which the overhead lights shine on the visitors in stead of the paintings. If you are from California, or have been there, you may have seen gardens where every bush has its own colored—light—blue, amber yellow—with bright green ones up in the tree branches.

[9] On the plus side, genuine showmanship is often encountered in architectural lighting, particularly in the use of exterior flood-lighting at night.⑦ This last, which has only recently begun to be used widely, has dramatically changed our cityscapes. Also on the plus side is the growing recognition on the part of architects that the shapes of their buildings, especially when the walls consist so widely of glass, are defined to a considerable extent by the lighted interiors.⑧ Midtown Manhattan, for instance, seen at dusk on a winter day, when the office lights are going on, is a wonderland of jeweled beauty. The architect who fails to use the versatile tool of lighting has very severely limited his possible effects, while the one who uses it sensitively adds immeasurably to the joy of his creativity.

New Words and Expressions

illumination * [i,lju:mi'neiʃən]	n.	照明，照（明）度
squint [skwint]	vi.	斜着眼看，眯眼看
persuasive [pə'sweisiv]	a.	劝诱的，有说服力的
auditorium [ɔdi'tɔ:riəm]	n.	音乐厅，礼堂
foot-candle	n.	英尺烛光
colloquially [kə'ləukwiəli]	ad.	用通俗口语地
booth [bu:ð]	n.	小室（房），小亭
watt * [wɔt]	n.	瓦（电功率单位）
cosmetic [kɔz'metik]	n.	化装品
terminal ['tə:minl]	n.	终点（站），终端
slip [slip]	n.	纸条，板条
deposit slip	n.	存款单
mascara [mæs'kɑ:rə]	n.	染眉毛（或睫毛）油
texture * ['tekstʃə]	n.	纹理，结构
cast shadow		投影
glare [glɛə]	n.	眩光，刺目的强光
	v.	发强烈的光，发眩光
retina ['retinə]	n.	视网膜
dimness ['dimnəs]	n.	昏暗
cone [kəun]	n.	圆锥，锥体
receptor [ri'septə]	n.	感（接）受器
acute * [ə'kju:t]	a.	尖锐的，敏锐的
headlight ['hedlait]	n.	（汽车等的）前灯；桅灯
legitimately [li'dʒitimitli]	ad.	合法地，合理地
ambiance ['æmbiəns]	n.	气氛，环境
acoustics * [ə'ku:stiks]	n.	（礼堂、剧院等的）音响装置；音响效果
ablaze [ə'bleiz]	a.	闪耀
flood light	n.	泛光灯，聚光灯
amber ['æmbə]	n.	琥珀，琥珀色
cityscape ['sitiskeip]	n.	城市景观
versatile * ['və:sətail]	a.	多方面的，多才多艺的
wonderland [wʌndəlænd]	n.	奇境
showmanship ['ʃəumenʃip]	n.	招揽生意，吸引公众注意之技巧
immeasurably [i'meʒərəbli]	ad.	无法计量地；无边无际地

Notes

① "Too much" 意为 "with too much illumination," 后文的 "too little" 省去同样部分;"coming on" 意为 "starting", 这里作宾语 a headache 的补语。

② 动词不定式短语 to be followed perhaps by a marriage proposal 此处做前面从句的状语, 表示目的。

③ foot-candle 英尺烛光系光照单位, 光照强度更常用光通量单位 "流明"(lumen)表示, 一流明＝一英尺烛光。

④ 这是一个省略了许多成分的含有比较状语从句的句子, 原句应为 The reflective surfaces play a major role with light exactly the same as the reflective surfaces play a major role with sound.

⑤ 句中形容词短语 severe enough to stimulate both sets of receptors at once 作主语 any lighting contrast 的后置定语, 而 as glare 则是主语的补语。

⑥ Cry out for 意为 "迫切需要"、"急需"。e. g. It has not rained for two weeks and the garden is crying for it 两个星期没下雨了, 花园急需雨水。

⑦ on the plus side＝on the positive side, 此处意为: "此外"、"另一方面"。

⑧ 本句系例装句, 主语是 recognition, 后边由 that 引导的从句是主语的同位语从句。

Exercises

Reading Comprehension

I. Identify the main ideas for each paragraph by matching the following statements with their appropriate paragraph numbers.

1. Lighting is the mechanical medium by which the forms of architecture can be visible. (1, 2, 3, 4)
2. A successful architect must be aware of the fact that architectural lighting can greatly change the look of cityscape, even affect commercial effects. (6, 7, 8, 9)
3. The proper degree of illumination in different cases. (1, 2, 3, 4)
4. Architectural environments require proper lighting. (6, 7, 8, 9)
5. The unit of illumination. (3, 4, 5, 6)
6. The reasons why you have "glare". (4, 5, 6, 7, 8)
7. General lighting and local lighting. (4, 5, 6, 7)
8. The reflective surfaces play an important role in lighting. (2, 3, 4, 5)

II. Choose the best answer according to the text

1. "Sometimes there is more truth to be found in the dark" may probably mean _____.
   A. you can think of more truth of lighting when it gets dark.

B. the darker it is, the quicker your thought becomes.

C. more truth of lighting can be easily found at night because nobody would disturb you.

D. your mind may be easily concentrate and work more effectively when the surroundings are dark.

2. According to "it is the mechanical medium by which architecture communi-cates", which of the following is true?

   A. Architecture can communicate by means of mechanical tools.

   B. By means of lighting architecture possesses the function as communications.

   C. Mechanical medium is something like advertisement.

   D. Architecture can find expressions for itself by means of lighting.

3. The type of lighting distribution is classified as _____.

   A. high level and low level.

   B. bright light and dim light.

   C. general lighting and local lighting.

   D. ordinary light and special light.

4. In Para. 5, "... even when the immediate intensity is high.", "immediate" here means _____.

   A. nearest   B. at once   c. quickest   D. middle

5. From the text we know that _____ would cause "glare".

   A. looking at strong light such as sunlight on snow

   B. coming out of a theater in daytime into the bright outside

   C. facing the headlights of an approaching car at night

   D. All above

6. In Para. 8, the author mentions the colored-lights in gardens of California to _____.

   A. show his love for California

   B. praise the colored-lights of California

   C. show ambiance of lighting in one case

   D. show a model of standardized cityscape

7. "genuine showmanship is often encountered in architectural lighting" is closest in meaning with _____.

   A. genuine showmanship is often expressed by architectural lighting

   B. genuine showmanship often meets architectural lighting

   C. genuine showmanship often has difficulties in architectural lighting

   D. architectural lighting depends on one's genuine showmanship

8. An architect without a sense of lighting _____.

   A. is a genuine architect

   B. has severely limited his possible professional effects

   C. adds greatly to the joy of his creativity

   D. fails to do everything in his work

Vocabulary

Ⅰ. Complete the following sentences with the words given blow, changing the form where necessary:

dimness	texture	booth	wonderland
ablaze	cityscape	cast shadow	versatile

1. Sculptures and street gardens add considerable interests to the _____ of the new town.
2. The number of public telephone _____ has greatly increased in that small town since the past few years.
3. The material used for interior sound absorption is generally of rough _____.
4. In the _____ of moonlight, we can see nothing but the outline of the far mountains.
5. The survey indicates that over 90 percent of the residents prefer to have their outdoor activities on the sunny south-faced front sides of the houses instead of the back sides where the houses _____.
6. The city hall was _____ with colored lights on the National Day's Eve.

Ⅱ. Match the definitions in Column A with the proper words in Column B:

A	B
1. the strength of light.	a. persuasive
2. having the power to influence others into believing or doing what one wishes	b. glare
3. a hard, unpleasant effect given by a strong light.	c. illumination
4. the character, quality, feeling ect. of a place	d. ambiance
5. a large electric light that produces a very powerful and bright beam of light.	e. showmanship
6. the skill in drawing public attention.	f. flood light

Ⅲ. Now use the words above to complete the following sentences, changing the form if necessary.

1. An angled fixture is an example of indirect lighting: no bright sources of _____ are visible to the eye, and illumination is soft and uniform.
2. Every good restaurant keeps each table as a separate pool of light, knowing that this contributes to a private and intimate _____.
3. Places where small lights do break down even _____, but do not correspond in any real way with the places where people tend to gather, which is a failure of creating functioning pools of light.
4. It is obvious that any entrance must be systematically lighter than its surroundings with

_____ there, so that its intensity becomes a natural target.
5. Usually a bright-lit and well-displayed shopwindow can be of much help to a _____ for the shop.
6. Skillful lighting design can have a _____ effect on people's activities in a particular space.

Reading Material A

Pools of Light

Uniform illumination—the sweetheart of the lighting engineers—serves no useful purpose whatsoever. In fact, it destroys the social nature of space, and makes people feel disoriented and unbounded.①

Look at this picture. It is an egg-crate ceiling, with dozens of evenly spaced fluorescent lights above it.② It is meant to make the light as flat and even as possible, in a mistaken effort to imitate the sky.

But it is based on two mistakes. First of all, the light outdoors is almost never even. Most natural places, and especially the conditions under which the human organism evolved, have dappled light which varies continuously from minute to minute, and from place to place.

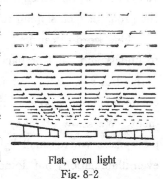

Flat, even light
Fig. 8-2

More serious, it is a fact of human nature that the space we use as social space is in part defined by light.③ When the light is perfectly even, the social function of the space gets utterly destroyed: it even, becomes difficult for people to form natural human groups. If a group is in an area of uniform illumination, there are no light gradients corresponding to the boundary of the group, so the definition, cohesiveness, and "existence" of the group will be weakened.④ If the group is within a "pool" of light, whose size and boundaries correspond to those of the group, this enhances the definition, cohesiveness, and even the phenomenological existence of the group.

One possible explanation is suggested by the experiments of Hopkinson and Longmore, who showed that small bright light sources distract the attention less than large areas which are less bright. These authors conclude that local lighting over a work table allows the worker to pay more attention to his work than uniform background lighting does. It seems reasonable to infer that the high degree of person to person attention required to maintain the cohesiveness of a social group is more likely to be sustained if the group has local lighting, than if it has uniform background lighting.⑤

On-the-spot observation supports this conjecture.⑥ At the International House, University of California, Berkeley, there is a large room which is a general waiting and sitting lounge for guests and residents. There are 42 seats in the room, 12 of them are next to lamps. At the two times of observation we counted a total of 21 people sitting in the room; 13 of them chose to sit next to lamps. These figures show that people prefer sitting near lights. Yet the overall light level in the room was high enough for reading. We conclude that people do seek "pools of light".

Everyday experience bears out the same observation in hundreds of cases.⑦ Every good restaurant keeps each table as a separate pool of light, knowing that this contributes to its private and intimate ambience. In a house a truly comfortable old chair, "yours", has its own light in dimmer surroundings-so that you retreat from the bustle of the family to read the paper in peace.⑧ Again, house dining tables often have a single lamp suspended over the table—the light seems almost to act like glue for all the people sitting round the table. In larger situations the same thing seems to be true. Think of the park bench, under a solitary light, and the privacy of the world which it creates for a pair of lovers. Or, in a trucking depot, the solidarity of the group of men sipping coffee around a brightly lit coffee stand.⑨

One word of caution. This pattern is easy to understand; and perhaps it is easy to agree with. But it is quite a subtle matter to actually create functioning pools of light in the environment. We know of many failures: for example, places where small lights do break down even illumination, but do not correspond in any real way with the places where people tend to gather in the space.

pools of light

Fig. 8-3

Place the lights low, and apart, to form individual pools of light which encompass chairs and tables like bubbles to reinforce the social character of the spaces which they form. Remember that you can't have pools of light without the darker places in between.

Notes

①采光工程师们所钟爱的均匀照明，无论用于哪种目的都毫无意义。事实上，它破坏了空间的社会性质，让人感到迷失方位，不着边际。

②看看这幅图。它是一个菱形格子天花板，上面有几十支均匀分布的荧光灯。

③更严重的是，出于人类的本性，人们用于社会活动的空间部分地受灯光限制。

④如果一群人处在一个照明均匀的空间，那么，光线就缺乏与人群规模相应的明暗梯度。于是该群体的界线、内聚力和"存在"就会受到削弱。

⑤看来有理由推断，采用局部照明，而不是均匀的背景照明，更有利于维持人与人之间的高度关注，而这种关注是保持一个社会群体的内聚力所必须的。

⑥On-the spot observation… 现场观察……

⑦Everyday experience bears out… 日常经验证明……

⑧要是家里有一把归你专用的舒适的老式椅子，椅子跟前有一盏灯，周围显得比较昏暗，那么，你就可以躲开家中的纷乱，静静地坐在那儿看报。

⑨或着想想货车场上，一群人围着灯光明亮的咖啡亭啜饮咖啡时所表现出的友好情景吧。本句省略了上句出现过的 think of. coffee stand 意为"咖啡亭"。

Reading Material B

Acoustics

Since the architect can affect us so profoundly through his handling (or mishandling) of the question of sound, it becomes his obligation to consider a knowledge of acoustics to be a necessary part of his professional training. Un-fortunately, up until very recently, architecture was thought of as almost entirely a visual art, with such considerations as acoustics at best peripheral.①

Yet, while the solution to a complex acoustical problem is extremely difficult, requiring expert assistance, the principles involved are fairly simple; with these well in hand, the architect can be fairly sure of not committing major errors. The factors involved are:

Volume. Volume, or intensity or loudness, is concerned with the level of sound involved. This is measured in decibels. A whisper, or the rustle of leaves, is about 10 decibels. A quiet home is 40. A busy office, with typewriters going, rates around 80. Subways, 100. Pneumatic drills, 110. Jet planes at takeoff, 120. 125 decibels is the threshold of pain.

With regard to volume, therefore, it is the first job of the architect to protect the people in his buildings from the battering of noise. He reduces sound conduction through walls by using doubled shells and heavy, sound-absorbing material. He is especially careful about noisy machinery, within and outside the building.

Reverberation. When sound waves bounce back and forth between walls, floors and ceilings, they strike the ear not once, but many times, decreasing in intensity until they fade out entirely. The time it takes for an initial sound to fade out is called the reverberation time, familiarly known, as t. A certain amount of t is desirable; it augments volume, so that in a theater, for example, you can hear an actor speaking in a normal voice.② It also adds fullness and richness to tones, much as a touch of echo helps a recording.③ In a "dead" room, one with little t, the speaker can barely be heard and music sounds dinky. On the other hand, in a hall that is too "live," has too much t, individual syllables or notes will overlap, causing blurring and incomprehension.

Generally, halls used for speaking should have less t than concert halls, since spoken words tend to blur more easily than does music. In any case, the happy fact is that t can be calculated quite exactly for any given hall, room, or auditorium. A rather simple formula relates the volume of the space with the sound-absorptive capacity of the enclosure (walls, floor, ceiling) resulting in a value for t in seconds. ④ If, say, your hall requires a t of one and a half seconds and your calculations show that it will come out at three seconds, you can reduce the t by adding sound-absorptive materials, such as fabrics, carpeting, porous plaster, and so forth. ⑤ Or if the t is too small, you do the opposite. You reduce the sound-absorptive materials and replace them with glass, tile, marble, or other materials with sound-reflecting quality.

Echo. If a sound is repeated in less than 1/16th of a second, the average human ear cannot distinguish one from another; the repetition seems to be merely an extension of the first sound, and therefore is classified as reverberation. If, however, the repetition occurs at intervals longer than 1/16th of a second, it is heard separately, and is then called an echo. Now, echoes may be lots of fun when played with in caverns or among mountains, but in a concert hall or theater they are murder. How can you tell when you will be likely to get an echo? The clue is in the time element. During 1/16th of a second sound travels about 90 feet; so that if a reflected sound follows a path 90 feet or more longer than the same sound on its direct line, the listener will hear it twice. ⑥

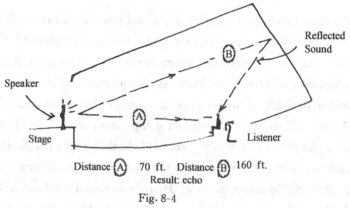

Fig. 8-4

Obviously, the cure is to change the shape of the interior outline so that such patterns of reflection are eliminated, or, if that is impossible for some reason or other, the reflecting surface can be broken up by perforations, serrations, or zigzags, so that it no longer reflects. ⑦

Focusing. When the space is rounded, either in plan or in section (as with a domed roof), there is always the danger that reflected sounds, instead of spreading evenly throughout the hall, will tend to focus on single spots. This can sometimes happen also when the side walls are slanted in so that most reflections go to the center of the hall.

Thus, there may be places in the hall where the sound is exceptionally loud, and others that are pretty much dead, since they receive only the direct sound, which, in a fairly large hall, is not enough.

With the use of microphones and electrical amplification many acoustic problems can be solved, but others come into being. For example, there is the question of sound quality. Sophisticated equipment, expertly manned, can produce amazingly good sound, with a degree of faithfulness that will satisfy the most exacting musician. ⑧ Unfortunately, this is an ideal that is seldom realized. Most often amplified sound is unmistakably amplified, and much of the per-

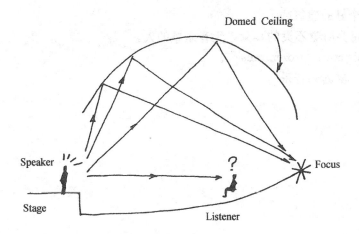

Fig. 8-5

sonal effect of a "live" performance is lost, as well as some of the musical nuances and tonal subtleties.

In short, sound—its efficiency, its quality—is a functioning element in architecture. It is doubtful if a man with a tin ear can be a good architect; equally, it is not surprising that many architects are music lovers.⑨ After all, wasn't it Goethe who called architecture "frozen music"?⑩

Notes

①…with such considerations as acoustics at best peripheral.

……认为声学最多也不过是外围问题。

②适当的回响时间是需要的,它能增加音量,比如,在戏院,演员用普通声音说话,你也能听见。

"t"回响时间。

③回响还可增加声调的圆润性和丰富性,正如按下音响装置有益于录音效果。

echo: 此处意为:"振谐器,回音箱,下文中则意为"回音(声)"。

④空间体积与围合结构(墙壁、地面、天花板)吸声能力的关系式颇为简单,可用每次回响几秒钟的数值表示。

"to relate…with (to) …"意为"建立……与……的关系式"。

⑤如果说大厅所需要回响时间是1秒半,而你计算的结果显示它的回响时间将是3秒钟,你可以通过增加诸如织物,地毯,多孔墙灰等这类的吸声材料,来减少回响时间。

⑥声音穿行90米需1/16秒钟,因此,如果反射回来的声音传播的途径比直接传来的声音途径长90米以上,听众将两次听见同一声音。

⑦补救的办法显然是改变内部轮廓的形状,以便减少这种反射形式,或者因为某种原因而不可能的话,则可通过打孔、成锯齿状(即之字形)等手段破坏反射面。

⑧内行操作的高级设备,可以产生出惊人的声音,其可信度令最苛求的音乐家也会满意。

⑨it is doubtful if a man with a tin ear can be a good architect… 很难让人相信一个无音乐感

的人会是一个好的建筑师……

　　tin ear 意为听觉不灵的耳朵，无音乐感的人。

⑩…called architecture "frozen music".

　　……建筑是"凝固的音乐"。

UNIT NINE

Text   The Evolution of Cluster Housing

[1] The cluster housing environment is the most fundamental and enduring form of human settlement. It may be simply described as housing that is joined together so that individual units share common walls, floors, and ceilings. More importantly, the individual units share common open spaces and common facilities. Historically, cluster configuration and scale have been limited only by the material resources and the ingenuity of the society building them.

The cluster housing environment is the most enduving form of human settlement

Fig. 9-1

[2] Traditionally, the scale and organization of the cluster settlement described not only the physical setting, but the social setting as well. In a culture whose settlement form was refined over thousands of years, the physical organization became highly structured.① This certainly did not mean that house form became rigid; rather each culture conceived order based on its own values.

[3] Planning new cluster housing environments requires a perspective view of their history. Studying the evolution of cluster housing environments through the ages reveals that they flourished in many stable cultures. Thus, the basic planning principles of cluster housing can most easily be understood by studying the housing environments of these cultures.

[4] Cluster housing is primarily an urban house form that is adaptable to many different community scales. By drawing upon the best of a rich tradition, it has the potential to become the enlightened compromise between conventional suburban and urban housing environments.

[5] In primitive cultures the village was often defined by the organization of individual dwelling units into groups to enclose a community space and simultaneously form a defensible enclosure. The main entry of each unit faced into the community space. In some cultures the

units were connected to actually form the enclosure, whereas in others they were aligned (not quite connected) to define, but not formally enclose, the community space. Depending upon available material resources and technological skills, the units were one or two stories high.

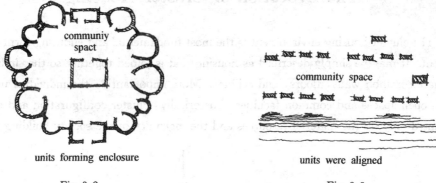

units forming enclosure   units were aligned

Fig. 9-2   Fig. 9-3

[6] In time, as the population increased, the village became the town. Al-though many of the village characteristics remained, the houses were more isolated from the main public spaces. The entry no longer fronted on the main community space, the town center, but on a secondary community space in the form of a pathway or street leading to the town center.② The house no longer formed the village wall. It either opened onto an interior court or was surrounded on all but one side by adjacent units. Moreover, improved technology allowed multiple story dwellings to be built to a height of four or five stories.

[7] As urbanization throughout the world led to still greater concentrations of population, the urban single-family house cluster reached a high level of refinement and sophistication. In medieval European cities it became still more compact with very narrow frontage on the street and heights of four to five stories.③ This basic model is the genesis of contemporary European urban housing.

[8] As the city began to be planned, the informal pattern of incremental growth yielded to more formal, large-scale preconceptions of total city organization. Regardless of topography city streets were arranged in regular geometric patterns, with the rectilinear grid being dominant.④ The city "block" thus formed became the standard. The cluster form, which had previously been the generator of informal growth and change, was subdued and had to yield to the discipline of the block.

[9] With the beginning of the industrial revolution and the great influx of rural population into the city, this formal massing combined with improved technology in the development of taller residential buildings. Many walk-up tenements, composed of flats, were built to heights of six to eight stories. With this trend the basic values of cluster housing environments were set aside and many of the advantages of urban lifestyle were greatly compromised for those living in tenement housing. The contemporary tenement housing environment, i. e. , the apartment house complete with elevators, is a stepchild of the industrial revolution.

[10] The squeezing upward of housing can almost always be correlated with the great de-

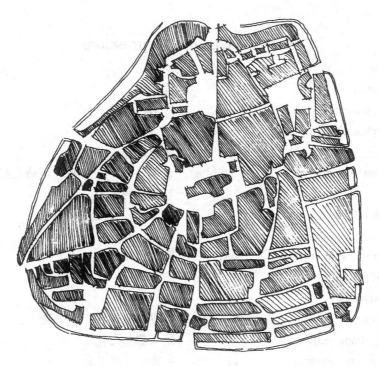

main public space and secondary communi ty spaces

Fig. 9-4

mand for land near the urban core, and the land management practices of a given culture. High-rise housing continues to be built in spite of overwhelming evidence that it spawns and sustains many social problems. Efforts to improve upon it seem only to further intensify the problem. Perhaps then, the problem is the basic assumption that high-rise housing is a humane environment. Interestingly, some ancient civilizations managed to build very large-scale residential environments which seem to be more humane than their contemporary equivalents. Perhaps because our ancestors could not conceive of the technological means to build vertical structures of great height and in great quantity, they were spared the social problems associated with high rise living.[5]

[11] For reasons of cultural tradition, climate, landform, materials, and technology, some civilizations built a complex of patio and terrace house clusters as their basic house type. Most of these civilizations continue to build in these forms. The patio house form is still the basic type throughout the hot/dry climate zones. The terrace house form naturally evolved in all the hilly portions of the world. Since many early civilizations chose to build in inaccessible places for defense, there are many enduring examples. The terrace house continues to be the dominant houseform in the hilly portions of the world, but its many advantages are making it an attractive alternative in many other parts of the world.

New Words and Expressions

cluster * ['klʌstə]	n.	群，组
configuration [kənfigu'reiʃən]	n.	外形；构造
ingenuity [indʒi'nu(:)iti]	n.	创造性；巧妙
refine [ri'fain]	vt.	精选；加工
perspective [pəs'pektiv]	a. & n.	透视（画、法）的；正确观察事物相互关系的能力
draw upon (on)		动（利、引）用；吸收
enlighten [in'laitn]	v.	启迪；开导
simultaneously * [siməl'tænjəsli]	ad.	同时地；一齐地
defensible [di'fensəbl]	a.	能防御的
whereas * [wɛə'ræz]	conj.	而；却
align * [ə'lain]	v.	排成一条直线；使一致
urbanization [ə:bənai'zeiʃən]	n.	城（都）市化
sophistication * [sə,fisti'keiʃən]	n.	完善化，复杂化
frontage ['frʌntidʒ]	n.	临街面
incremental * [inkri'mentəl]	a.	增长的，增值的
preconception [pri:kən'sepʃən]	n.	预想，先入之见
topography [tə'pɔgrəfi]	n.	地形，地势
rectilinear [rekti'linjə]	a.	直线的，由直线围起的
medieval [medi'i:vəl]	a.	中世纪的，中古时代的
subdue ['sʌbdju:]	v.	征服
influx [in'flʌks]	n.	流入，川流不息
walk-up	a.	无电梯的，直接走上去的
correlate ['kɔrileit]	v.	相互关联
spawn [spɔ:n]	v.	大量生产；酿成
sustain [səs'tein]	v.	遭受，蒙受
assumption * [ə'sʌmpʃən]	n.	前提；假设
intensify * [in'tensifai]	v.	使更剧烈，加强
humane [hju'mein]	a.	人道的，仁慈的
landform ['lændfɔ:m]	n.	地形，地貌
patio ['pɑ:tiə]	n.	庭院，天井
hilly ['hili]	a.	有斜坡的，丘陵的
inaccessible [,inək'sesəbl]	a.	不能接近的，不能达到的

Notes

① the physical organization 此处指的是住宅群的结构、布局。

② 句中 fronted 是动词，front on (to) 意为"面对（向）……"，"朝着……"；the town center 系 the main community 的同位语。

③ (1) medieval 欧洲中世纪指的是公元 1100～1500 年。

(2) …with very narrow… 此处介词 with 的含义是"由于"、"因为"。

④ …, with the rectilinear grid being dominant.

在这个介词短语中，分词短语 being dominant 是介词宾语 the rectilinear grid 的补语，有着强烈的逻辑上的主谓关系，因而这种带有宾补的介词短语常常可视作为一个句子来理解，在整个句子中起补充说明作用。

⑤ …they were spared the social problems associated with high-rise living.

在这个被动语态的句子结构中，the social problems associated with high-rise living 是保留宾语；动词 spare 此处含义是"赦免"，"不受牵连"。

Exercises

Reading Comprehension

Ⅰ. Say whether the following statements are true (T) or false (F) according to the text, making use of the paragraph numbers.

1. In the cluster housing environment, the houses are usually connected to share common walls, floors and ceilings, but not to share common facilities. (Para. 1)   (   )
2. In primitive cultures, whether the dwelling units were connected or aligned there would be a community space. (Para. 5)   (   )
3. One of the differences between the towns and the villages is that in the town, the houses are farther away from the main common open spaces. (Para. 6)   (   )
4. The contemporary European urban housing has nothing to do with that of medieval European cities. (Para. 7)   (   )
5. "Block" formed by regular geometric patterns with rectilinear grid was the discipline of city planning. (Para. 8)   (   )
6. Although taller apartment houses were constructed during the industrial revolution, the basic values and advantages of cluster housing environments were completely kept. (Para. 9)   (   )
7. High-rise building produces and suffers a lot of social problems, so people try to solve them and it seems that they are on their was to success. (Para. 10)   (   )
8. The terrace house remains the main type in the mountainous areas and is likely to be

adopted by many other places of the world. (Para. 11)   ( )

Ⅱ. According to your understanding of the text, fill in the blanks with the one best choice from the four suggestions.

1. "physical setting" in the second paragraph probably means _____.
   A. construction site   B. natural environment
   C. open space   D. natural resources

2. "This certainly did not mean that house form became rigid; rather each culture conceived order based on its own values" From the sentence we may know _____.
   A. each culture had a social order different from that of others.
   B. different cultures made different laws according to their own values.
   C. the relation between housing clusters of different cultures was not quite close.
   D. the house forms of different cultures might not be the same.

3. From Paragraph Three we can learn _____.
   A. a stable culture helped cluster housing environments develop healthily
   B. stable cultures are helpful to draw up the basic planning principles
   C. a perspective view is, in fact, the base of planning principles
   D. studying the evolution of cluster housing environments means studying the housing environments of various cultures

4. "By drawing upon" in the second sentence of Paragraph Four can be replaced by _____.
   A. By applying   B. By bringing forth
   C. By reaching   D. By pulling up

5. All of the followings are mentioned in Paragraph Five except _____.
   A. Gates or doors of each dwelling unit opened into the community common space.
   B. There were more than two ways for the units to form the community space.
   C. The height of the units was one or two stories.
   D. The primitive villages had a function of defense.

6. From Paragraph Six _____ can be deduced.
   A. The dwelling houses became higher.
   B. The community space became larger in size.
   C. There would be at least one neighbor always adjacent to a house.
   D. The residents contacted less frequently with each other than those in a village.

7. The word "Preconceptions" in the phrase "more formal, large-scale preconceptions of total city organization" may be replaced by _____.
   A. prejudices   B. foresights   C. plans   D. predictions

8. According to Paragraph Nine we know that the author probably _____.
   A. is in favor of taller residential buildings
   B. prefers walk-up tenements of heights of six to eight stories
   C. is not satisfied with the contemporary tenement housing environment

D. is pleased with the trend that the basic values of cluster housing environments were set aside.

9. From the last paragraph we may draw a conclusion that _____.

   A. a complex of patio and terrace house cluster is the basic house type all over the world.
   B. there is no definite model as the basic house type to be followed throughout the world
   C. patio house cluster is the ideal house type used everywhere
   D. terrace house is naturally the best house type used everywhere

Vocabulary

I. Match the words in Column A with their corresponding definitions or descripfions in Column B.

A	B
1. cluster	a. to line up or to bring into straight line
2. align	b. a number of things of the same sort gathered
3. sophistication	c. to make more intense
4. incremental	d. courtyard open to the sky
5. intensify	e. becoming greater or larger
6. inaccessible	f. impossible to reach or enter
7. tenement	g. state of being highly complex, refined.
8. patio	h. a large dwelling house for many families at low rent, especially the one that is overcrowded

II. Complete the following sentences with some of the words listed below, changing the forms where necessary.

perspective	flourish	adaptable to
yield to	configuration	adjacent
regardless of	residential	correlate

1. When brightly lit at night, the _____ of that famous building looks even more beautiful.
2. With more available material resources and improved technological skills, people have become increasingly _____ their environment.
3. For the sake of the price of land, the high-rise building may _____; and the single-family house cluster will _____ it.
4. The sixteen-story building _____ to the teaching building is the library of their school.
5. _____ the heavy snow, the students went skiing.
6. The evolution of cluster housing is _____ with a lot of factors, such as materials, technology, cultural tradition and climate, etc.

III. Complete each of the following statements with one of the four choices given below.
1. Today, a lot of the city dwelling units are _____ so that they can form a humane community.
   A. separated   B. aligned   C. overlapped   D. fitted
2. Generally speaking, the buildings with _____ on the streets are preferred by the tradesmen.
   A. pathways   B. dwellings   C. frontages   D. patio
3. I am fond of architecture, but not good at it. Can you _____ me on this subject?
   A. enlighten   B. teach   C. instruct   D. conduct
4. Being _____ the ancient terrace houses were easily to defend, so many of them have been well preserved.
   A. dominant   B. inaccessible   C. overwhelming   D. multiple

Reading Material A

House Cluster

People will not feel comfortable in their house unless a group of houses forms a cluster, with the public land between them jointly owned by all the householders.

When houses are arranged on streets, and the streets owned by the town, there is no way in which the land immediately outside the houses can reflect the needs of families and individuals living in those houses. The land will only gradually get shaped to meet their needs if they have direct control over the land and its repair.

This pattern is based on the idea that the cluster of land and homes immediately around one's own home is of special importance. It is the source for gradual differentiation of neighborhood land use, and it is the natural focus of neighborly interaction. ①

Consider the following diagram—one like it can be made for almost every house in a tract. ② There is a house on either side, one or two across the street, and one directly behind, across a garden fence.

On a typical block each home is at the center of its own cluster

Fig. 9-5

Ninety-three percent of all the neighborhood visiting engaged in by the subjects is confined to this spatial cluster. ③ And when asked "Whom do you visit most?" Ninety-one percent said the people they visit most are immediately across the street or next door. The beauty of this finding is its indication of the strength of the spatial cluster to draw people together into neighborly contact. ④

What about the size of the cluster? What is the appropriate size? In our investigation, we found it is better for each home to stand at the center of a cluster of five or six other homes. But this is certainly not a natural limit for a housing cluster since many block layouts are so confining. In our experience, when the siting of the homes is attuned to the cluster pattern, the natural limit arises entirely from the balance between the informality and coherence of the group.⑤

The cluster seem to work best if they have between 8 and 12 houses each. With one representative from each family, this is the number of people that can sit round a common meeting table, can talk to each other directly, face to face, and can therefore make wise decisions about the land they hold in common. With 8 or 10 households, people can meet over a kitchen table, exchange news on the street and in the gardens, and generally, without much special attention, keep in touch with the whole of the group. When there are more than 10 or 12 homes forming a cluster, this balance is strained. We therefore set an upper limit of around 12 on the number of households that can be naturally drawn into a cluster. Of course, the average size for clusters might be less, perhaps around 6 or 8; and clusters of 3, 4, or 5 homes can work perfectly well.

Now, assuming that a group of neighbors, or a neighborhood association, or a planner, wants to give some expression to this pattern, what are the critical issues ?

On the one hand, the issue of geometry. There may be various shapes of clusters. For example, a cluster with the houses built around or to the side of common land; or a cluster with a core to it that gradually tapers off at the edges.⑥ These are all quite dramatic ones.

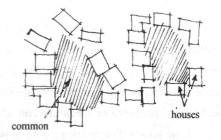

Fig. 9-6

In all cases common land which is shared by the cluster is an essential ingredient. It acts as a focus and physically knits the group together. This common land can be as small as a path or as large as a green.⑦

On the other hand, care must be taken not to make the clusters too tight or self-contained, so that they exclude the larger community or seem too constricting and claustrophobic. There needs to be some open ends and over lapping among clusters.

Along with the shape of the cluster, the way in which it is owned is critical. If the pattern of ownership is not in accord with the physical properties of the cluster, the pattern will not take hold.⑧ Very simply, the cluster must be owned and maintained by its constituent households. The households must be able to organize themselves as a corporation, capable of owning all the common land they share.

Notes

①它是街区公用土地用途逐步演变的根源，也是邻里间人们进行交往的自然而然的中心。
②——one like it can be made for almost every house in a tract.

——像图中这样的布局几乎适用于一块地面上每幢住宅。

句中 like 系介词，it 指的是 the following diagram。

③调查对象所从事的邻里间互访中，有93％都局限在这种住宅范围。

④这个发现的妙处在于它指出了住宅群吸引人们进行邻里接触的力量。

⑤…from the balance between the informality and coherence of the group.

……照顾了（平衡了）它们的随意性和凝聚力。

⑥…or a cluster with a core to it that gradually tapers off at the edges.

……，或者住宅群有一个中心部位，房舍由此往边缘逐渐扩散。

⑦…or as large as a green.

……或大至草坪。

⑧如果占有的方式和住宅群的实际所有权不对口，那么这种方式就维持不住。

Reading Material B

Low-rise, Medium-density Cluster Housing①

This article addresses itself to only one scale of cluster housing. It is the scale of the multi-celled clusters associated with suburban and low-scale urban housing environments.② The scale is limited to low rise and medium density. Low rise limits the height to four stories, while medium density is set at an average net density of 15 dwelling units per acre. The many reasons for this choice of focus are considered below.

Low Rise—The four-story limit was established by several determinants, the most critical one being the problem of stair climbing. Climbing three stories of stairs is currently thought to be the maximum for healthy adults and excessive for children and elderly. In addition, behavioral studies indicate that we become disengaged from the land if we go any higher. This disengagement causes a host of human problems such as anonymity, indifference, fear of safety, loneliness, lack of community interest, and insensitivity toward natural processes in general.③ Some very practical determinants to the four-story limit are that the building can be constructed of most conventional building systems and still meet structural and fire safety requirements, and that unit cost compares favorably with both low-and high-density housing. And finally, four-story stacking allows for development of open spaces in medium-density housing environments.④

Medium Density-Reestablishing human density for housing environments is, at best, an approximation. A suitable maximum density can only be determined during the site planning process, since each site, and the way it is developed, suggests its own optimum density. However, by drawing upon the long history of cluster housing environments similar in scale and by assessing the density in the community surrounding the site, we can establish a density range. The density will also be influenced by physical limitations of low-rise cluster housing. Once again, this does not fix density, but does set some broad limits.

By examining many examples of low-rise, medium-density housing throughout the world—America and Western Europe in particular—the average density of 15 D. U. /acre was established.⑥ This far exceeds the existing single-unit suburban density of 4.5 D. U. /acre, but falls well below the hundred D. U. /acre density in urban high-rise housing environments.⑦ We should bear in mind that it is possible to cram over 40 two-story row houses on an acre if there is absolutely no open space except for very small private gardens.

The distinction between gross and net density is important.⑧ Gross density usually covers a large area, and includes all land, roads, parking, services, and nonresidential uses, while net density usually refers to a smaller segment within the gross area. Net density is usually higher than gross density since it covers a smaller land area and includes few nonresidential uses.

In cluster housing, the gross (overall) density may be 10 D. U. /acre while the net density of each cluster may vary from 2 D. U. /acre to 20 D. U. /acre. Thus, variable density within a development has the advantage of responding to different physical conditions and household types.⑨

All land has some allowable density recorded in the zoning ordinance. Because increasing density increases land value, most developers evaluate the problems associated with, increasing density before assigning a final density figure. For instance, as density increases, the cost of services (parking, water, gas, fire protection, etc.) increases to a point where adding one more unit may throw off the budget balance.⑩

We often use the term Planned Unit Development from time to time. A Planned Unit Development (also known as PUD, Planned Unit, Planned Development, Planned Community) is a parcel of land planned as a single unit rather than as an aggregate of individual lots, with design flexibility from traditional siting regulations (setbacks, height restrictions) or land use restrictions (such as mixing land uses.⑪) The greater flexibility in locating buildings and combining land uses often makes it possible to achieve an economy of construction as well as to preserve open space and to maintain a reasonably high density.

Notes

①低层中密度住宅群。
②本文讨论的规模是与郊区住宅群、低层的市区住宅群有关的多单元住宅群。
③这种脱离地面会引起许多与人有关的问题，诸如不为他人所知，冷漠，不安，孤独，对社区缺乏兴趣等。总之，对自然进程显得迟钝。
④four-story stacking=four-story building
⑤不过通过引用规模相似的住宅群环境的悠久历史，以及评估这一住宅基地周围社区的密度，我们可以确立"密度范围"。
⑥…the average density of 15 D. U. /acre.

……每英亩 15 个住户的平均密度。

  D. U. =Dwelling Unit

⑦…but falls well below…

  ……但是远远低于……

⑧gross density 总密度；net density 有效密度。

⑨所以，在一个开发区内不同的密度具有适应不同的具体情况和住户类型的优点。

⑩所以，随着密度的增大，各项服务费用（停车费、水费、煤气费、防火费等）都会随之增加到这样一种程度：多加一个单元都会打破预算的平衡。

⑪一个规划型住宅开发区（也称 PUD，或规划型住宅，规划型开发区、规划型社区等）是规划来作为独户住宅区的一部分土地，而不是组合起来的零散住宅基址。比起现行的传统条例（建筑边界限制，高度限制）或土地使用限制（如土地的综合用途），规划型住宅开发区拥有设计上的灵活性。

UNIT TEN

Text Where do We Go from Here—Architecturally

[1]   Developments of the 1970s may presage the new developments of the '80s and '90s. Zoning effects on the density of tall buildings and solar design may raise ethical questions. ① Energy limitations will continue to be a unique design challenge. A combined project of old and new buildings may bring back human scale to our cities. Owners and conceptual designers will be challenged in the 1980s to produce economically sound, people-oriented buildings. ②

[2]   In 1980 the Lever House, designed by Skidmore, Owings and Merrill (SOM) received the 25-year award from the American Institute of Architects "in recognition of architectural design of enduring significance. "③ This award is given once a year for a building between 25 and 35 years old. Lewis Mumford described the Lever House as "the first office building in which modern materials, modern construction, modern functions have been combined with a modern plan". At the time, this daring concept could only be achieved by visionary men like Gordon Bunshaft, the designer, and Charles Luckman, the owner and then-president of Lever Brothers. The project also included a few "firsts": (1) it was the first sealed glass tower ever built; (2) it was the first office building designed by SOM; and (3) it was the first office building on Park Avenue to omit retail space on the first floor. Today, after hundreds of look-alikes and variations on the grid design, we have reached what may be the epitome of tall building design: the nondescript building. ④ Except for a few recently completed buildings that seem to be people-oriented in their lower floors, most tall buildings seem to be a repetition of the dull, graph-paper-like monoliths in many of our cities. Can this be the end of the design-line for tall buildings ? Probably not. There are definite signs that are most encouraging. Architects and owners have recently begun to discuss the design problem publicly. Perhaps we are at the threshold of a new era. The 1980s may bring forth some new visionaries like Bunshaft and Luckman. If so, what kinds of restrictions or challenges do they face ?

Zoning

[3]   Indications are strong that cities may restrict the density of tall buildings, that is , reduce the number of tall buildings per square mile. In 1980 the term grid-lock was used for the first time publicly in New York City. It caused a terror-like sensation in the pit of one's stomach. ⑤ The term refers to a situation in which traffic comes to a standstill for many city blocks in all directions. The jam-up may even reach to the tunnels and bridges. Strangely enough, such an event happened in New York in a year of fuel shortages and high gasoline prices. If we are to avoid similar occurrences, it is obvious that the density of people, places, and vehicles must be drastically reduced. Zoning may be the only long-term solution.

[4]   Solar zoning may become more and more popular as city residents are blocked from the sun by tall buildings. Regardless of how effectively a tall building is designed to conserve energy, it may at the same time deprive a resident or neighbor of solar access.⑥ In the 1980s the right to see the sun may become a most interesting ethical question that may revolutionize the architectural fabric of the city. Mixed-use zoning, which became a financially viable alternative during the 1970s, may become commonplace during the 1980s, especially if it is combined with solar zoning to provide access to the sun for all occupants.

Renovation

[5]   Emery Roth and Sons designed the Palace Hotel in New York as an addition to a renovated historic Villard house on Madison Avenue. It is a stri king example of what can be done with salvageable and beautifully detailed old buildings. Recycling both large and small buildings may become the way in which humanism and warmth will be returned to buildings during the '80s. If we must continue to design with glass and aluminum in stark grid patterns, for whatever reason, we may find that a combination of new and old will become the great humane design trend of the future.

Conceptual Design

[6]   It has been suggested in architectural magazines that the Bank of America office building in San Francisco is too large for the city's scale. It has also been suggested that the John Hancock Center in Boston is not only out of scale but also out of character with the city.⑦ Similar statements and opinions have been made about other significant tall buildings in cities throughout the world. These comments raise some basic questions about the design process and who really makes the design decisions on important structures-and about who will make these decisions in the 1980s.

[7]   Will the forthcoming visionaries-architects and owners-return to more humane designs? Will the sociologist or psychologist play a more important role in the years ahead to help convince these visionaries that a new, radically different, human-scaled architecture is long overdue? If these are valid questions, could it be that our "best" architectural designers of the'60s and'70s will become the worst designers of the '80s and '90s? Or will they learn and respond to a valuable lesson they should have learned in their "History of Architecture" course in college-that "architecture usually reflects the success or failure of a civilized society"? Only time will tell.

New Words and Expressions

presage ['presidʒ]　　　　　　　　　　*vt.*　　　　　　预示，预言

ethical ['eθikəl]	a.	道德的，伦理的
conceptual * [kən'septjuəl]	a.	概念的；理性的
daring ['dɛəriŋ]	a.	大胆的
visionary ['viʒənəri]	a.	想象的；好幻想的
retail ['ri:teil]	n.	零售，零卖
look-like	n.	外观相似
grid * [grid]	n.	柱网；格栅
epitome [i'pitəmi]	n.	梗概；缩影
nondescript ['nɔndiskript]	a.	（因无特征而）难以归类的，难以形容的
monolith ['mɔnəuliθ]	n.	（柱状或碑状的）独块巨石，独石柱
design-line	n.	设计行业
threshold * ['θreʃhəuld]	n.	开端；门槛
bring forth		产生
sensation [sen'seiʃən]	n.	感觉；轰动
standstill * ['stændstil]	n.	停止，停滞不前
drastically ['dræstikəli]	ad.	猛烈地，激烈地
conserve [kən'sə:v]	vt.	保存，保养
deprive [di'praiv] (of)		剥夺，使丧失
revolutionize [ˌrevə'lu:ʃnaiz]	vt.	彻底改革，使革命化
viable * ['vaiəbl]	a.	可行的；能生存的
commonplace * ['kɔmənpleis]	a.	平凡的；陈腐的
occupant ['ɔkjupənt]	n.	居住者；占用者
renovation [ˌrenəu'veiʃən]	n.	整修，革新
salvageable ['sælvidʒəbl]	a.	可救的，可抢救的
striking ['straikiŋ]	a.	显著的；惊人的
recycle [ˌri:'saikl]	vt.	（使）再循环
humanism ['hju:mənizəm]	n.	人情，人性
stark [stɑ:k]	a.	僵硬的，刻板的
forthcoming [fɔ:θ'kʌmiŋ]	a.	即将到来的，即将出现的
radically * ['rædikəli]	ad.	根本地，基本地
overdue [ˌəuvə'dju:]	a.	期待已久的，早就成熟的
valid ['vælid]	a.	正确的；有根据的

Notes

①solar design 指考虑到阳光因素的自然采光方案。
②people-oriented buildings 适合于人的建筑物。
 oriented 一词在现代英语中常在其前边加一名词构成复合形容词，可作定语或表语。基本含意是"适合于……的"、"有利于……的"，但确切译文要视具体情况而定。

③SOM 是美国现代一所著名建筑师事务所，由 Louis Skidmore，Nathaniel Owings 和 John Merrill 三人于 1939 年在芝加哥创建，其分事务所分布于美国许多大城市。Skidmore 是 SOM 中最有权威的设计者，Merrill 是有实践经验的工程师，而 Owings 则是出色的管理者。SOM 造就了一大批建筑人才，其作品遍布世界，包括 1978 年建成的我国香港的"新世界"。

④grid 一词本意是"格栅、网格"，在本文此处则是"柱网"。

⑤in the pit of one's stomach 本意是"胸口、心窝、腹上部"，这里则是"在人们的心中"，等于 in one's mind。

⑥…deprive a resident or neighbor of solar access 其中 deprive sb. of St. 是一习惯用语，意为"剥夺某人的什么权"，更常用的形式是…is deprived of…，即某某人（或物）被剥夺了（或失去了）什么。

⑦…is not only out of scale but also out of character with the city. 其中词组 to be out of…with…意为"与……在……方面不一致"。

Exercises

Reading Comprehension

Ⅰ. Say whether the following statements are true (T) or false (F) according to the text, making use of the paragraph number given.
1. A combination of old and new buildings may make our cities more suitable for people to live in. (Para. 1) ( )
2. Buildings between 25 and 35 years old are likely to be awarded once a year. (Para. 2) ( )
3. The Lever House is regarded as the first in three respects. (Para. 2) ( )
4. Since tall buildings are in grid forms, we can hardly see their difference. (Para. 2) ( )
5. People are afraid of grid-lock, for it means a jam-up in many blocks in all directions within a city. (Para. 3) ( )
6. Palace Hotel serves as a good example of a combination of old and new buildings. (Para. 5) ( )
7. People's judgment may change with the time, therefore, the "best" designers in the '60s are always the worst of the '80s. (Para. 7) ( )
8. Only time can prove whether the designers would have understood and practiced the idea that architecture usually reflects the success or failure of a civilized society. (Para. 7) ( )

Ⅱ. Fill in the missing words or expressions for the following sentences from the text.
1. If we must continue to design with _____ in stark grid patterns, we may find that a combination of new and old will become the great _____ of the future.

2. A combined project of _____ building may _____ to our cities.
3. Lewis Munford _____ the Lever House as "the first office building in which modern materials, modern construction, modern functions have been _____ with a modern plan".
4. Except for a few recently completed buildings that seem to be _____ in their lower floors, most tall buildings seem to be a _____ of the dull, graph—paper—like monoliths in many of our cities.
5. Regardless of how effectively a tall building is designed to _____ energy, it may at the same time deprive a resident or neighbor of _____.

Vocabulary

I. Complete the following sentences with some of the words listed below, changing the form where necessary.

standstill	deprive…of	variation
function	trend	limitation	scale
renovation	conserve	design-line

1. This building is of mixed-use for office and residential _____.
2. High buildings have no genuine advantages, for they _____ the occu-pants _____ many opportunities in social life.
3. Energy _____ will restrict the urban development.
4. _____ of historic buildings will contribute _____ human civilization.
5. A building with any function must have a reasonable human _____ other-wise it will be nondescript.
6. With the depression of housing development, _____ will naturally slump.
7. Without the policy of Transformation and Opening, _____ would have occurred in our state economy.

II. Complete each of the following statements with one of the four choices given below.
1. The _____ of buildings refers to the number of buildings per square mile.
   A. dense   B. density   C. cluster   D. scale
2. The ground level of a tall building is usually for _____ and the upper levels are either for residential or office spaces.
   A. shopping centre   B. recreational centre
   C. retail space   D. open space
3. Tall buildings damage lighting, as they _____ city residents from the sun.
   A. protect   B. take   C. divide   D. block
4. Living in a high-rise building, one's connection to the ground and to the _____ of the town becomes weak.

A. fabric   B. streets   C. buildings   D. construction

5. High-rise buildings are always designed with glass and aluminum in _____ patterns.

A. square   B. grid   C. flat   D. rectangle

III. Match the words in Column A with their corresponding definitions or descriptions in Column B.

A	B
1. zoning	a. able to exist
2. conceptual	b. beginning point of something; wood or stone placed beneath a door
3. look-like	c. system of dividing areas
4. epitome	d. St. which shows, on a small scale, the characteristics of St. much larger
5. threshold	e. of concepts
6. viable	f. likeness in appearance
7. commonplace	g. well-based on evidence
8. radically	h. ordinary or usual
9. occupant	i. from the base, fundamentally
10. valid	j. person who occupies a house, room or position

Reading Material A

Structural Systems for Multi-use High-rise Buildings[①]

Industrial urbanization created high-density living in urban spaces in city centers. These spaces were most often intermixed with each other in such a way that neighborhood stores, offices, and apartments were all in the same building at different levels. The ground level was mostly stores and commercial functions and the upper levels were mixed-use with offices and residential functions. The automobile was not a part of urban life, and therefore parking was never a requirement for these buildings. The nineteenth century urban centers in Europe, such as London, Paris, Prague, and Vienna, were very much of this kind of development. Industrial development during the late nineteenth and early twentieth centuries, combined with land speculation, forced a new kind of urban settlement pattern in which the living and working spaces became more and more separated in urban areas. The rise of downtowns and city centers consisting of office buildings and other commercial facilities created separate residential areas outside these urban centers.[②] And even when some special residential centers were built near the urban centers, they were distinctly separate buildings in no way connected with the commercial or office building complexes.[③] The architectural/engineering solutions for such specialized buildings were therefore quite different from each other. The office and commercial buildings used larger-span structural systems consistent with the space requirements for offices and other commercial functions; whereas the housing and apartment buildings used relatively smaller-span structural systems consistent with residential room sizes. Although both reinforced concrete and structural steel were used for office buildings as well as residential buildings, the structural systems werequite different. The office building, requiring longer spans as well as much more complicated mechanical and electrical systems, almost invariably used fake ceilings; whereas the residential buildings, with less complicated mechanical and electrical systems, did not require the use of false ceilings except for special cases. ④ Flat-plate, reinforced-concrete-slab construction therefore became the most accepted floor system for residential buildings; whereas beams, joists, or grid beam (waffle) systems were used more frequently for office and commercial floors. ⑤ Masonry bearing-wall construction almost always was used only for residential buildings of medium height. ⑥

In the 1960s, concerns about urban quality of life and better utilization of national energy resources raised questions about the earlier trend of total separation of office, commercial, and living spaces in the urban areas. Sociologists, economists, and citizens in general began to rediscover the great advantages of working and living within the same urban environment. As a result, multi-use projects became increasingly attractive to developers from an economic and marketing point of view. The 100-story John Hancock Center in Chicago is an excellent example.

One of the largest such projects built in the middle 1960s, it combines commercial, office, parking, residential, and recreational spaces into one large structure. Such a combination of spaces in one building created a 24-hour use of the land, rather than the 9-to-5 downtown environment of major cities. The John Hancock Center not only became a successful development; its success also encouraged a large number of similar projects that were developed around the same area of the city. The multi-use projects, often incorporated into a megastructure, raised new challenges and required new disciplines in formulating the overall building mass and a complimentary structural system. ⑦ The earlier efficient structural systems that were developed only for the office building or the residential building could not be used in their pure forms to satisfy the multi-use requirements of such a project. New structural modifications and variations had to be developed to satisfy, within the same structure, the space requirements for both office buildings and apartment and parking.

Innovations leading to more economical and efficient buildings are only possible through a comprehensive understanding of the nature and behavior of various structural systems, an awareness of the relationship of the structure with other disciplines such as the mechanical system, and a practical sense of construction problems. ⑧ A multi-use building is much more complex architecturally because of the different requirements for each use. For example, the maximum building width required for apartment space is generally much less than that required for an efficient office space; and the optimum column spacings for a residential building, as well as its plan flexibility, are distinctly different from those for commercial or office buildings.

For multi-use buildings it is therefore necessary to develop structural systems that respond effectively to the needs of the different functions. In developing such systems, the first step is to select an appropriate structural material. The selection process must start with the most commonly used structural materials (steel or reinforced concrete, both normal and lightweight; composite systems; and so forth). Although local relative economies must be considered, the selection process is much more difficult than it is for a single-use building. The different requirements of the different functions and their relative importance in the overall project will be the most important consideration.

Notes

①Structural Systems for Multi-use High-Rise Buildings
  多功能高层建筑的结构系统
②商业区和由办公楼以及其它商用设施组成的市中心的兴起，创造了在这些中心之外的住宅区。
③而且，即使在市中心附近修建某种专用住宅中心，它们也是与那些商用或办公综合楼群毫无联系的、截然分开的建筑物。
④The office building, requiring…almost invariably used false ceilings…
  由于办公楼需要更长的跨度、相当复杂的机械和电气设备，因而它们几乎总是采用吊顶……
⑤reinforced-concrete-slab：钢筋混凝土楼板；joists：托梁；grid beam：框梁。
⑥Masonry bearing-wall construction：砖石承重墙结构
⑦(1) megastructure 一词意为"巨型结构"或"超大型建筑结构"。
  (2) new disciplines in formulating the overall building mass and a complimentary structural system.
    ……确定总建筑物和辅助结构的新规则。
⑧只有通过对各种结构系统的本质和特征的综合理解才能有导致更经济实用的建筑物的新方法。所谓综合理解就是认识到结构与其它学科（如机械系统）的关系和实际辩别出诸多施工问题。

Reading Material B

Four-story Limit

High buildings have no genuine advantages, except in speculative gains for banks and land owners.① They are not cheaper and do not help create open space. They destroy the townscape and social life. They promote crime. They make life difficult for children. They are expensive to maintain. They wreck the open spaces near them. And they damage light, air and view. But quite apart from all of this, which shows that they aren't very sensible, empirical evidence shows that they can actually damage people's minds and feelings. ②

D. M. Fanning gives strong evidence in "Families in Flats". He shows a direct correlation between incidence of mental disorder and the height of people's apartments. The higher people live off the ground, the more likely are they to suffer mental illness. And it is not simply a case of people prone to mental illness choosing high-rise apartments. ③ Fanning shows that the correlation is strongest for the people who spend the most time in their apartments. Among the families he studied, the correlation was strongest for women, who spend most time in their apartments. It was less strong for children, who spend less time in the apartments. And it was weakest for men, who spend the least amount of time in their apartments. This strongly suggests that sheer time spent in the high-rise is itself what causes the effect.

The reason for this is that high-rise living takes people away from the ground, and away from the casual, everyday society that occurs on the sidewalks and streets and on the gardens and porches. It leaves them alone in their apartments. The decision to go out for some public life becomes formal and awkward. Unless there is some specific task which brings people out in the world, the tendency is to stay home alone. The forced isolation then causes individual breakdowns.

A Danish study by Jeanne Morville adds more evidence to Fanning's findings: ④

Children from the high blocks start playing out of doors on their own at a later age than children from the low blocks. Among the children aged five years in the high point blocks 29% do not as yet play on their own out of doors, while in the low blocks all the children aged five do so. Among the children aged one, two and three years, 86% from the low blocks have daily contact with playmates; this applies to only 29% from the high blocks.

Moreover, we noticed the fact that the crime rate in the high-rise was roughly twice that in the three-story walk-ups.

At what height do the effects described by Fanning and Morville begin to take hold ? It is our experience that in both housing and office buildings, the problems begin when buildings are more than four stories high.

At three or four stories, one can still walk comfortably down to the street, and from a window you can still feel part of the street scene. You can see details in the street-the people, their faces, foliage, shops. From three stories you can yell out, and catch the attentions of someone below. Above four stories these connections break down. The visual detail is lost; people speak of the scene below as if it were a game, from which they are completely detached. ⑤ The connection to the ground and to the fabric of the town becomes tenuous. The building becomes a world of its own, with its own elevators and cafeterias.

We believe, therefore, that the "four-story limit" is an appropriate way to express the proper connection between building height and the health of people. Of course, it is the spirit of the pattern which is most essential. Certainly, a building five stories high, perhaps even six, might work if it were carefully handled. But it is difficult. On the whole, we advocate a four-story limit, with only occasional departures, throughout the town.⑥

Notes

①高层建筑除了给银行家和地产主带来投机利益外，并没有带来什么真正的好处。
②然而，除了显示出这些不合理外，经验也表明，高层建筑实际上还能够损害人们的心理和感情。
③这种情况不能简单地看作是由于易患精神病的人选择了高层公寓而造成的。
④丹麦的珍妮·莫维尔的研究进一步证实了范宁的发现。
⑤外面那生动的景象就领略不到，当人们谈起楼下的情况时，似乎那是一种与他们毫不相干的游戏。
⑥总之，除了个别情况例外，我们提倡在整个城市实施四层限度。

UNIT ELEVEN

Text Tall Building

[1]   Tall towers and buildings have fascinated mankind from the beginning of civilization, their construction being initially for defense and subsequently for ecclesiastical purposes.① The growth in modern tall building construction, however, which began in the 1880s, has been largely for commercial and residential purposes.

[2]   Tall commercial building are primarily a response to the demand by business activities to be as close to each other, and to the city center, as possible, thereby putting intense pressure on the available land space.② Also, because they form distinctive landmarks, tall commercial buildings are frequently developed in city centers as prestige symbols for corporate organizations. Further, the business and tourist community, with its increasing mobility, has fueled a need for more, frequently high-rise, city center hotel accommodations.③

[3]   The rapid growth of the urban population and the consequent pressure on limited space have considerably influenced city residential development. The high cost of land, the desire to avoid a continuous urban sprawl, and the need to preserve important agriculture production have all contributed to drive residential buildings upward. In some cities, for example, Hon Kong and Rio de Janeiro, local topographical restrictions make tall buildings the only feasible solution for housing needs.

[4]   Tall building are designed primarily to serve the needs of an intended occupancy, whether residential, commercial, or, in some cases, a combination of the two. The dominant design requirements is therefore the provision of an appropriate internal layout for the building. At the same time, it is essential for the architect to satisfy the client's expectation concerning the aesthetic qualities of the building's exterior. The main design criteria are, therefore, architectural, and it is within these that the engineer is usually constrained to fit his structure. Only in exceptionally tall buildings will structural requirements become a predominant consideration.

[5]   The basic layout will be contained within a structural mesh that must be minimally obtrusive to the functional requirements of the building. Simultaneously, there must be an integration of the building structure with the various service systems—heating, ventilating, air-conditioning, water supply and waste disposal, electrical supply, and vertical transportation—which are extensive and complex, and constitute a major part of the cost of a tall building.

[6]   Once the functional layout has been established. the engineer must develop a structural system that will satisfy established design criteria as efficiently and economically as possible, while fitting into the architectural layout. The vital structural criteria are an adequate reserve of strength against failure, adequate lateral stiffness, and an efficient performance during the service life of the building.

[7]   Radical changes in the structural form of tall buildings occurred in the construction peri-

od that followed World War II. Over the same period, a major shift occurred in design philosophy, and the Code formats have progressed from the earlier working stress or ultimate strength deterministic bases to modern more generally accepted probability-based approaches. The probabilistic approach for both structural properties and loading conditions has led to the limit states design philosophy, which is now almost universally accepted. The aim of this approach is to ensure that all structures and their constituent components are designed to resist with reasonable safety the worst loads and deformations that are liable to occur during construction and service, and to have adequate durability during their lifetime.④

[8]　　The entire structure, or any part of it, is considered as having "failed" when it reaches any one of various "limit states," when it no longer meets the prescribed limiting design conditions.⑤ Two fundamental types of limit state must be considered: (1) the ultimate limit states corresponding to the loads to cause failure, including instability, since events associated with collapse would be catastrophic, endangering lives and causing serious financial losses, the probability of failure, must be very low; and (2) the serviceability limit state, which involve the criteria governing the service life of the building, and which, because the consequences of their failure would not be catastrophic, are permitted a much higher probability of occurrence. These are concerned with the fitness of the building for normal use rather than safety, and are of less critical importance.

[9]　　A particular limit state may be reached as a result of an adverse combination of random effects. Partial safety factors are employed for different conditions that reflect the probability of certain occurrences or circumstances of the structure and loading existing. The implicit objective of the design calculations is then to ensure that the probability of any particular limit state being reached is maintained below an acceptable value for the type of structure concerned.

New Words and Expressions

initially [i'niʃəli]	ad.	最初地；开始地
ecclesiastical [i͵kli:zi'æstikəl]	a.	基督教会的
subsequently ['sʌbsikwəntli]	ad.	随后地；后来地
thereby ['ðɛə'bai]	ad.	因此；从而
distinctive [dis'tiŋktiv]	a.	有特色的；与众不同的
prestige [pres'ti:ʒ]	n.	威望；声望
mobility [məu'biliti]	n.	运动性；变动性
consequent ['kɔnsikwənt]	a.	作为结果的；随之发生的
topographical [͵tɔpə'græfikəl]	a.	地形的
feasible ['fi:zəbl]	a.	可行的；可用的
criterion [krai'tiəriən]	n.	标准；尺度
constrain [kn'strein]	vt.	强使；强制
predominant [pri'dɔminənt]	a.	主要的；占优势的

exceptionally *	[ikˈsepʃənəli]	ad.	例外地；特殊地
minimally	[ˈminiməli]	ad.	最低限度地；最小地
obtrusive	[əbˈtruːsiv]	a.	强入的；强迫别人接受的
integration *	[ˌintiˈgreiʃən]	n.	综合；集成；积分
reserve	[riˈzəːv]	n.	储备；保存
lateral *	[ˈlætərəl]	a.	侧面的；横向的
stiffness *	[sˈtifnis]	n.	刚度；硬度
format	[ˈfɔːmæt]	n.	格式；尺寸；形式
deterministic *	[ditəˌmiˈnistik]	a.	确定的；决定的
deterministic base			定限；判据
probability	[prɔbəˈbiliti]	n.	可能性；概率
probabilistic approach			概率法
constituent	[kənstitjuənt]	a.	构成的；组成的
deformation	[ˌdiːfɔːˈmeiʃən]	n.	变形
durability	[ˈdjuərəˈbiliti]	n.	耐久性
prescribe	[prisˈkraib]	n.	指令；规定
instability	[ˌinstəˈbiliti]	n.	不稳定性
catastrophic	[ˌkætəˈstrɔfik]	a.	大灾难的；大祸的
serviceability	[ˌsəːvisəˈbiliti]	n.	操作性能；适用性
adverse	[ˈædvəːs]	a.	相反的；逆的；不利的；
random	[ˈrændəm]	a.	任意的；偶然的
implicit	[implisit]	a.	绝对的；固有的

Notes

①句中分词独立结构 their construction being initially for defense and subsequently for ecclesiastical purpose 作状语，表示补充说明。

②句中动词不定式短语 to be as close to…as possible 作 business activities 的后置定语；分词短语 thereby putting …land space. 作状语，表示结果。

③…has fueled a need for …
fuel 作为动词本意为"给……加燃料"，此处转意为"加剧……"或"给……火上加油"。

④本句的主要结构是 The aim of this approach is to ensure . . . and to have adequate durability during their lifetime.
另外，句中介词短语 with reasonable safety 是动词 resist 的状语，意为"可靠地经受住"。

⑤本句包含了两个由主从连接词 when 引导的时间状语从句，其中第二个从句 when it no longer meets …是对第一个从句含意的明确化、具体化，可看作是第一个从句的"同位语"。

Exercises

Reading Comprehension

I. Say whether the following statements are true (T) or false (F) according to the text, making use of the paragraph number.

1. Tall buildings were initially built for religious purposes and the efficient use of land. (Para. 1) ( )
2. Tall commercial buildings are frequently constructed in city centers, one of the reasons is that they symbolize some commercial organizations. (Para. 2) ( )
3. People tend to build high residential buildings to restrict the expansion of urban area and to preserve farm land. (Para. 2) ( )
4. The main design criteria is to provide suitable internal design for the buildings. (Para. 4) ( )
5. Structural requirements are usually a predominant consideration for tall buildings. (Para. 4) ( )
6. Service systems form a small part of the cost of a tall building. (Para. 5) ( )
7. The ultimate limit states are vital factors to be considered. (Para. 8) ( )
8. The serviceability limit states are as equally important as the ultimate limit states. (Para. 8) ( )

II. Classify the reasons listed below, for the growth of tall buildings and then fill in the following table with the corresponding numbers according to the groups they belong to. (Some have been done for you)

1. commercial purpose
2. defence purpose
3. residential purpose
4. religious purpose
5. rapid growth of the urban population
6. increasing mobility
7. pressure on limited space
8. high cost of land
9. demand by business activities to be close to each other and to the city center
10. the need to preserve farm land
11. as prestige symbols
12. the desire to avoid a continuous urban sprawl
13. local topographical restrictions

groups of various tall buildings		numbers of corresponding reasons
A.	ancient tall buildings and towers	4.
B.	modern tall buildings began in 1880's	1.
C.	tall commercial buildings	6.
D.	tall residential buildings	12. 13.

Vocabulary

I. Match the words in Column A with their corresponding definitions or descriptions in column B

    A   B

1. criterion   a. forming a whole
2. exceptionally   b. change in form
3. consequent   c. following as a result or proceeding in logical order
4. integration   d. not ordinary
5. stiffness   e. standard by which St. can be judged
6. formal   f. rigidity
7. durability   g. ability to last for long time
8. constituent   h. contrary or unfavorable
9. abverse   i. shape, size and general arrangement
10. deformation   j. combination of parts

II. Complete the following sentences with some of the words listed below, changing the form where necessary.

residential	criteria	accommodations
occupancy	performance	contribute
layout	restriction	instability

1. The building is described as the first commercial building in which modern materials, modern construction and efficient _____ have been combined with a modern plan.

2. One of the design _____ is to provide residents with solar access.

3. The rapid growth of residential areas is a response to the needs of an increasing _____.

4. The internal _____ for a mixed-use building with commercial and residential functions is a complex.

5. In order to reduce _____ of the structure a self-supporting system is usually applied to

the lateral walls.

6. The campus of Georgia State University was asked to provide a _____ of 10 000 athletes during the Olympic Games, Atlanta.

III. Complete each of the following statements with one of the four choices given below.

1. The rapid growth of the urban population has stimulated city _____ development.
   A. terrace housing   B. high-rise building   C. residential   D. living

2. The continuous urban _____ should be avoided to preserve farm land.
   A. sprawl   B. shrinkage   C. extension   D. development

3. The _____ life of an ordinary building is usually more than 50 years.
   A. serving   B. service   C. living   D. working

4. Service systems such as water supply, waste disposal, and _____ transportation are usually placed in the centre of a tall building.
   A. high-rise   B. outdoor   C. long-distance   D. vertical

5. The _____ of many tall building look much the same, resulting in the forms of monoliths with little variations.
   A. outdoors   B. outside   C. outlook   D. exterior

Reading Materials A

Design Criteria of Tall Building

The following sections are considered as some of the criteria that apply in particular to the design of tall buildings.

Loading

The structure must be designed to resist the gravitational and lateral forces, both permanent and transient, so that it will be called on to sustain during its construction and subsequent service life. These forces will depend on the size and shape of the building, as well as on its geographic location, and maximum probable values must be established before the design can proceed.

The probable accuracy of estimating the dead and live loads, and the probability of the simultaneous occurrence of different combinations of gravity loading, both dead and live, with either wind or earthquake forces, is included in limit states design through the use of prescribed factors.①

Strength and Stability

For the ultimate limit state, the prime design requirement is that the building structure should have adequate strength to resist, and to remain stable under the worst probable load actions that may occur during the lifetime of the building, including the period of construction.

This requires an analysis of the forces and stresses that will occur in the members as a result of the most critical possible load combinations, including the augmented moments that may arise from second-order additional deflections. ② An adequate reserve of strength, using prescribed load factors, must be present. Particular attention must be paid to critical members, whose failure could prove catastrophic in initiating a progressive collapse of part of or the entire building. Any additional stresses caused by restrained differential movements due to creep, shrinkage, or temperature must be included.

In addition, a check must be made on the most fundamental condition of equilibrium, to establish that the applied lateral forces will not cause the entire building to topple as a rigid body about one edge of the base. ③ Taking moments about that edge, the resisting moment of the dead weight of the building must be greater than the overturning moment for stability by an acceptable factor of safety. ④

Human Comfort Criteria

There are as yet no universally accepted international standards for comfort criteria, although they are under consideration, and engineers must base their design criteria on an assessment of published data. It is generally agreed that acceleration is the predominant parameter in determining human response to vibration, but other factors such as period, amplitude, body orientation, visual and acoustic cues, and even past experience can be influential. Threshold curves are available that give various limits for human behavior, ranging from motion perception through work difficulty to ambulatory limits, in terms of acceleration and period. ⑤ A dynamic analysis is then required to allow the predicted response of the building to be compared with the threshold limits.

Fire

The design considerations for fire prevention and protection, smoke control, fire-fighting, and escape are beyond the scope of a book on building structures. However, since fire appears to be by far the most common extreme situation that will cause damage in structures, it must be a primary consideration in the design process.

The characteristic feature of a fire, such as the temperature and duration, can be estimated from a knowledge of the important parameters involved, particularly the quantity and nature of combustible material present, the possibility and extent of ventilation, and the geometric and thermal properties of the fire compartment involved. Once the temperatures at various surfaces have been determined, from the gas temperature curve, it is possible to estimate the heat flow through the insulation and structural members. A knowledge of the temperature gradient across the member, and the degree of restraint afforded by the supports and surrounding structure, enables the stresses in the member to be evaluated. The mechanical properties of the structural materials, particularly the elastic modulus or stiffness and strength, may deteriorate rapidly as the temperature rises. and the resistance to load is greatly reduced. For example the yield stress of mild steel at a temperature of 700 ℃ is only some 10~20% of its value at room temperature.⑥ Over the same temperature range, the elastic modulus drops by around 40%~50%。 The critical temperature at which large deflections or collapse occurs will thus depend on the materials used, the nature of the structure, and the loading conditions.

The parameters that govern the approach are stochastic in nature, and the results of any calculation can be given only in probabilistic terms. The aim should be to achieve a homogeneous design in which the risks due to the different extreme situations are comparable.

Notes

① 通过使用规定的因素，把估计的死荷载和活荷载的可能精确度以及同时出现的重力荷载（死荷载或活荷载）分别与风力或地震力结合的概率都包括在极限状态设计范围之内。
② 这就要求要对构件中将出现的若干力及应力进行分析，这些力是若干最关键的可能荷载相结合的结果，包括在二级新增变形中可能出现的力矩增大。
③ 另外，必须对最基础的平衡状况进行检查，以确定外加侧向力不会导致整个建筑物作为刚性体向其基础的一边倒塌。
④ 就基础的这一边力矩而言，建筑物自重的抗力矩必须比保持稳定的倾覆力矩大一个安全系数。
⑤ 可以获得以加速度和周期的形式所表示出的各种限制人类行为范围的临界曲线，人类行为指的是从工作难度的运动感觉到步行范围。
⑥ 例如，软钢在 700 ℃下的屈服应力值只有室温下的 10%~20%。

Reading Material B

Stiffness and Drift Limitation①

The provision of adequate stiffness, particularly lateral stiffness, is a major consideration in the design of a tall building for several important reasons. As far as the ultimate limit state is concerned. lateral deflections must be limited to prevent second-order P-Delta effects due to gravity loading being of such a magnitude as to precipitate collapse. ② In terms of the serviceability limit states, deflections must first be maintained at a sufficiently low level to allow the proper functioning of nonstructural components such as elevators and doors; second, to avoid distress in the structure, to prevent excessive cracking and consequent loss of stiffness. and to avoid any redistribution of load to non-load-bearing partitions, in fills, cladding, or glazing; and third, the structure must be sufficiently stiff to prevent dynamic motions becoming large enough to cause discomfort to occupants, prevent delicate work being undertaken, or affect sensitive equipment. In fact, it is in the particular need for concern for the provision of lateral stiffness that the design of a high-rise building largely departs from that of a low-rise building. ③

One simple parameter that affords an estimate of the lateral stiffness of a building is the drift index, defined as the ratio of the maximum deflection at the top of the building to the total height. ④ In addition, the corresponding value for a single story height, the interstory drift index, gives a measure of possible localized excessive deformation. ⑤ The control of lateral defections is of particular importance for modern buildings in which the traditional reserves of stiffness due to heavy internal partitions and outer cladding have largely disappeared. It must be stressed, however, that even if the drift index is kept within traditionally accepted limits, such as 1/500, it does not necessarily follow that the dynamic comfort criteria will also be satisfactory.

The establishment of a drift index limit is a major design decision , but, unfortunately, there are no unambiguous or widely accepted values, or even, in some of the National Codes concerned, any firm guidance. The designer is then faced with having to decide on an appropriate value. The figure adopted will reflect the building usage, the type of design criterion employed (for example, working or ultimate load conditions), the form of construction, the materials employed, including any substantial infills or claddings, the wind loads considered, and, in particular, past experience of similar buildings that have performed satisfactorily.

Design drift index limits that have been used in different countries range from 0.001 to 0.005. To put this in perspective, a maximum horizontal top deflection of between 0.1 and 0.5m would be allowed in a 33-story, 100-m high building, or, alternatively, a relative deflection of 3 to 15 mm over a story height of 3 m. ⑥ Generally, lower values should be used for hotels or apartment buildings than for office buildings, since noise and movement tend to be more disturbing in the former. Consideration may be given to whether the stiffening effects of any internal partitions, infills, or claddings are included in the deflection calculations.

The consideration of this limit state requires an accurate estimate of the lateral deflections that occur, and involves an assessment of the stiffness of cracked members, the effects of shrinkage and creep and any redistribution of forces that may result, and of any rotational foundation movement. In the design process, the stiffness of joints, particularly in precast or prefabricated structures, must be given special attention to develop adequate lateral stiffness of the structure and to prevent any possible progressive failure. The possibility of torsional deformations must not be overlooked.

In practice, non-load-bearing infills, partitions, external wall panels, and window glazing should be designed with sufficient clearance or with flexible supports to accommodate the calculated movements.

The drift criteria apply essentially to quasistatic conditions. When extreme force conditions are possible, or where problems involving vortex shedding or other unusual phenomena may occur, a more sophisticated approach involving a dynamic analysis may be required.

If excessive, the drift of a structure can be reduced by changing the geometric configuration to alter the mode of lateral load resistance, increasing the bending stiffness of the horizontal members, adding additional stiffness by the inclusion of stiffer wall or core members, achieving stiffer connections, and even by sloping the exterior columns. In extreme circumstances, it may be necessary to add dampers, which may be passive or active type.

Notes

①Stiffness and Drift Limitations：刚度与位移极限。
②就最终极限状态而言，必须限制侧向变形以防止由于重力荷载过大造成的倒塌而导致的二级 P-Delta 后果。
③实际上，就是在提供侧向刚度的特别需要上，高层建筑设计与低层建筑设计有很大差异。
④提供估计建筑物侧向刚度的简单参数是侧向指数，定义为建筑物最高点的最大变形与总高度之比。
⑤此外，单层建筑的相应值，即层际位移系数，可以测出可能的定位过度变形。
⑥用透视来表示，对于 33 层楼高的建筑物（100m），水平顶部的最大变形是在 0.1 至 0.5 米之间，换言之，每增高一层楼（3m），相对变形在 3 至 15 mm 之间。

UNIT TWELVE

Text   Parking

[1]   The design of parking projects today and in the future must be integrated with the various design considerations of the high-rise building development. From the initial concept through the final design, each phase of the project should be geared to mesh with the other.

[2]   There are certain conditions that should be incorporated in the design of any structure that is intended to have an area set aside for parking. The premise is that the parking is necessary in this particular situation and is economically feasible to construct.

[3]   Parking facilities may be part of high-rise office towers, residential towers, or shopping complexes, or they may be stand-alone structures. ① Therefore, each facility will have a set of conditions and an environment that will be unique; and each will have to be analyzed from many aspects to determine if it is meeting the present need and if it is flexible enough to accommodate future change.

[4]   For example, office towers are generally a Monday-to-Friday, 9 a.m.-to-5 p.m. proposition. ② The tenancy of the tower will dictate the amount of space that will be required for parking; that is, multicorporate tenancy will mean many executives who will more than likely drive to work, whereas single corporate tenants will likely have large clerical staffs who will normally use mass transit if available or even car-pool where possible. ③ Moreover, office tower tenants are usually all-day parkers with little in-and-out activity. However, adding shops, restaurants, and theaters—either in the toweritself or in the immediate surrounding area—creates a demand for short-term parking, with attendant turnover in space utilization.

[5]   The requirements for residential towers, on the other hand, will depend on the age and mix of the tenants. The parking facility will be either a constant in-and-out operation, having continuous space for transient parkers or be primarily for retired tenants with little in-and-out movement, having a lower availability of space for transients.

[6]   Shopping centers usually have short-term occupancy that runs two-and-a-half hours per stay for the average shopper. Turnover of space should be very high. However, depending on the proximity to mass transportation, turnover can be very low if the facility becomes a convenient place for commuters to park. In this case, safeguards would have to be built in to restrict such abuse; prevention can be easily achieved by matching the facility with shopper's hours and not opening before 10 a.m., or by establishing a rate structure favorable to the shopper but unattractive to the commuter. ④

[7]   Stand-alone parking facilities are wholly dependent on their feeder sources. Therefore, it must be possible to predict the needs of the immediate area—the number of spaces required, the length of stay, the rates that are competitive, the method of operation, and the required hours of operation. ⑤ It is equally important to consider actual design aspects for parking facili-

ties, as described in the following sections. ⑥

Signage

[8]   Is the parking facility open to the public, and recognizable as such, or is it restricted to tenants of the supporting structure? Is the interior signage clear and limited in the length of message conveyed? Simply stated, can the driver find his way to a space, and then go from that space to the facility exit without becoming confused or lost?

Columns

[9]   Are columns arranged to provide for the clear space required by today's vehicles ? Can a vehicle drive through the facility with a minimum number of turns ? Are clearances sufficient to permit two-way traffic ? If one-way traffic is desirable—as it would be in a high turnover facility—are the columns arranged so that there is limited dead space ?

[10]   In addition, we are now in a transition period with respect to vehicle size. It is estimated that by 1985 at least 70% of the vehicles on the road will be in the compact or small-car group. Consideration must be given to the redesign of the facility to accommodate the smaller car and the possible increase in the number of cars.

Concrete

[11]   As a minimum, 4 000 psi concrete should be specified. ⑦ It should be air entrained, and the concrete cover over the top reinforcing steel should not be less than 1 1/2 in. If possible, the reinforcing steel for the facility decks and driveways should be mill coated to reduce the possibility of rusting and the attendant deterioration of the slab. ⑧

Drainage

[12]   There should be positive drainage to the nearest floor drain. Moreover, climatic conditions impose special requirements. For example, in the snow belt, large amounts of snow and ice will be brought into the facility and, of necessity, equally large amounts of snow melting chemicals and salts will be deposited on its floor. In such a case, the faster the runoff flows to the drain, the less time the water has to penetrate the slab and start its destructive action.

Lighting

[13]   Good lighting is essential for the safe operation of the facility. It is most important in driveways and in the entrance and exit areas where it should be equal to the exterior light con-

ditions to minimize eye adjustment time.

Interior layout

[14]   It is important to consider spaces for the handicapped. The federal government has established guidelines on the number of such spaces that must be included, especially in projects that receive federal funds. Where will they be located? Are there obstacles that prohibit the free movement of the handicapped? Handicapped parking areas should be located in the safest possible section of the facility, away from vehicular traffic lanes, if possible.

New Words and Expressions

integrate ['intigreit]	vt.	使结合
gear [giə]	v.	使配合；传动
mesh [meʃ]	v.	紧密结合；啮合
	n.	网孔；网状结构
incorporate [in'kɔːpəreit]	vt.	体现，使合并
premise ['premis]	n.	前提
	v.	提出……为前提
stand-alone	a.	独立的
accommodate [ə'kɔmədeit]	vt.	使适应，容纳
proposition [prɔpə'ziʃən]	n.	建议，命题
dictate [dik'teit]	v.	规定，要求
multicoporate ['mʌlti'kɔpərit]	a.	多元的，多单位的
clerical ['klerikəl]	a.	办事员的，办公室工作的
corporate ['kɔːpərit]	a.	共同的，全体的
transit ['trænsit]	n.	公共交通系统，运输
car-pool	n.	车辆合用组织
attendant ['tendənt]	a.	伴随的
transient ['trænziənt]	n.	暂时居住的人，过客
	a.	短暂的，过路的
proximity [prɔk'simiti]	n.	接近度，邻近
clearance ['kliərəns]	n.	（建）净空，间隙
two-way	n.	双向交通，相向的交通
with respect to		关于
compact [kəm'pækt]	n.	小型汽车；压制品
	a.	紧密的，结实的
entrain [in'trein]	vt.	使（空气）以气泡状存在于混凝土中
deck [dek]	n.	楼层面；盖板

deterioration [ditiəriə'reiʃən]	n.	损坏，恶化
slab [slæb]	n.	混凝土楼板；平板
drainage ['dreinidʒ]	n.	排水；排水系统，排水管
of necessity		不可避免地，必然地
runoff ['rʌnəf]	n.	（雨水、融雪等的）径流，流量
handicapped ['hændikæpt]	a.	残废的，身体有缺陷的
prohibit [prə'hibit]	v.	禁止，阻止，妨碍

Notes

①(1) Parking facilities…

facility 为复数时，一般作"设施"、"装置"等解，此处和下句中的 facility 一律作为"停车场"讲。

(2) …high-rise office towers, residential towers…

在现代英语中，office tower，residential towers 常表示"高层办公楼""高层住宅楼"，有无 high-rise 或 tall 修饰无关紧要。

②…a Monday-to-Friday, 9 A.M.-to-5 P.M. proposition.

proposition 本意"主张"、"命题"等，此处指"上班"、"办公"等。proposition 前的两个复合词均系定语。

③car-pool：系美国社会上一种轮流为其它成员提供自用车的自发性组织。

④…a rate structure favorable to the shopper but unattractive to the commuter.

这部分也可能是指在建筑物里留给购物者停车的空间大于留给过往车辆停车的空间，造成过客停车的拥挤不便，因而不愿在此停车。另一种理解见参考译文。

⑤…the rates that are competitive…

此处 rates 意为进出停车场的车辆流量。由于流量是 competitive（具有竞争性），因而译为"流量高峰"。

⑥…as described in the following sections.

这是一个由关系代词 as 引导的修饰前边整个主句的特种定语从句（special attributive clause）从句中省略了助动词 is 。

⑦PSI 即 pounds per square inch.

⑧mill 作为名词本意为"轧钢机"、"轧制设备"等，这里作"轧钢"解，系物质名词，因而没有数的变化；过去分词 coated 作 mill 的后置定语。

Exercises

Reading Comprehension

I. The followings are the main ideas of some paragraphs. Read each and then find out the corresponding number of the right paragraph from the four suggested.

1. Any structure which is intended to build a parking area should take account of the premise that the parking is necessary and economically feasible to construct. (3, 2, 5, 4)
2. Parking space serving shopping centers should have a very high turnover. (1, 5, 6, 4)
3. Parking facilities may be either part of the tall buildings they serve or a separate structure. (1, 2, 3, 4)
4. The design of parking facilities must be associated with the design considerations of tall building developments. (1, 2, 3, 4)
5. Good lighting is essential for the safe operation of the facilities. (10, 11, 12, 13)
6. The amount of parking space for office tower is determined by the tenancy. (4, 6, 3, 7)
7. In a parking structure there should be efficient drainage on the floor. (10, 12, 8, 13)
8. The requirements for the parking facilities of residential towers are based on the age and mix of the tenants. (4, 5, 6, 7)
9. Separate parking facilities are entirely dependent on their parkers. So it is significant to predict the needs of the nearby areas. (5, 6, 7, 8)
10. Consideration must be given to the redesign of facility to admit the smaller car and the possible increase in the number of cars. (5, 7, 8, 10)
11. Signage in and outside a parking facility must be brief and clear. (8, 9, 11, 12)
12. Considerable attention must be given to the arrangement of columns in parking structures. (14, 13, 12, 9)

II. Choose the best answers according to the text.

1. In the first sentence of Para. 1, "be integrated with" can be replaced by _____.
   A. be combined with
   B. be explained as
   C. be interfered with
   D. be mixed with
2. In the last sentence of Para. 2, "in this particular situation" refers to _____.
   A. certain conditions should be incorporated.
   B. to have an area set aside for parking.
   C. economically feasible to construct.
   D. what it means in the first sentence.
3. According to the second sentence of Para. 4, _____ of the following is true.
   A. Car-pool is a favorite to many executives.
   B. The executives prefer to drive to work.
   C. Large clerical staffs are naturally to occupy more parking space.
   D. The executives are normally in favour of mass transit.
4. In the last sentence of Para. 4, "with attendant turnover in space utilization" actually means _____.
   A. with overcrowded occupancy of parking space

B. having attendant obstruction in space utilization

C. with accompanying shift in space utilization

D. with considerable insufficiency in space utilization

5. It is inferred from Para. 6, that in the parking structures of shopping centers _____.

    A. the more parkers the better

    B. the lower turnover the better

    C. commuters from mass transportation are not welcomed

    D. shoppers are not welcomed either

6. In the last sentence of Para. 6, "a rate structure" means _____.

    A. a high-rise building

    B. a structure with its space proportionally divided in function

    C. a place where parking fee is paid

    D. a structure used as safeguards

Vocabulary

Ⅰ. Complete the following sentences with some of the words or expressions listed below, changing the form if necessary.

integrate	gear	with respect to
deck	premise	accommodate
attendant	incorporate	of necessity

1. Double _____ buses used to be seen in Hong Kong and now you can see them frequently in some of the inland cities.

2. In learning a science, it is always essential to _____ theory with practice. The same is true for architecture.

3. Besides having reasonable interior layout, an office tower must _____ itself to the immediate surroundings.

4. A building at high cost is not _____ a structure of high quality.

5. That ancient temple on the hill _____ typical architectural style of Tang Dynasty.

6. Prof. Smith is invited to give us a lecture on the History of Western Architecture, especially _____ the modern period.

Ⅱ. Complete each of the following statement with one of the four choices given below:

1. In downtown areas the underground garage may be the only _____ solution to the problem of parking since land price there is terrible high.

    A. favourite   B. common   C. feasible   D. attractive

2. The supply of parking space for the _____ is a sign of the advancement in social civilization.

A. handicraft   B. handicapped   C. handiwork   D. handiness

3. It is required that we take the frequent _____ vehicle into account while designing parking facilities for shopping centers.

   A. transit   B. temporary   C. transient   D. transform

4. As the turnover is very high, the parking space needs to leave _____ enough to permit two-way traffic.

   A. columns   B. accommodation   C. clearance   D. drainage

5. Stand-alone parking facilities tend to be the _____ utility used by the immediate surroundings.

   A. cooperate   B. corporate   C. commune   D. corporation

6. The _____ to be used in the floor of high buildings have to undergo tension test or will be regarded as unqualified products.

   A. deck   B. drain   C. runoff   D. slabs

7. As far as the traffic conditions and the consuming power of Chinese citizens are concerned, _____ is the best choice for the taxi business.

   A. compact   B. luxurious cars   C. larger cars   D. buses

8. Being air _____, soft concrete is relatively porous and is suited to floor finish.

   A. broken into   B. breaking into   C. entrained   D. entraining

Reading Material A

Nine Percent Parking

Very rough empirical observations lead us to believe that it is not possible to make an environment fit for human use when more than 9 percent of it is given to parking.

Our observations are very tentative. We have yet to perform systematic studies—our observations rely on our own subjective estimates of cases where "there are too many cars" and cases where "the cars are all right."① However, we have found in our preliminary observations, that different people agree to a remarkable extent about these estimates. This suggests that we are dealing with a phenomenon which, though obscure, is nonetheless substantial.②

An example of an environment which has the threshold density of 9 percent parking, is shown in our key photograph: a quadrant of the University of Oregon.③ Many people we have talked to feel intuitively that this area is beautiful now, but that if more cars were parked there it would be ruined.

What possible functional basis is there for this intuition? We conjecture as follows: people realize, subconsciously, that the physical environment is the medium for their social intercourse. It is the environment which, when it is working properly, creates the potential for all social communion, including even communion with the self.④

We suspect that when the density of cars passes a certain limit, and people experience the feeling that there are too many cars, what is really happening is that subconsciously they feel that the cars are overwhelming the environment, that the environment is no longer "theirs," that they have no right to be there, that it is not a place for people, and so on. After all, the effect of the cars reaches far beyond the mere presence of the cars themselves. They create a maze of driveways, garage doors, asphalt and concrete surfaces, and building elements which people cannot use. When the density goes beyond the limit, we suspect that people feel the social potential of the environment has disappeared. Instead of inviting them out, the environment starts giving them the message that the outdoors is not meant for them, that they should stay indoors, that they should stay in their own buildings, that social communion is no longer permitted or encouraged.

We have not yet tested this suspicion. However, if it turns out to be true, it may be that this pattern, which seems to be based on such slender evidence, is in fact one of the most crucial patterns there is, and that it plays a key role in determining the difference between environment which are socially and psychologically healthy and those which are unhealthy. [5]

We conjecture, then, that environments which are human, and not destroyed socially or ecologically by the presence of parked cars, have less than 9 percent of the ground area devoted to parking space; and that parking lots and garages must therefore never be allowed to cover more than 9 percent of the land.

It is essential to interpret this pattern in the strictest possible way. The pattern becomes meaningless if we allow ourselves to place the parking generated by a piece of land A, on another adjacent piece of land B, thus keeping parking on A below 9 percent, but raising the parking on B to more than 9 percent. [6] In other words, each piece of land must take care of itself; we must not allow ourselves to solve this problem on one piece of land at the expense of some other piece of land. A town or a community can only implement the pattern according to this strict interpretation by defining a grid of independent "parking zones" — each zone 1 to 10 acres in area — which cover the whole community, and then insisting that the rule be applied, independently, and strictly, inside every parking zone.

The 9 percent rule has a clear and immediate implication for the balance between surface parking and parking in garages, at different parking densities. [7] This follows from simple arithmetic. [8] Suppose, for example, that an area requires 20 parking spaces per acre. Twenty parking spaces will consume about 7 000 square feet, which would be 17 percent of the land if it were all in surface parking. To keep 20 cars per acre in line with the 9 percent rule, at least half of them will have to be parked in garages. The table below gives similar figures for different densities:

Cars per acre	Percent on surface	Percent in two story garages	Percent in three story garages
12	100	—	—

17	50	50	—
23	50	—	50
30	—	—	100

What about underground parking? May we consider it as an exception to this rule? Only if it does not violate or restrict the use of the land above. If, for example, a parking garage is under a piece of land which was previously used as open space, with great trees growing on it, then the garage will almost certainly change the nature of the space above, because it will no longer be possible to grow large trees there. Such a parking garage is a violation of the land. Similarly, if the structural grid of the garage — 60 foot bays — constrains the structural grid of the building above, so that this building is not free to express its needs, this is a violation too.⑨ Underground parking may be allowed only in those rare cases where it does not constrain the land above at all: under a major road, perhaps, or under a tennis court.

We see then, that the 9 percent rule has colossal implications. Since underground parking will only rarely satisfy the conditions we have stated, the pattern really says that almost no part of the urban area may have more than 30 parking spaces per acre. This will create large changes in the central business district. Consider a part of a typical downtown area. There may be several hundred commuters per acre working there; and, under today's conditions, many of them park their cars in garages.⑩ But if it is true that there cannot be more than 30 parking spaces per acre, then either the work will be forced to decentralize, or the workers will have to rely on public transportation.

We must, therefore, keep in mind: Do not allow more than 9 percent of the land in any given area to be used for parking. In order to prevent the "bunching" of parking in huge neglected areas, it is necessary for a town or a community to subdivide its land into "parking zones" no larger than 10 acres each and to apply the same rule in each zone.⑪

Notes

①我们还需要做系统的研究。因为，我们的观察结果是建立在对一些情况的主观判断上，比方说："这里的车太多了"，又比如，"那儿的车还可以"。
　　observations 为复数时，可意为"观察结果"。
②这说明我们正在讨论一种现象，这种现象虽然还模糊，但各方面仍然很有价值。
　　nonetheless=nevertheless 仍然，依然
③本文前的照片（俄勒冈大学的一角）就是一个例子，表明停车达到百分之九这个临界密度的环境。（照片略——编注）
④是环境（当环境理想时）创造了所有社交的潜力，甚至包括与环境本身打交道的潜力。
　　the self 指环境"本身"。
⑤这只是一种猜测，然而，如果被证实，情况就可能是：这种模式（指停车密度不超过9%——编注）尽管它的证据似乎不足，但实际上是最具决定性的模式之一，它在决定哪种环境从社会角度和心理角度是健康的还是不健康的环境方面起着关键作用。

⑥如果我们允许自己把 A 地段上的停车场建在邻近的 B 地段上。这样，A 地段上的停车场占地不到百分之九，而 B 地段上的停车场却超过了百分之九。这种模式就没有什么意义了。

⑦百分之九的规则明显而直接地暗示一种平衡，一种在不同停车密度中露天停车和停车房里停车的平衡。

⑧This follows from… 这是根据……得出的。

⑨同样，如果地下停车房的层面结构凹下 60 米，限制了地面建筑物的层次结构，因而影响其它地面建筑物自由表现其作用，也同样是违反规则。

⑩commuters 在此处意为"往来停车者"。

⑪为了防止在一大片人们忽视的地区出现驻车聚集现象，每个城镇或社区有必要将其土地细分成不超过 10 英亩的停车范围，并在每个范围中应用本文中所提到的规则。

Reading Material B

Shielded Parking

Large parking structures full of cars are inhuman and dead buildings — no one wants to see them or walk by them. At the same time, if you are driving, the entrance to a parking structure is essentially the main entrance to the building — and it needs to be visible.

In NINE PERCENT PARKING, we have already defined an upper limit on the total amount of parking in a neighborhood.① In SMALL PARKING lots we give the best size and the distribution of the lots when they are on the ground. But in certain cases it is still necessary to build larger parking lots or parking structures. The environment can tolerate these larger lots and structures, provided that they are built so that they do not pollute the land around them.②

This is a simple biological principle. In the human body, for example, there are waste products; the waste products are part of the way the body works, and obviously they must have a place. But the stomach and colon are built in such a way as to shield the other internal organs from the poisons carried by the wastes.③

The same is true in a city. At this moment in history the city requires a certain limited amount of parking; and for the time being there is no getting away from that.④ But the parking must be built in such a way that it is shielded — by shops, houses, hills of grassy earth, walls, or any other buildings of any kind — anything, so long as the interior of the parking structure and the cars are not visible from the surrounding land. On ground level, the shield is especially critical. Shops are useful since they generate their own pedestrian scale immediately.⑤ And since the need for parking often goes hand in hand with commercial development, shops are often very feasible economically.

And of course, the houses themselves can serve the same function. In Paris, many of the most charming and beautiful apartment houses are arranged around courtyards, which permit parking inside, away from the street. There are few enough cars, so that they don't destroy the courtyard, for the houses; and the street is left free of parked cars entirely.

Along with the need to shield parking structures there is the equally pressing need on the part of a driver to be able to spot the parking structure quickly — and see how it is connected to the building he is headed for.⑥ One of the most frequent complaints about the parking near a building is not that it is too far away, but that you don't know where you can go to find a parking spot and still be sure of how to get back into the building.

This means that

1. Parking, which is specifically for the use of visitors, must be clearly marked from the directions of approach, even though the structure as a whole is shielded.⑦ The person who is coming by car will be looking for the building, not the parking lot. The entrance to parking must be marked as an important entrance — a gate — so that you can see it automatically, in the process of looking for the building. And it must be placed so that you find it about the same time that you see the building's main entrance.

2. While you are parking your car you must be able to see the exit from the parking area which will lead you into the building. This will let you search for the closest spots, and will mean that you don't have to walk around searching for the exit.

Therefore, we may draw conclusions as following:

Put all large parking lots, or parking garages, behind some kind of natural wall, so that the cars and parking structures cannot be seen from outside. The wall which surrounds the cars may be a building, connected houses, or housing hills, earth berms, or shops.

Make the entrance to the parking lot a natural gateway to the buildings which it serves, and place it so that you can easily see the main entrance to the building from the entrance to the parking.⑧

Notes

①在"百分之九的停车场面积"一文中，我们已经确定了一个街区停车场总面积的极限。
②如果这些大型停车场和建筑不污染周围的土地；那么环境就允许它们存在。
③而胃和结肠的构造就可以保护体内其他器官不受粪便携带毒物的影响。
④…and for the time being there is no getting away from that.
　……目前，还不能摆脱这种情况。
⑤开商店的益处在于只要有商店，就能立即招来一定数量的行人。
⑥除了需要隐蔽停车场建筑物外，从司机角度来说，也有一个同样迫切的要求，即希望能够迅速地辨认出停车场并看出停车场与他要去的建筑物之间的路线。
　spot v. 认出，识别。
⑦即使整个停车场都遮蔽住，但为客人专用的停车场必须清楚地标出路向。
⑧使停车场的入口成为通往停车场所从属的建筑物的天然通路，它应设置在刚一进停车场就能很容易看见建筑物的主要入口的地方。

UNIT THIRTEEN

Text   Ornament

[1]   We usually think of ornament or decoration as being applied to something, added to its surface—in a sense even removable①. Actually, though, from the most primitive eras onward, ornament has been part of the very essence and substance of the object being designed, be it a spear, a piece of fabric, or a building. ② An arrow, for instance, would have feathers not only to keep its flight straight but to please the god of hunting — who was mad about feathers — while the shaft would be painted or carved to express some slogan or other, such as "Keen sight makes dead enemy. " Fabrics often bore designs and patterns which meant "Happy Motherhood " or the like, while buildings, from the most elementary to the most advanced, carried emblems, forms, and carvings upon which, in the minds of the people, the entire validity of the structure depended.

[2]   Very often elements with ritualistic meaning would persist beyond the period in which they were so used to become permanent parts of their structures even though the "meaning" had disappeared in the changing social vocabulary. ③For instance, acanthus leaves tied to the columns of ancient temples at certain holidays were eventually carved permanently into stone and applied to buildings having no connection with those holidays. Sheaves of wheat appearing on Egyptian pillars soon became carved and gilded, and put into buildings having nothing to do with harvests whatsoever.

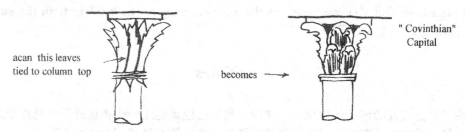

Fig. 13-1

[3]   But even when the original ritualistic or religious meaning of the ornament is long forgotten it still may function legitimately in architect as a way of expressing something about the nature or quality of the structure on which it is used. It may speak of wealth, of importance, of elegance — or it may be no more than a tribute to the good taste of possessor. In any case, the ornament continues — and this is the point — to be an integral part of the architect rather than something "pretty-pretty" put on the surface.

[4]   Of course, this is a somewhat idealistic way of putting it. The fact is, unfortunately, that a great many people, including some architects who should know better, have the attitude that ornament is not integral, but is something really superfluous, only perhaps useful for "show". Perhaps some of this approach is due to the many years of the stark, functionalist

phase of modern architecture, during which all ornament or decoration came to be regarded as sentimental, traditionalistic, and, at its worst, reactionary.④ The swing in the latter part of the twentieth century is the other way, and we are once more allowing ourselves, as did our parents and grandparents the luxury of patterns, colors, and carvings.⑤ The main difference is that manual craftsmanship having been largely replaced by machine processes, the ornament has a different quality — a mass produced feeling that is enhanced rather than reduced by the use of materials that are often synthetic.⑥

[5] In view of these considerations, then, it becomes evident that a good architect should understand not merely the stylistic uses of ornament, but much more importantly, the social origins and functions that ornament involves. Ornament is language, part of the language of architecture; if it is to be more than pretty prattle it must have meaning.⑦ To those who would understand architecture, some grasp of the meanings to be found in ornament is necessary.

[6] **Orientation** If it is agreed that ornament is integral with, not separate from, architectural form, then the two together, form and ornament, give the viewer his initial impression of the building, telling him what sort of place it is , and what it means in relation to himself. For example, if he sees a colonnaded facade, topped by a sculptured pediment, with steps flanked by stone lions, he does not take long to decide that it is an institutional building — museum, courthouse, city hall, etc. — of a conservative, tradition-alistic persuasion.

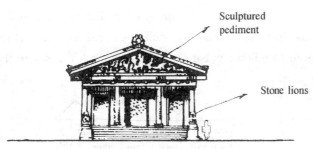

Fig. 13-2

[7] Note that the character of the ornament, the style and subject matter of the sculpture, must all be consistent with this basic statement, or the whole thing will look like a caricature.

[8] If, in contrast, he sees a contemporary structure, even if it is still "institutional" in character, in which the decorative elements are of the time and the sculpture modern, he will tend to identify the building as a progressive college, an arts center, an agency of the U. N. or something equally up-to-date. Note, again, that it is the ornament, as much as the structural shapes, that tells the story.

[9] To hit the extreme of the contrast, let us imagine a discotheque on Hollywood's Sunset strip.⑧ The forms used are intentionally bizarre, while the decoration follows the approved fashion of running across the forms capriciously, in a manner suggestive of the multimedia art being practiced within — a mixture of electronic music, film, and psychedelic lights. The point, at the risk of being redundant, is that the ornament, being part of the architectural statement, is inseparable from the whole and must be consistently conceived.

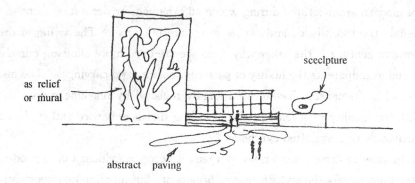

Fig. 13-3

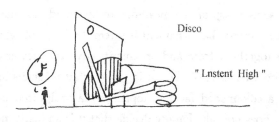

Fig. 13-4

[10]   Direction. Your eye tends to slide rapidly over plain surfaces and linger, or at least pause, at places of visual interest — murals, sculpture, and so forth. And where your eye goes your feet are inclined to follow; or, if the feet cannot go, as. say to the painting on the ceiling, your attention goes.

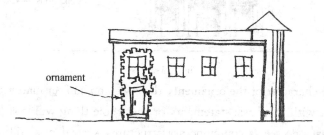

Fig. 13-5

Thus the architect can use ornament to direct the eye, the attention, and the potential movement of the people using his building. From the outside, for instance, ornament can tell you where the entrance is, so that you are spared the uncomfortable hesitation which you would otherwise — especially on a first visit — especially on a first visit — experience.

New Words and Expressions

removable * [ri'muːvəbl]   a.   可拆装的；可移动的
onward ['ɔnwəd]   a., ad.   向前（的）；在前面（的）

essence *	[ˈesns]	n.	本质；精华
shaft *	[ʃɑːft]	n.	箭杆；柱身，塔尖
emblem	[ˈemblem]	n.	标志，象征
validity *	[vəˈliditi]	n.	有效性；真实性
ritualistic	[ritjuəˈlistik]	a.	仪式的
acanthus	[əˈkænθəs]	n.	莨苕叶形装饰
acanthus leaves			叶板
sheaves	[ʃiːvz]	n.	捆
pillar	[ˈpilə]	n.	支柱
gild	[gild]	v.	镀金于；漆成金色
legitimately	[leˈdʒitimeitli]	ad.	合法地；正统地
elegance	[ˈeligəns]	n.	雅致，优美
tribute	[ˈtribjuːt]	n.	称赞，颂词
integral *	[ˈintigrəl]	a.	完整的，整个的
superfluous	[sjuːˈpəːfluəs]	a.	多余的，不必要的
functionalist	[ˈfʌŋkʃənəlist]	n.	建筑实用（功能）主义者
sentimental	[ˈsentimәntl]	a.	感情的，情绪的
stylistic	[staiˈlistik]	a.	风格上的
prattle	[ˈprætl]	n.	空谈，废话
colonnaded	[kɔləˈneidid]	a.	设有柱廊的
pediment	[ˈpedimənt]	n.	山花（墙）
flank	[ˈflæŋk]	v.	位于……侧面的（两侧的）
institutional	[instiˈtjuːʃənəl]	a.	社会事业性的，公共机构的
persuasion	[pəˈsweiʒən]	n.	信念；集团
conservative	[kənˈsəvətiv]	a.	保守的，守旧的
caricature	[kærikəˈtjuə]	n.	漫画，讽刺画
bizarre	[biˈzɑː]	a.	希奇古怪的；异乎寻常的
capriciously	[kəˈpriʃəsli]	ad.	变化莫测的
psychedelic	[saikəˌdelik]	a.	颜色鲜艳的；引起幻觉的
redundant	[riˈdʌndənt]	a.	多余的；累赘的

Notes

①being applied to something 和 (being) added to its surface 系作介词 as 的两个并列的动名词短语。

②be it a spear, a piece of fabric, or a building

这是一种含有让步、选择成份的状语从句,相当于 whether it was a spear, a piece of fabric, or it was a building.

③element 一词除了本身在词典中的一些含义之外，在建筑学领域中也表示建筑物中形成固

定格式的构件；在城市规划中则指一个特定区域内各个相关的建筑物或设施。在这种情况中，一般译作"建筑符号"或"建筑要素"、"要素"。

④(1) approach 此处含义同上句中的 attitude。

(2) functionalist：建筑实用主义者，也叫"功能主义者"，是建筑学的一个流派，主张形式服从功能、用途、材料。

⑤The swing in the latter part of …

swing 一词此处意为"周期性交替"，也可引申为"轮回"。

⑥本句的主要结构是 The main difference is that…the ornament has a different quality… manual craftsmanship having been largely replaced by machine processes 系分词独立结构，在表语从句中作状语，表示原因。

⑦…; if it is to be more than pretty prattle, it must have meaning.

其中 is to be more 系谓语动词 to be to do (be) 现象，表示将来的概念（将来时）。但必须注意，这种将来时一般都是计划、规定、打算好的，翻译时要适当加词。如本句可成"如果要想不是空谈，……"。

⑧Hollywood's Sunset strip：好莱坞的日落街是一条林荫大道，两边有许多娱乐设施和酒吧间等。

Exercises

Reading Comprehension：

I. Say whether the following statements are true (T) or false (F) according to the text, making use of the paragraph numbers.

1. From the very ancient time, ornament has been part of the main factors of the object being designed. (Para. 1) ( )

2. No matter what kinds of emblems, forms or carvings a building carried, it stood in the minds of people. (Para. 1) ( )

3. Very often ornament with ritualistic meaning would persist as permanent elements even though the real meaning had already vanished as time went by. (Para. 2) ( )

4. Whatever an ornament was used on a structure, it would has completely lost its original meaning and only serves as a way to express something about the structure. (Para. 3) ( )

5. It may be inferred from Paragraph 4 that the author is in favor of the ornament made by manual craftsmanship. (Para. 4) ( )

6. To be a qualified architect, it is necessary and possible of for architects to master the meanings in ornament, since it is part of architectural language. (Para. 5) ( )

7. To be specific, the word orientation in the text means for a building to tell you what sort of place it is and what it means in relation to you. (Para. 6) ( )

8. If the character of the ornament, the style and subject of the sculpture fail to be consis-

130

tent with the basic statement, the whole thing will become an actual caricature. (Para. 7)   (   )

9. To be specific again, the word direction in the text means for people ornament to direct your eye, your attention and the potential movement of the using the structure. (Para. 10)   (   )

II. According to your understanding of the text, complete the following statements by choosing the best answers from those suggested.

1. You may learn _____ from Paragraphs One and Two.
    A. Ornament elements can be permanent part of the structures they belong to
    B. It is often the case that ornament might gradually loose its original meaning
    C. Ornament must not be thought as removable
    D. All above

2. The following can be indicated by ornament except _____.
    A. the possessor's wealth
    B. the possessor's habit
    C. the possessor's social position
    D. the possessor's ability to enjoy beauty

3. The worst attitude towards ornament is to consider it as being _____.
    A. removable   B. not integral
    C. reactionary   D. superfluous

4. The swing in latter part of the twentieth century is the other way. The word "swing" here is referred to _____.
    A. periodic alternation   B. crossing through
    C. turnover   D. relaxed motion

5. According to the text _____ is not mentioned as the function of ornament.
    A. Language of architecture   B. defense
    C. orientation   D. direction

6. From the text we know the author probably think that ornament is _____ to structures.
    A. unnecessary   B. not essential
    C. significant   D. most essential

Vocabulary

I. Match the words in Column A with their corresponding definitions or descriptions in Column B.

    A   B
    1. removable   a. the inner nature

2. essence b. whole or complete
3. shaft c. vary strange
4. validity d. opposed to great or sudden change
5. integral e. sigh; object that for something else
6. orientation f. able to remove
7. conservative g. long stem of an arrow or spear
8. bizarre h. awareness of one's environment
9. gild i. the state or quality of being true
10. emblem j. coat with gold; make bright as if with gold

II. Fill in the missing words or expressions for the following sentences from the text.
1. It is obvious that a good architect should understand not only the _____ uses of ornament, but much more importantly, the _____ of functions that _____ involves.
2. It is the _____ and _____ that give the viewer his initial impression of the, building.
3. The character of the ornament, the _____ and the matter of the _____ must all be consistent with this basic statement.
4. The architect can use ornament to direct the eye, the _____ and the potential _____ of the people using his building.

Reading Material A

Architecture is the Ornament of Human Environment

In an interior, the placement of ornament is equally critical. Consider, for example, how strongly a decorative mantelpiece dominates a room, and how much less eye-impelling an untrimmed fireplace is.① In a public building the efficient operation of the lobby and entrance hallways may depend largely on the ornament.

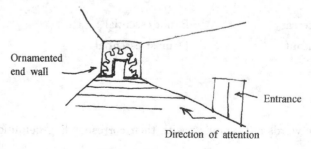

Fig. 13-6

If, as sometimes happens when the function of ornament has not been well enough understood, the painting or sculpture appears around or close to the entrance doors, the result is unfortunate. People about to leave the building do not need to be directed; psychologically they are already oriented towards the outdoors and their next activities. For those entering, if the ornament is sufficient interesting, it is a cause for slowing down, delaying the next step, and , thus, helping clog the passage. Also, though this is a relatively minor point, the light level usually shifts considerably between outdoors and in; the eyes of the entering person need a moment of adjustment, so that ornament at this point is at best poorly seen.

In large areas, such as public buildings, malls, and plazas, ornament can serve to establish a center of interest, which will then help to keep the viewer's eyes from wandering about at random, with the consequent slight sensation of being lost. A statue in a garden, a fountain in a park, a mural in the lobby of courthouse-all of these do a good day's work, architecturally, every day.② To think of them as "pretty-pretty," or as useless sentiment, is not only unjust, but betrays a sad lack of understanding of the real function of ornament. Of course, getting the painter or sculptor to see why the architect wants the ornament here and not there, and so big instead of larger or smaller, is another matter, involving occasionally bruised egos, to put it gently. Quite a few architects, who have had awkward experiences of this kind, tend to avoid using ornament at all, except for the kind which is built-in to the material.

Built-in ornament.③ Many material are decorative in themselves, requiring no hassles with painters and sculptors. Marble, for instance, can be found in an infinite variety of colors and veining. A fine marble wall is not beautiful in itself; it seems to repel any idea of fussing with it. Anyone who would paint over good marble is in obvious need of psychotherapy. Then, of course, there are woods with enchanting grains and tiles offering endless colors and patterns.④ These, and others like them, we might call natural ornament. But other kinds of built-in ornament. But other kinds of built-in ornament can be realized by using, say, precast concrete blocks, or terra cotta blocks, in which a pattern has been set by the mold.⑤ Among modern enthusiasts of this kind of ornament are Edward Durrell Stone and the late Frank Lloyd Wright. Again, however, the responsibility for the correct scale, character, and placement of the ornament falls directly on the architect.

Taste. For the purposes of this chapter it is assumed that the taste of the architect is impeccable; that of his client, though, can be pretty unpredictable.⑥ Who knows? He may be mad about gilded cherubim, while nursing a violent hatred for nonrepresentational painting. He may insist on using his grandfather's collection of cartwheels as a wall motif in a formalbanquet room. Some architects, after taking a stomach pill, will shrug and do what the client wants. Others, of stauncher caliber (or weaker stomachs) will shame or cow the client into submission. Architects of the gentleman-aesthete type are particularly good at this. A convincing tantrum, thrown at the right moment, can do wonders. In short, the question of taste in ornament, unless the architect and his client are unusually en rapport, becomes a conflict of wills.⑦ If the wrong one wins, if there is a compromise, the result can be even worse, for a consistent decorative approach, however misguided, is not as bad as one which contains inherent contradictions, and a compromise can be defined as the acceptance of contradictions.⑧

Total ornament. If it is agreed that ornament is an integral part of architecture, then it must be conceded that it is possible to consider an entire building as an ornament. Indeed, many architects have so thought through the ages. Perhaps the most obvious example is the period we call Baroque, when architecture was used as a plastic medium, its forms molded and turned until it become impossible to say what was structure and what was ornament. (It also become difficult to say what was good and what was not.)

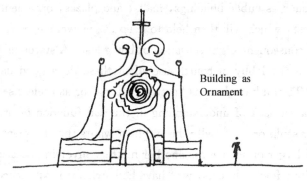

Fig. 13-7

In the largest sense of all, architecture is ornament for the human environment. The urban scene, or the village one, for that matter, is adorned by its buildings. This is perhaps why the citizens of any community feel a sense of personal relationship to their buildings, even though, individually, they have had nothing to do with their conception, design, execution, or decoration. It perhaps explains why New Yorkers, for instance, beam fondly at Lever House, while, so far, their eyes glaze when by chance they see the World Trade Center. They want their city, like they want their women, to look its best.

Ornament, in the end, is a question of pride. Speaking of which, it is interesting to notice how many slum dwellers have begun to paint gay designs on the dingy outside walls of their decrepit tenements. Pride, clearly, is a universal emotion.

Notes

①例如，考虑一下，一件装饰罩单是多么强列地支配着房间，而对于杂乱的壁炉人们又是多么不愿多看一眼。

②…all of this do a good day's, architecturally, every day. ……所有这一切，从建筑学角度讲，每天都在干着良好的工作。

③Built-in ornament—固有装饰

④woods with enchanting grains：带有迷人的木纹的木材

⑤但是，通过使用现浇水泥块和用模子制作的生陶块可以认识到其它种类的固有装饰。

⑥为了达到本文的目的，我们假定建筑师的情趣是没有问题的；而客户的情趣则很难预料了。

⑦…unless the architect and his client are unusually en rapport，…

……除非建筑师与他的客户的关系十分密切，……。

⑧en rapport：关系密切

⑨如果错误的一方获胜，或者有一个折中办法，后果会更糟。因为一个前后一致的装饰观点，无论如何误导都不会比包含着内在矛盾更坏。折中办法可以定义为"可接受的矛盾。"

Reading Material B

The Function of Ornament

All people have the instinct to decorate their surrounding.

But decorations and ornaments will only work when they are properly made. For ornaments and decorations are not only born from the natural exuberance and love for something happy in a building; they also have a function, which is as clear and definite as any other function in a building. The joy and exuberance of carvings and color will only work, if they are made in harmony with this function. And further, the function is a necessary one—the ornaments are not just optional additions which may, or may not be added to a building, according as the spirit moves you.① A building needs them just as much as it needs doors and windows.

In order to understand the function of ornament, we must begin by understanding the nature of space in general. Space, when properly formed, is whole. Every part of it, every part of a town, a neighborhood, a garden, or a room, is whole. It is both an integral entity, in itself, and at the sometime, joined to some other entities to form a larger whole. This process hinges largely on the boundaries. It is no accident that so many of the ideas in this article concern the importance of the boundaries between things.②

A thing is whole only when it is itself entire and also joined to its outside to form a larger entity.③ But this can only happen when the boundary between the two is so thick, so fleshy, so ambiguous, that the two are not sharply separated, but can function either as separate entities or as one larger whole which has no inner cleavage in it.

In the left-hand diagram where there is a cleavage that is sharp, the thing and its outside are distinct entities, they function individually as wholes, but they do not function together as a larger whole. In this case the world is split. In the right-hand diagram where there is ambiguous space between them, the two entities are individually entire, as before, but they are also entire together as a larger whole. In this case the world is whole.

This principle extends throughout the material universe, from the largest organic structures to the very atoms and molecules. The main purpose of ornament in the environment—in buildings, rooms, and public spaces—is to make the world more whole. As far as specific ways of doing it are concerned, there are hundreds, of course.

Here is a more complicated case—the entrance to a Romanesque church.

The ornament is built up around the edge of the entrance. It creates a unifying seam be-

split ... and whole

Fig. 13-8

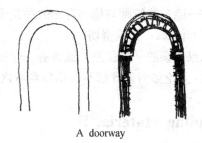

A doorway

Fig. 13-9

tween the entrance space and the stone. Without the ornament, there would be a gap between the arch of the entry and the passage itself. The ornament works on the seam, between the two, and holds them together. It is especially lavish and developed in this place, because just this seam—the boundary of the entrance to the church—is so important, symbolically, to the people who worship there.

In fact, doors and windows are always important for ornament, because they are places of connection between the elements of buildings and the life in and around them. It is very likely that we shall find a concentration of ornament at the edges of doors and windows, as people try to tie together these edges with the space around them.

And exactly the same happens at hundreds of other places in the environment: in rooms, around our houses, in the kitchen, on a wall, along the surface of a path, on tops of roofs, around a column—in fact, anywhere at all where there are edges between things which are imperfectly knit together, where materials or objects meet, and where they change.④

Most generally of all, the thing that makes the difference in the use of ornament is the eye for the significant gap in the continuum: the place where the continuous fabric of interlock and connectivity is broken.⑤ When ornament is applied badly it is always put into some place where these connections are really missing, so it is superfluous, frivolous. When it is well used, it is always applied in place where there is a genuine gap, a need for a little more structure, a need for what we may call metaphorically "some extra building energy," to knit the stuff together where it is too much apart.⑥

Notes

①另外，建筑装饰物的这种功能之所以是必不可少的，是因为它们并不根据人们的情绪变化而成为可有可无。
②本文中许多概念涉及分界线的重要性，这是决不是偶然的。
③物体只是自成一体，并且也与其外部的事物连接起来形成一个更大的整体时才是完整无缺的。
④……in fact, any where at all …and where they change.
——事实上，任何物体间的边缘拼接得不理想的地方，任何材料或物体衔接在一的地方

以及它们发生的变化的地方,装饰都是用得上的。

⑤一般说来,之所以对装饰物存在不同的态度,是由于对连续结构中具有重大意义的间隙的看法不同而导致。所谓间隙是指建筑结构内在联系和衔接中断的地方。

⑥如果装饰使用恰当,那么它一定是用在存在真正间隙、需要再增加一点结构的地方,一个需要我们隐喻地称之为"某种附加能量"的地方,从而在相隔过分远的地方将材料拼接起来。

UNIT FOURTEEN

Text   The Development of a Low-rise Urban Housing Alternative

[1]   A group of Chicago architects, planners, and other professionals has begun Ran investigation into what they believe is an effective alternative to the high-rise model of urban housing. This group, known as Urbs in Horto, adopted its name from Chicago's motto, which means "City in a Garden" and reflects the aspirations of a significant segment of the urban population concerning the kind of environment in which they want to live. ① Urbs in Horto came together in response to a challenge set forth in March of 1981 by Peter Land, an architect and educator, who called for undertaking the planning and building of a different urban habitant to demonstrate new ideas and point the way for housing in the future. Chicago has been a proving-ground and showcase of the world's most impressive concentration of tall buildings, many of which have served as prototypes for structures throughout the world.

[2]   Urbs in Horto has chosen to focus on Chicago to test the viability of this idea — the renewal of neighborhoods through low-rise housing that has the benefits of high-rise density. ② Successfully tested in Chicago, the concept could then be adapted to other urban areas worldwide. ③

[3]   Despite a population loss of over 600 000 in the course of the past 20 years, Chicago has a shortage of housing, particularly of dwelling units suited to moderate-income households. A significant percentage of existing stock is either in need of major upgrading or must be replaced altogether. ④ The inadequate supply of housing of the type required in urban neighborhoods today has resulted in continued migration to the suburbs and further deterioration of inner city areas. The rehabilitation of inner city neighborhoods will depend on the response to the challenge of providing alternative types for affordable housing. And, economic pressure has never been a stronger impetus.

[4]   Bearing this sense of urgency in mind, Urbs in Horto has begun an investigation of one possible solution to this housing problem. Great strides in high-rise technology have made the modern high-rise building an affordable and practicable solution; nevertheless, the public-at-large seeks a variety of housing options. Currently, there are few variable alternatives within the inner areas of cities. Comparable research in other types of high-density housing has been limited to date, but recent studies indicate that there are housing types that have the potential for achieving densities that equal those provided by many high-rise buildings (Fig. 14-1). It is the pursuit of one building type as an urban housing option to which Urbs in Horto presently addresses itself.

[5]   The first major objective of the group is to advance the state of knowledge concerning low-rise, high-density housing — to bring it up to date with the art and technology of its high-

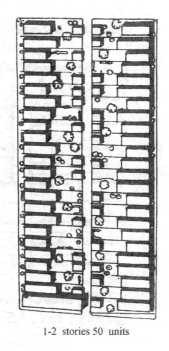 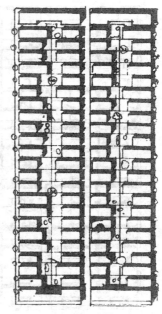

1-2 stories 50 units   1-2 stories 100 units

Fig. 14-1　Existing residenticu densities on typical Chicago bloek (330×660 ft. o. c)

rise counterpart.[5] This will require the cooperation of professionals from many disciplines: architecture, engineering, urban planning, finance, building technology, law, sociology, psychology, and others. Urbs in Horto has begun to examine this approach to the housing problem, but a great deal of work remains to be accomplished.

[6]　The goals that the group is striving to achieve in the design of low-rise, high-density housing are numerous and certainly include the accommodation of lifestyles not well suited to the high-rise building. It is necessary to examine how design can advance this goal more fully and how it can facilitate personal expression in the face of significant constraints.

[7]　In responding to the requirements of inner city neighborhoods, low-rise housing must be truly economical and efficient. Initial indications of the group's work suggest that structures would need to be two-, three-, and four-story walk up units clustered together in combinations adapted to the Chicago grid. (Fig. 14-2) Floorplan layouts would probably be simple, with flexible living areas and more compact and efficient bedrooms and bathroom facilities. The allocation of space is a reflection of usage — of lifestyle by the occupants. The clustering of units could also produce economic benefits in the form of energy savings — a particularly urgent requirements today. Units could be played or designed to utilize the benefits of the sun and wind in providing natural lighting, solar heating, as well as crossventilation. Building materials will need to be studied, as well as prefabrication techniques, if substantial economies are to be realized. In order to meet changing needs, the adaptability of units will prove to be an important factor in the long-term economy of low-rise high-density structures. The aspects of

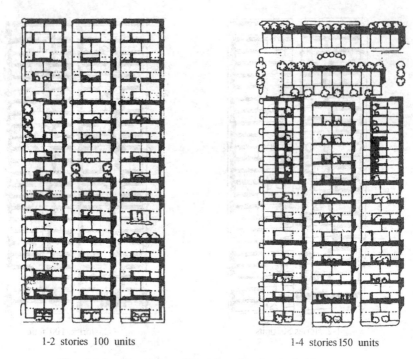

1-2 stories 100 units   1-4 stories 150 units

Fig. 14-2 Alternate residential studies for garden houses
on typical Chicago block (330×660 ft. o. c)

housing that have been identified above are typical of many areas requiring research.

[8]　The second major objective of the group is to study methods of integrating this type of housing into the existing pattern of Chicago neighborhoods. In view of the lack of success in this area over the last several decades, this is an especially important purpose. The goal of creating innovative moderate-income housing must be pursued with the objective of revitalizing total neighborhoods.

[9]　It is premature at this stage to try to identify specific Chicago neighborhoods where the proposed mode of housing could be successfully incorporated and tested. The neighborhoods investigated should, however, satisfy several fundamental conditions. They should be viable communities in need of new housing with essential infrastructure and service in place, including public transportation, schools, hospitals, recreation facilities, and the like. Neighborhoods without some or most of these ingredients could jeopardize the success of the project regardless of the merit of the housing prototypes themselves.

[10]　The third objective of Urbs in Horto is to go beyond merely theoretical studies to the building of an actual neighborhoods.⑥ An actual neighborhood would demonstrate in built form high-density, walk-up living as a viable housing alternative.⑦ The question remains why the concept must be studied at the scale of a neighborhood. The new urban habitat must be of a size that will permit it to be a competitive form of housing with respect to other options.⑧ At this time, the group believes an appropriate site area in Chicago to be twelve to fifteen blocks, but the size may vary after further investigation.

New Words and Expressions

motto	['mɔtəu]	n.	箴言，座右铭
segment	['segmənt]	n.	部分；扇形体
habitat	['hæbitæt]	n.	住（场）所，栖息地
proving-ground		n.	检验场，试验场
showcase	['ʃəukeis]	n.	橱窗，陈列窗
prototype	['prəutətaip]	n.	典型，样品，原型
viability	[vaiə'biliti]	n.	耐久性，生存性
renewal	[ri'nju:əl]	n.	更新，重建
moderate	['mɔdərit]	a.	中等的，适度的
upgrade	[ʌp'greid]	v.	改良，提高（等级）
deterioration	[ditiəriə'reiʃən]	n.	变坏，变质
rehabilitation	[ri:həbili'teiʃən]	n.	重（改）建，更新
affordable	[ə'fɔ:dəbl]	a.	买得起的
impetus *	['impitəs]	n.	（原）动力；促进
urgency	['ə:dʒənsi]	n.	迫切
stride	[straid]	n.	大步，阔步
address oneself to			致力于，着手
pursuit	[pə'sju:t]	n.	研究，从事
counterpart	['kauntəpa:t]	n.	对应物，对方
facilitate	[fə'siliteit]	vt.	便于，使容易（便利）
constraint	[kən'streint]	n.	约束，制约
allocation	[ælə'keiʃən]	n.	部署，分配
prefabrication	[pri:fæbrikeiʃən]	n.	预制
adaptability	[ə,dæptə'biliti]	n.	适应（用）性，灵活性
pursue	[pə'sju:]	vt.	追随；进行
innovative	[,inəu'veitiv]	a.	革新的，富有创造精神的
revitalize	['ri:'vaitəlaiz]	vt.	使新生，使有新的活力
premature *	[pri:mə'tjuə]	a.	过早的，不成熟的
infrastructure	['infrəstrʌktʃə]	n.	下部（基础）结构
jeopardize	['dʒepədaiz]	v.	危害

Notes

①Urbs in Horto

　　Horto 一词的含义与"园林"、"园艺"有关，所以 Urbs in Horto 相当于 City in a garden。

②…high-rise density.

density 此处指的是高层住宅中的住户密度。

③Successfully tested …could then be adapted to …

这是一个带有省略成分的虚拟语气句子，但并非表示与现实不符的假设，而是语气上的委婉。

④stock 一词本意"存货"等，此处指现有的住房。

⑤to bring …up to date with…

使……达到和……一样的现代程度（水平）。

⑥to go beyond …to …：超出……去……

⑦…would demonstrate in built form high-density, walk-up living…

其中 high-density, walk-up living 是动词 demonstrate 的宾语，而 in built form 则是该动词的状语。

⑧短语 with respect to 有几个含义，此处意为"相对于……"、"与……相比"。

Exercises

Reading Comprehension

Ⅰ. The following are the main ideas of some paragraphs. Read each and then find out the corresponding number of the right paragraph from the four suggested.

1. To bring the knowledge about low-rise, high-density housing up to date with that of high-rise building is the group's first major objective. （1, 3, 5, 7）

2. To study the methods of integration of the new type of housing with the existing pattern of Chicago neighborhoods is the second major objective of the group. （2, 8, 9, 10）

3. To build a true neighborhood to show a viable housing alternative is the group's third objective. （7, 8, 9, 10）

4. A group of professionals in Chicago are devoting themselves to searching for an alternative of high-rise urban housing. （4, 3, 2, 1）

5. The group has tried to work out a possible solution to the housing problem and it seemed to have found a potential housing type. （2, 3, 4, 6）

6. There has been a housing shortage in Chicago, which has caused deterioration of urban conditions. （3, 4, 5, 6）

7. The group has got a lot of goals in their research. （4, 6, 8, 10）

8. Economy and efficiency are the requirements of inner city neighborhoods. （2, 4, 5, 7）

9. The neighborhoods should satisfy a number of fundamental conditions. （9, 7, 5, 6）

Ⅱ. According to your understanding of the text, fill in the blanks on the left with the number of the proper information on the right. The first one has been done for you.

1. Urbs in Horto have _____ in their researching work.
2. A group of Chicago professionals have sought for _____.
3. Urbs in Horto was named after _____.
4. Peter land is _____.
5. Urbs in Horto have chosen _____ to test the life power of their new idea.
6. _____ is particularly in need during the housing shortage in Chicago.
7. The majority of the citizens prefer _____ to high-rise dwelling units.
8. To realize the groups, objectives needs _____ from many scientific fields.
9. In the structures _____ should be fiexible.
10. The arrangement of space reflects _____.
11. The combination of dwelling units can produce economic benefits _____.
12. A viable community needing new housing should have _____.

a. Chicago
b. an alternative to the hight-rise model of urban housing
c. a Chicago motto
d. three objectives
e. houses for moderate-income families
f. an architect and educator
g. cooperation of professionals
h. living areas
i. in the form of energy saving
j. a variety of housing alternatives
k. necessary infrastructures and proper service facilities
l. the life style of the occupants

Vocabulary

I. Pick out the suitable words or expressions from the four suggested answers which have the meanings close to the parts underlined, according to the content of the text.

1. The allocation of space is a reflection of usage — of lifestyle by the occupants.
   A. function   B. relation   C. rearrangement   D. distribution
2. The goal of creating innovative moderate-income housing must be pursued with the objective of revitalizing total neighborhoods.
   A. followed   B. pressed   C. combined   D. replaced
3. "City in a Garden" reflects the aspiration of a significant segment of the urban population concerning their environment.
   A. division   B. part   C. group   D. number
4. A significant percentage of existing stock is either in need of major upgrading or must be

143

replaced altogether.

   A. money   B. goods   C. structures   D. investment

5. Economic pressure has never been a stronger impetus.

   A. significance   B. reason   C. motive force   D. decisive factor

6. It is necessary to examine how design can facilitate personal expression in the face of significant constraints.

   A. restrictions   B. compression   C. controls   D. threats

7. The new urban habitat must be of a size that will permit it to be a competitive form of housing with respect to other options.

   A. about   B. regardless of C. as for   D. compared with

8. It is premature at this stage to try to identify specific Chicago neighborhoods.

   A. right time   B. earlier   C. already late   D. impossible

Ⅱ. Complete the following statements with the proper words listed below, changing the form where necessary.

renewal	upgrade	prototype	showcase
viability	jeopardize		rehabilitation
deterioration	prefabrication		incorporate

1. Suzhou Gardens are praised as _____ of typical Chinese traditional garden architecture.

2. Twenty years after the big earthquake, the city of Tangshan has emerged as a modernized city after _____.

3. Mass-produced houses can not do without structural members of _____.

4. With the rapid development of science and technology in construction, our people's living conditions are also _____.

5. Along the river, many village-run paper mills were set up one after another, which has resulted in serious _____ of the water.

6. In addition to comfort and pleasing the eye, _____ is a significant standard concerning building quality.

7. Because of the delay of the funds for construction, it will be a long way to _____ the blue-print into an actual structure.

8. The Northern Part of Shanxi Province, with a lot of cave dwellings, used to be regarded as a _____ of the natural-earth structure (生土建筑).

Reading Material A

Magic of the City

There are few people who do not enjoy the magic of a great city. But urban sprawl takes it away from everyone except the few who are lucky enough, or rich enough, to live close to the largest centers. ①

This is bound to happen in any urban region with a single high density core. Land near the core is expensive; few people can live near enough to it to give them genuine access to the city's life; most people live far out from the core. To all intents and purposes, they are in the suburbs and have no more than occasional access to the city's life. ② This problem can only be solved by decentralizing the core to form a multitude of smaller cores, each devoted to some special way of life, so that, even though decentralized, each one is still intense and still a center for the region as a whole.

The mechanism which creates a single isolated core is simple — urban services tend to agglomerate. ③ Restaurants, theaters, shops, carnivals, cafes, hotels, night clubs, entertainment, special services, tend to cluster. They do so because each one wants to locate in that position where the most people are. As soon as one nucleus has formed in a city, each of the interesting services — especially those which are most interesting and therefor require the largest catch basin — locate themselves in this one nucleus. ④ The one nucleus keeps growing and the downtown becomes enormous. It becomes rich, various , fascinating. But gradually, as the metropolitan area grows, the average distance from an individual house to this one center increases. And land values around the center rise so high that houses are driven out from there by shops and offices — until soon no one, or almost no one, is any longer genuinely in touch with the magic which is created day and night within this solitary center.

If we are to resolve the problem by decentralizing centers, we must ask what the minimum population is that can support a central business district with the magic of the city.

From some investigations, we believe it is quite possible to get very complex and rich urban functions at the heart of a catch basin which serves no more than
300 000 people. Since it is desirable to have as many centers as possible, we propose that the city region should have one center for each 300 000 people, with the centers spaced out widely among the population, so that every person in the region is reasonably close to at least one of these major centers.

To make this more concrete, it is interesting to get some idea of the range of distances between these centers in a typical urban region. At a density of 5 000 persons per square mile (the density of the less populated parts of Los Angeles) the area occupied by 300 000 will have a diameter of about nine miles; at a higher density of 80 000 persons per square mile (the density of central Paris) the area occupied by 300 000 people has a diameter of about two miles.⑤ We therefore take these crude estimates as upper and lower bounds. If each center serves 300 000 people, they will be at least two miles apart and probably no more than nine miles apart.

One final point must be discussed. The magic of a great city comes from the enormous specialization of human effort there. It would be absurd if the new downtowns, each serving 300 000 people, in an effort to capture the magic of the city, ended up as a multitude of second-class hick towns.⑥

This problem can only be solved if each of the cores not only serves a catch basin of 300 000 people but also offers some kind of special quality which none of the other centers have, so that each core, though small, serves several million people and can therefor generate all the excitement and uniqueness which become possible in such a vast city.

Thus, as it is in Tokyo or London, the pattern must be implemented in such a way that one core has the best hotels, another the best antique shops, another the music, still another has the fish and sailing boats. Then we can be sure that every person is within reach of at least one downtown and also that all the downtowns are worth reaching for and really have the magic of a great metropolis.

Notes

①但市区的延伸是使得除少数人非常幸运或非常富有的人能住在都市的市区中心外，其他所有的人均领略不到这种都市的魅力。
②实际上，他们住在郊区，最多不过偶尔一下接触城市生活。
　　词组 to all intents and purposes 意为"实际上"，"实质上"。
③产生独一而又孤立的市中心的原因很简——城市服务业有聚集成群的倾向。
　　mechanism 原意："作用机理"、"途径"等，此处译为"原因"。
④nucleus＝center；catch basin 原意"流域"、"区域"，此处指"服务范围"。
⑤密度为每平方英里5 000人（这相当于洛杉矶人口较稀的地区），则3 000 000人口的地区的直径约为9英里；如果密度达到每平方英里80 000人（这相当于巴黎市中心），则300 000人的地区的的直径就是2英里左右。
⑥如果每个为300 000人提供服务的新商业区都企图具备整个城市的所有魅力，那是荒唐可笑的。其结果只能造成一大批土里土气的二流城镇。
　　hick 一词在美国口语中指"乡下佬"。

Reading Material B

Activity Nodes

One of the greatest problems in existing communities is the fact that the available public life in them is spread so thin that it has no impact on the community.① It is not in any real sense available to the members of the community. Studies of pedestrian behavior make it clear that people seek out concentrations of other people, whenever they are available. To create these concentrations of people in a community, facilities must be grouped densely round very small public squares which can function as nodes, with all pedestrian movement in the community organized to pass through these nodes.② Such nodes require four properties.

First, each node must draw together the main paths in the surrounding community. The major pedestrian paths should converge on square, with minor paths funneling into the major ones, to create the basic star-shape of the pattern.③ This is much harder to do than one might imagine. To give an example of the difficulty which arises when we try to build this relationship into a town, we show the following plan — a scheme of ours for housing in Peru — in which the paths are all convergent on a very small number of squares.④

This is not a very good plan—it is too stiff and formal. But it is possible to achieve the same relationship in far more relaxed manner. In any case the relationship between paths, community facilities, and squares is vital and hard to achieve. It must be taken seriously, from the very outset, as a major feature of the city.

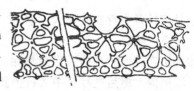

Fig. 14-3 Public paths converge on centers of action

Second, to keep the activity concentrated, it is essential to make the squares rather small, smaller than one might imagine. A square of about 45 × 60 feet can keep the normal pace of public life well concentrated.

Third, the facilities grouped around any one node must be chosen for their symbiotic relationship.⑤ It is not enough merely to group communal functions in so-called community centers. For example, church, cinema, kindergarten, and police station are all community facilities, but they do not support one another mutually. Different people go to them, at different times, with different things in mind. There is no point in grouping them together. To create intensity of action, facilities which are placed together round any one node must function in a cooperative manner, and must attract the same kinds of people, at the same times of day. For example, when evening entertainments are grouped together, the people who are having a night out can use any one of them, and the total concentration of action increases. When kindergartens and small parks and gardens are grouped together, young families with children may use either, so their total attraction is increased.

Fourth, these activity nodes should be distributed rather evenly across the community, so that no house or workplace is more than a few hundred yards from

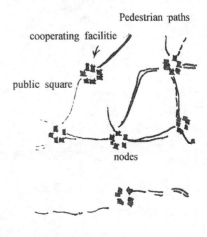

Fig 14-4

one. In this way a contrast of "busy and quiet" can be achieved at a small scale — and large dead areas can be avoided.

The following is our suggestion:

Create nodes of activity throughout the community, spread about 300 yards apart. First identify those existing spots in the community where action seems to concentrate itself. Then modify the layout of the paths in the community to bring as many of them through these spots as possible.⑥ This makes each spot function as a "node" in the path network. Then, at the center of each node, make a small public square, and surround it with a combination of community facilities and shops which are mutually supportive.

Notes

①目前社区中存在的最大问题之一就是人们可以参与的公共活动太分散，因而对社区没有什么影响。

②为了在社区中创造人们聚集在一起的机会，公共设施必须集中在能起中心作用的小型广场周围，然后把社区中人行道路线安排好，使之经过这些中心。

③主要的人行道应该集中到广场上，而小巷、便道则汇集到主要的人行道上，基本形成星形布局。

④为了举例说明我们试图在城镇中建立这种道路关系的困难，我们展示下面的设计方案——一个我们替秘鲁设计的住房建筑方案。在这些设计图中，道路都汇集在为数很少的广场上。

⑤symbiotic relationship：协作关系。

⑥接着改造社区中的道路分布，使尽可能多的道路通过这些点。

UNIT FIFTEEN

Text   The Architecture of Hospital
             ——Breaking the paradigm

[1]   The hospital is one of society's most important civic buildings. It is most often where we are born and where we die, and it is the place of much in between.① As such, the architecture of a hospital must respond both to his emotional content of hope and tragedy and to the functional requirements of treatment and technology. Unfortunately, the design process is often overwhelmed by the functional needs of medical science, and too often, the soul of the patient is completely overlooked while the body is treated. In our work we have tried to move past the perceived tyranny of the hospital program in order to explore the full potential of space and design in the effort to aid the healing process.②

[2]   The architecture of a hospital is a permanent backdrop for varying scenes and acts. As a theater, it is the site of human experiences ranging from joyful to horrific and as a museum, it must provide the broadest possible canvas for performance. Its form and materials must allow for the rapid and continual evolution of technology and science, each of which provokes constant change in program and function. A hospital's ability to change must extend from its smallest department to its overall massing and contextual relationships, particularly as new types of healthcare facilities and treatment style are established. At the same time, its stature as a permanent place of excellence in medical treatment and public concern must never waver.

[3]   Within our projects, the recognition that the idea of the institution is more permanent than the building itself has led to architectural strategies such as open-ended circulation, long-span structures, and specific choices of site development.③ In addition, we are continually reevaluating the formal and programmatic needs of current healthcare policies and treatment. By analyzing political, scientific, and cultural patterns we are better able to be fully informed about the real functions of a hospital. Given the complexities in the relationships within and between medical departments, this knowledge helps us to manipulate spaces in both a functional and formally effective manner and allows us to move architecture beyond the role "technological skin", even with the most demanding programs.④

[4]   Achieving clarity of massing and organization in the hospital is as important as building in flexibility. People are often in a state of high agitation when they enter a hospital. Though necessary and helpful, interventionist treatments performed on patients often serve to exacerbate feelings of victimization and disorientation. It is therefore crucial that at all times the sequence of reaching treatment must be clearly understood. This clarity begins with the placement of the hospital within its context.⑤ It is important for the healthcare campus, often a part of a hospital, to create a hierarchy of public spaces and entries which may be easily navigated.⑥ In addition, the placement of medical buildings must be considered in terms of distri-

bution of staff, scarce and expensive technological resources, and mobility of patients. The circulation and organization within the hospital must be equally clear and perceptible from both the interior and the exterior of the building. In our work, this has led to the use of urban design principles such as boulevards, galleries, and courtyards to establish hierarchy within internal, as well as external, circulation. Public and private spaces are then placed off of these spines and nodes in strong, axial relationships, providing visual clues for movement within what are often complex buildings. ⑦ Ultimately, we hope that when a simplicity of organization is achieved and buildings provide simple identification of circulation and function, the architecture is able to aid in the demystification of the process of healing.

[5]   Significant events in the circulation and massing within the hospital are often highlighted with the introduction of natural light. ⑧ Courtyards, single-loaded corridors, clerestories, skylights, and light shelves are filtered between departments, offering interruptions into the poche of a section. ⑨ Within the patient room, varying conditions of natural light and the ability of the patient to control this light are even more fully explored. This control, particularly for patients who may be physically disabled, is a crucial element in dignifying the treatment process.

[6]   In addition to offering clarity of function and flexibility, a hospital must provide a strong sense of care and service. A patient, like a guest in any premier hotel, must feel that the staff is available to take care of both physical and psychological needs. The design must enhance communication with the staff, both visually and aurally. Extensive internal glazing, public libraries, living rooms, and solariums, and other public and semi-public spaces allow patients areas to gather and communicate. ⑩ In addition, extensive use of internal glazing allows physicians and nurses to be in visual contact with patients and their families at all times, preventing any sense of isolation. At the same time, within the complexities of a hospital, the patient room should be seen as a sanctuary of privacy and safety, the place in which the patient is the one in control of his or her life. In our work, ornament is kept to a minimum. We allow the play of light and shadow, the sound of water, and the fragrance of the garden to provide a sense of aesthetic delight. The rich use of indoor and outdoor courtyards, flowers, pools, and the multi-hued filtering of various types of natural light provide a sense of tranquility. Color and texture tends to be keyed to organic references, weaving together the themes of growth and integration within a larger system. ⑪ This emphasis on the celebration of natural materials seems to complement our efforts to create a simple and elegant space for the healing process.

New Words and Expressions

paradigm [ˈpærədaim]	n.	范例，示例
tyranny [ˈtirəni]	n.	暴虐，残暴的行为
backdrop [ˈbækdrɔp]	n.	（舞台后部的）背景，彩画幕布
horrific [həˈrifik]	a.	极其可怕的

canvas ['kænvəs]		n.	背景，画布
provoke [prə'vəuk]		vt.	引起，诱发
contextual [kɔn'tekstʃuəl]		a.	上下文的
stature [ˌstætʃə]		n.	重要性
waver [weivə]		vi.	摆动，动摇
institution [insti'tju:ʃən]		n.	（慈善，宗教性质的）公共机构，协会，学校
programmatic [prəugrə'mætik]		a.	纲领性的，计划性的
manipulate * [mə'nipjuleit]		v.	熟练地使用，利用
agitation * [ˌædʒi'teiʃən]		n.	激动不安，焦虑
interventionist * [intə'venʃənist]		a.	干涉主义的
exacerbate [ek'sæsə:beit]		vt.	使（病，痛）加剧，激怒
hierarchy * ['haiərɑki]		n.	层次，体系
disorientation [disɔ:rien'teiʃən]		n.	迷失方向
perceptible [pə'septəbl]		a.	可领悟的，可理解的
boulevard ['bu:livɑ:d]		n.	宽阔的大路，林荫大道
spine [spain]		n.	地面隆起地带
node [nəud]		n.	交叉点，中心
axial * ['æksiəl]		a.	轴的，轴向的
demystification [diˌmistifi'keiʃən]		n.	使非神秘化
highlight * [hailait]		v.	以强烈光线照射；使…突出（显著）
clerestory * ['kliəstəri]		n.	天窗，高侧窗
dignify ['dignifai]		vt.	使显得有价值，使增光
aurally ['ɔ:rəli]		adv.	听觉上，听力方面
solariums [sɔ'lɛəriəm]		n.	日光浴室
sanctuary ['sæŋktjuəri]		n.	圣所，圣堂
fragrance ['freiʒrəns]		n.	芬芳，香味
multi-hued ['mʌlti'hju:d]		a.	有多种颜色的
tranquility [træŋ'kwility]		n.	安静，宁静
clarity * ['klæriti]		n.	清晰度，明确性

Notes

①between 在此是名词，in between 意为"在……期间"。
②hospital program 此处指医院的建筑设计方案。
③open-ended circulation（开放式通道）此处指的是端头不封闭的通道。
④"technological skin" 指医院建筑只体现医疗技术，成了包装医疗技术的一张"皮"。
　"demanding" 意为"过分要求的"、"苛求的"，这里指传统的、常规的医院建筑项目。
⑤…within its context. 根据上下文 context 此处应理解为医院的建筑结构。
⑥"campus" 意为"校园"、"营地"等，healthcare campus 此处指"健康管理部门"。而 hierarchy

意为"层系"、"科目分类"。

句中 often a part of hospital 是 healthcare campus 的同位语。

⑦public and private spaces are then placed off of these spines and nodes in strong axial relationship…

(1) 这里 public space（共用空间）指挂号室、登记处、病人休息室等，而 private space（私用空间）则指办公室、病房等。

(2) be placed off 意为"安置（排列）在……两侧（或前后）"。

(3) spines 此处与上下文中 circulation 同意，即各科通道。

⑧massing 此处指的是大面积的建筑空间。

⑨(1) are filtered 此处等于 scatter about 即"散布"之意。

(2) poche 法语词，等于 pocket，此处指"小范围的环境"。

(3) "interruption 此处意为"缓松一下"。

⑩…allow patients areas to…

动词 allow（允许的）后带间接宾语 patients 和直接宾语 areas。

⑪分词短语 weaving together the themes of growth and integration within a larger systems 在句中作状语，表示补充说明，其逻辑主语是 color and texture.

Exercises

Reading Comprehension

Ⅰ. Identity the main ideas for each paragraph by matching the following statements with the corresponding numbers of the right paragraphs.

1. The design of a hospital should aid the fact that patients must be provided with a strong sense of care and service and aid to create a simple and elegant space for healing process. （4，5，6，7）

2. Clarity of various spaces and organization in a hospital is very important. （2，3，4，5）

3. While being a permanent place of fine medical treatment and public healthcare, a hospital must be adapted to the rapid and continual advancement of science and technology. （1，2，3，4）

4. The architecture of a hospital must respond both to the emotional needs of patients and functional requirements of treatment. （1，3，5，7）

5. The knowledge that the function of a hospital is more important than its buildings has led to flexibility in the architectural spaces of hospital rather than "technological skin." （1，3，5，7）

6. Natural light is a crucial element in the treatment process. （2，5，6，7）

Ⅱ. Choose the best answers according to the text.

1. "move past" in the last sentence of Para. 1 means _____.

   A. move farther   B. move beyond   C. go up to   D. go by

2. "Its form and material…" in the third sentence of Para. 2, "its" indicates _____.

   A. the museum　　　　　　　　B the theater

   C. the architecture of hospital　　D. the hospital

3. The key point of the third sentence of Para. 2 is that _____.

   A. the constant change allows for the evolution in technology and science.

   B. the evolution provokes constant change in program and function.

   C. when considering the form and the material of the architecture of hospital, you should also consider the rapid and continual evolution in technology and science.

   D. hospital's form and material make the evolution of technology and science possible.

4. "its overall massing" in Sentence 4, Para. 2 indicates _____.

   A. all the architectural structures and spaces of a hospital.

   B. all the medical staff in a hospital.

   C. all the patients staying in a hospital.

   D. both B and C.

5. In Para. 3, the word "circulation" refers to _____.

   A. water supply　　　　　　　　B. passage system

   C. power supply　　　　　　　　D. air ventilation

6. It is emphasized in Para. 4 that "the sequence of reaching treatment must be clearly understood" _____.

   A. otherwise the patients would not accept the treatment.

   B. because the doctors would be misunderstood.

   C. otherwise it would induce the patients to produce a feeling of victimization and disorientation.

   D. because the patients are often in a state of high agitation.

7. The phrase " to create a hierarchy of public spaces and entries which may be easily navigated" essentially means _____.

   A. to distribute the public spaces and their entries among the medical staff according to their ranks.

   B. to distribute the public spaces and their entries to the patients according to their social status.

   C. to arrange the public spaces according to their functions and make clear mark for each entry.

   D. to arrange the public spaces into different grades according to the treatment fees and make clear marks for their entries.

8. In addition to…a hospital must provide a strong sense of care and service. Here "care and service " is what made _____.

   A. by medical staff for patients.

   B. by patients for each other.

   C. by the members of medical staff for each other.

D. by patients for medical personnel.
9. According to the last paragraph, the following senses are all appreciated except _____.
   A. sense of care and service
   B. sense of isolation
   C. sense of aesthetic delight
   D. sense of tranquility

Vocabulary

I. Find the definition in column B which matches the word in column A.

A	B
1. agitation	a. along or round an axis
2. hierarchy	b. anxiety or excitement from mind
3. node	c. combination as a whole
4. axial	d. level or system
5. highlight	e. point of crossing; center
6. integration	f. state of calmness
7. clarity	g. give brightest light to
8. tranquility	h. clearness

II. Conplete the following sentences with words or expressions given below. Changing the forms where necessary.

clerestory	disorientation	paradigm
allow for	demystification	backdrop
place off	agitation	provoke
fragrance	boulevard	dignify

1. A successful architect should have a creative mind to break _____ in traditional architecture.
2. Because of windy and wet weather for the most of time in winter, Scandinavians used to build narrow _____ in their houses to prevent wind and moisture while let natural light in.
3. It is quite a fresh idea to compare the architecture of a hospital to a permanent _____ for varying scenes and acts.
4. It takes about an hour to get there, _____ possible traffic jam.
5. The clever conception of the Falling Water in Pittsburgh, Pennsylvania by F. L. Wright _____ many visitors', especially architects, great interest.

6. The news of the sudden bankruptcy of the bank immediately raised disturbance and _____ among its depositors.
7. With no signage, the poorly planned neighborhood often caused _____ among the new comers, sometimes, even among the native small children.
8. Shops and restaurants _____ new highways have brought about a lot of conveniences to motor vehicle drivers.
9. After transformation, in the suburbs of the old city there have appeared many _____ which are quite convenient to traffic as well as to pedestrians.

Reading Material A

Theater

Theater is a structure used for the performance of a play or other dramatic presentation. A theater includes a stage or performing area and an auditorium or viewing place for the audience. The stage may be completely separated from the audience by a proscenium arch, as in the typical 20th-century theater, or it may extend into the auditorium, as in the popular playhouses of England in the 16th and 17th centuries. Some stages are designed for maximum use of scenery, and others are designed for no scenery at all. Among these factors are the type of play to be performed, the dramatic conventions of the period, the physical relationship between the actors and the stage, and the kind of audience for whom the theater is intended.[①]

During the 18th century many theaters were built throughout Europe, and Italian theater architects achieved international fame. The typical theater of the period was characterized by the use of seats in the orchestra pit, heavy reliance on boxes and galleries for seating accommodations, and a proscenium arch.[②]

Most of the theaters and opera houses on the Continent in the 19th century continued to follow the traditional horseshoe design. An especially opulent example of the period is the enormous Paris Opera, opened in 1875. Its decorations are lavish and its stage machinery enormously complex. Many commercial theaters were constructed during the 19th century in England and the United States. Notable features of these playhouses were the absence of proscenium doors, a shorter stage apron, and reserved orchestra seats in place of the apron.[③]

The theaters of Europe and the United States that built during the early 20th century were generally modifications of the traditional horseshoe design or the new fan-shaped Bayreuth design.[④] The development of naturalism, with its emphasis on realistic picture-frame settings and on the actor's separation from the audience, discouraged experimentation in theater design. The development of naturalism, with its emphasis on realistic picture-frame settings and on the actor's separation from the audience, discouraged experimentation in theater design. In most theaters the proscenium arch remained standard. In the United States, experimentation in theater design was also hindered by the high cost of real estate in urban areas and by antiquated fire laws governing theater construction. ⑤

Oriental drama has traditionally depended on the skill of the actors and the imagination of the audience to create atmosphere and to indicate changes of locale. Realistic scenery as known in the West is seldom used. Musicians often sit on the stage, and stagehands or prop men move about in full view of the audience during the performance. The traditional Chinese theater consists of a raised stage surrounded on three sides by the audience. In modern Chinese theaters the stage is no longer surrounded by the audience; however, a curved apron extending into the audience maintains the atmosphere of closeness between performer and spectator. ⑥

During the early 20th century there was an increasing reaction against the naturalistic stage setting and the proscenium arch. The bold symbolic stage settings made imaginative use of the actors' playing area and stimulated efforts to design new playhouses that would restore contact between actors and audience. ⑦ Scholars studied the theaters of the past, as well as the Oriental theaters, for fresh alternatives to the traditional proscenium design.

Soon, many theaters departed sharply from 19th-century conventions. In some new theaters, such as the Vivian Beaumont Theater in New York City, the size and shape of the playing area can be varied mechanically from a conventional proscenium to a thrust platform stage. ⑧ Perhaps the most interesting development in modern theater design is the arena stage, a laying area surrounded on four sides by the audience.

Notes

①这些设计上的差别取决于几个因素，其中包括上演的剧种、当时的演剧习俗、演员与舞台的实际关系以及剧院所接待的观众类别等。

②这一时期的典型剧院有以下几个特点：利用乐池中的座位，大量的包厢、楼座，有一个拱形前台。

③这些剧院的明显特征是取削了前台门，幕前的舞台部分较短，空出来的地方专门留作乐队席。

④20世纪初期，欧洲和美国的剧院一般都是传统的马蹄形或新的白露丝扇形剧场的改进型。

⑤在美国，剧院设计的创新还受到城市房地产价格昂贵以及过时的管理剧院建筑的防火条例的限制。

⑥现代中国剧院的舞台不再围有观众。然而，伸向观众的曲线型前台仍然保持着演员与观众间的亲密气氛。

⑦大胆启用象征性舞台布景使得人们通过想象来利用演员的表演场地，因而激发了人们设计出恢复演员与观众之间相互联系的新型剧院。

⑧在一些新的剧院里，如纽约市的维维安·搏蒙特剧院，表演场地的大小和形状能够通过机械从传统式的前台调节成三面对着观众的舞台。

Reading Material B

Holy Ground

What is church or temple ? It is a place of worship, spirit, contemplation, of course. ① But above all, from a human point of view, it is a gateway. A person comes into the world through the church. He leaves it through the church. And, at each of the important thresholds of his life, he once again steps through the church.

The rites that accompany birth, puberty, marriage, and death are fundamental to human growth. Unless these rites are given the emotional weight they need, it is impossible for a man or woman to pass thoroughly from one stage of life to another. ②

In all traditional societies, where these rites are treated with enormous power and respect, the rites, in one form or another, are supported by parts of the physical environment which have the character of gates. ③ Of course, a gate, or gateway, by itself cannot create a rite. But it is also true that the rites cannot evolve in an environment which specifically ignores them or makes them trivial. ④ A hospital is no place for a baptism; a funeral home makes it impossible to feel the meaning of a funeral.

In functional terms, it is essential that each person have the opportunity to enter into some kind of social communion with his fellows at the times when he himself or his friends pass through these critical points in their lives. And this social communion at this moment needs to be rooted in some place which is recognized as a kind of spiritual gateway for these events.

What physical shape or organization must this "gateway" have in order to support the rites of passage, and in order to create the sanctity and holiness and feeling of connection to the earth which makes the rites significant? ⑤

Of course, it will vary in detail, from culture to culture. Whatever it is exactly that is held to be sacred — whether it is nature, god, a special place, a spirit, holy relics, the earth itself, or an idea — it takes different forms, in different cultures, and requires different physical environments to support it.

However, we do believe that one fundamental characteristic is invariant from culture to culture. In all cultures it seems that whatever it is that is holy will only be felt as holy, if it is hard to reach, if it requires layers of access, waiting, levels of approach, a gradual unappealing, gradual revelation, passage through a series of gates. ⑥ There are many examples: the Inner City of Peking; the fact that anyone who has audience with the Pope must wait in each of seven waiting rooms; the Aztec sacrifices took place on stepped pyramids, each step closer to the sacrifice; the Ise shrine, the most famous shrine in Japan, is a nest of precincts, each one inside the other.

Even in an ordinary Christian church, you pass first through the churchyard, then through the nave; then, on special occasions, beyond the altar rail into the chancel and only the priest himself is able to go into the tabernacle. The holy bread is sheltered by five layers of ever more difficult approach.

This layering, or nesting of precincts, seems to correspond to a fundamental aspect of human psychology. We believe that every community, regardless of its particular faith, regardless of whether it even has a faith in any organized sense, needs some place where this feeling of slow, progressive access through gates to a holy center may be experienced.⑦ When such a place exists in a community, even if it is not associated with any particular religion, we believe that the feeling of holiness, in some form or other, will gradually come to life there among the people who share in the experience.

Notes

①什么是教堂或庙宇？自然，它是人们进行礼拜、增灵和默祷的场所。

②除非人们对这些仪式付出一定的情感，否则，一个男子或女子就不可能彻底地通过生命的一个阶段而进入另一个阶段。

③在人们极为重视这些仪式的所有传统社会中，都有某种具有门槛特征的物质环境来支持这些仪式的举行。

④但同样正确的是，在一个特别忽视或完全不重视仪式的环境中，也不会孕育出隆重的仪式来。

⑤为了支持这种人生道路中的仪式，也为了使仪式变得庄重，从而产生庄严、神圣的气氛以及实实在在的感觉，这个"门槛"应当采用什么具体的形状或结构呢？

⑥在各种文化中，情况似乎是，神圣的事物之所以被感觉到是神圣的，正因为它是不能轻易接近的。它设置有层层的通道、等候的场所、高低不一的路径、逐渐展开和显露的空间、穿过了重重门口的通道等。

⑦我们认为，每一个社区，无论它的特殊信仰是什么，也无论它的信仰有没有组织，它都需要某种场所，在那里，人们可以体验到一种感受，即缓慢而逐步地穿过层层大门，到达一个神圣的中心。

UNIT SIXTEEN

Text   The Practice of Architecture (I)

[1]   In a period of rapidly accelerating change in every area of human activity — economic, industrial, scientific, professional, sexual, artistic, and so on — it would be foolhardy to pretend that any description could hold true for more than the moment.① We will therefore deal with the matter of architectural practice in two sections: how it is, or rather has been up until now, and second, how it appears to be changing and in what probable directions.

[2]   With this caution in mind, let us begin by repeating that architecture is a service profession — that is, the architect does not buy or sell land or buildings, nor does he get any profits out of the construction process, as, for instance, the contractor does. He sells his professional skill as advisor and designer. For this service he receives a fee, a fee that is generally based upon the cost of the building. For residential work (private) it runs somewhere about 10 percent. Thus, the fee for a $50 000 house would be about $50 000. It could be a good deal more, if the client insists upon a "name" architect, who turns away more commissions than he can handle. Alterations or remodeling come higher-say 15 percent in most cases. For large buildings, apartment houses, office buildings, and so on, where the cost may run into millions, the fees are much lower percentagewise, since the architectural work involved in designing a forty-story building is not much greater than for a twenty-story one, so many of the floor plans being duplicates. But 5 or 6 percent of $100 million is a substantial sum.② A few jobs like that each year and the architect will have income tax problems.

[3]   The service performed falls into three sections or stages:

[4]   **Schematic Design**   After consultations with the client, visits to the site, study of budgets, and so forth, the architect prepares sketches (and often a model) of plans and exteriors of the proposed building, to the satisfaction of the client. These, mind you, are sketches, not blueprints. They will often include pictorial drawings showing trees, clouds, people, cars and so forth, so that the client can visualize the finished product most easily. When the client is happy he instructs the architect to go ahead, and pays 10 to 15 percent of the fee, according to their agreement (in the case of the $50 000 house above, involving a total fee of $5 000, the amount due at this point is $500-750). If the client is not satisfied, he may ask the architect for more sketches, more ideas. Or, if no meeting of the minds is forthcoming, he gets another architect, in which case the first architect relinquishes the commission but receives his 10 to 15 percent anyway, as payment for work done.

[5]   **Preliminary Design**   This is an extension of the schematic design, which covers conceptually the basic ideas of the building-to-be. When the schematic design has been approved, the architect proceeds to work it out in considerable detail, so that everyone can be sure that all the parts-corridors, rooms, lobbies, etc. — work together as they should and that all the

needs of the client, functional and aesthetic, are satisfied within the budget. In this stage some revision of the approved schematic design may take place, and, indeed, it is largely to make certain that the schematic design is correct and that the preliminary design is correctly worked out too. When it is done and everyone is happy with it, the architect receives another 20 to 25 percent of his fee. In our imaginary case this would be $1 000 to $1 250.

[6]　Working Drawings. This is the hardest and most tedious part of the job. Every part of the building, every floor plan, every detail, has to be drawn carefully and dimensioned, so that the building may be built with these drawings as a guide. In addition, a written statement of the materials and workmanship required is added; this written statement is called the specifications. Taken together, the working drawings and the specifications are called the contract documents, on which the contractor makes his bid, and which he contracts to execute. When the contract documents are ready, the architect, in consultation with his client, will select several contractors whose reputations and completed work seem satisfactory and invite them to examine the contract documents and submit bids — sums of money for which they promise a finished building to match the plans.③ The sealed bids are due on a certain day, and on that day they are opened by the client and architect and one is accepted — not necessarily the lowest, for the lowest may be not quite as desirable, as, say, the next lowest, or, as sometimes happens, all the bids are rejected, and the project either scrapped or sent back to the drawing boards for revision. This type of bid, incidentally, is called a lump-sum bid, since it is a lump-sum that the contractor is proposing.④ Sometimes, for example in museums and such, where money is not as important as quality, or when speed of construction is essential, a cost-plus bid will be accepted, in which the client will pay whatever the contractor's costs have been, plus a fixed percent as the contractor's profit. (Needless to say, this type of contract is one every contractor dreams about.)⑤

[6]　In any case, at this stage, when the contract documents are finished, the architect receives a further 40 to 50 percent of his fee. (In the case of our $50 000 house, this will be another $2 000 to $2 500 of his fee.)

[7]　**Supervision**　The third, and perhaps most critical, part of the architect's service is to oversee the actual construction of the building. At well chosen times he visits the job and examines the work being done to make sure it is in strict accordance with the working drawings and specifications — the contract documents. Also he makes himself available to the contractor to clear up any points that he, the contractor, may not completely understand, and to furnish any additional detailed drawings that may be needed. For this work the architect usually gets 10 percent of his fee.⑥

New Words and Expressions

accelerating * [æk'seləreitiŋ]　　　a.　　加速的
foolhardy ['fu:l'hɑ:di]　　　　　　　a.　　莽撞的，蛮干的

hold true (for)		适用，有效
caution ['kɔːʃən]	n.	小心，谨慎
contractor [kən'træktə]	n.	承包商
commission [kə'miːʃn]	n.	委托（代理）事项
alteration [ɔːltə'reiʃən]	n.	改动；变动
remodel [ri'mɔdəl]	v.	改造，改型
percentagewise [pə'sentidʒwaiz]	n.	百分比；百分数
duplicate ['djuːplikeit]	n.	复制品
schematic * [ski'mætik]	n.	简图，略图
substantial [sʌb'stænʃəl]	a.	相当大的，显著的
consultation [kɔnzʌl'teiʃən]	n.	商量，磋商
budget ['bʌdʒit]	n.	预算
blueprint ['bluːprint]	a.	蓝图
pictorial [pik'tɔriəl]	a.	绘画的，用图片表示的
visualize * ['vizjuəlaiz]	v.	使可看见；使具体化
relinquish [ri'liŋkwiʃ]	v.	放弃，停止
conceptually [kən'septjuəli]	ad.	概念上
proceed [prə'siːd]	v.	继续进行
building-to-be		未来（要施工）的建筑物
lobby ['lɔbi]	n.	（剧院、旅馆的）门廊；门厅
tedious ['tiːdiəs]	a.	冗长乏味的，使人厌烦的
make one's bid		投标，出价
execute ['eksikjuːt]	v.	履行，执行
in consultation with		与…磋商
submit ['sʌbmit]	v.	提出
incidentally [ˌinsi'dentli]	ad.	顺便提一句；附带的
scrap * ['skæp]	v.	废弃，作废
lump-sum		（金额）一次总付的
cost-plus	a.	在实际成本之外加以一定比例费用的
supervision * [sjuːpə'viʒən]	n.	监督，管理
oversee ['ɔvəsiː]	v.	监督，监查
clear up		解除（疑虑）等

Notes

①hold true for—适用于说明……
②这个长句的主要结构是 For large buildings, apartment houses, office buildings, and so on …the fees are much lower percentagewise, …
　　so many of the floor plans being duplicates 是分词独立结构，作原因状语。

③本句的一个突出特点是动词的含量很大,阅读时要注意它们的含义,句中功能及相互关系如 to examine…and submit… 之间是并列关系,均作宾语 them 的补足语,等等。

④本句虽长,但却是由 5 个相关的并列分句组成。读者不妨试找出这几个分句(不含分句中的定语从句等)。

due 一词此处系形容词,表示"预定(期的)"。

⑤在牵扯到合同时,client 也可译作"甲方",contractor 也可译作"乙方"。

⑥to make oneself available to do…

使自己随时可去……

另外,在美国对于一项重要的工程,在施工期间建筑师要在工地上派一名常驻代表,以便随时解决问题或取得联系,而建筑师本人则定期去督察。

Exercises

Reading Comprehension

Ⅰ. Find out the main ideas for each paragraph by choosing the corresponding number from the four listed.

1. The first step of success for an architect is to prepare fine sketches which should please the client. (1. 2. 3. 4)

2. As an extension of the schematic design, the preliminary design must contain the basic concepts of the project which may be built. (2. 3. 4. 5)

3. Architecture is a service profession because architects make their money by showing their professional skill as advisors and designers. (2. 4. 6. 7)

4. Supervision is the final but the most critical part of the architect's service. (2. 3. 5. 7)

5. The article will discuss the matter of architectural practice in two sections. (1. 2. 3. 4)

6. The architect can receive a considerable sum of money when the contract documents are finished. (4. 5. 6. 7)

7. Working drawing and the specifications make up of the contract documents, on which contractors make their bids. (1. 3. 5. 7)

Ⅱ. According to your understanding of the text, fill in the blanks with the best choices from those suggested.

1. How much the fee an architect receives for his or her service depends on _____.

A. his or her ability to deal with the clients

B. the sum the client is willing to offer

C. the cost of the building to be built

D. his or her luck

2. For residential work it runs somewhere about 10 percent. The word somewhere here can

be replaced by _____.

   A. some place   B. to a point   C. at a price   D. somehow

3. _____ may be probably deduced according to the text.

   A. An architect prefers to do the service of the private work because he can receive a higher percentage of fees.
   B. The higher the cost of a building is, the less fees can an architect receive for his service.
   C. Because of the problem of income tax, architects are usually not willing to accept the service of large buildings.
   D. Regardless of the problem of income tax, the architect is definitely to receive a higher pay for a high-cost project though the fees are much lower percentagewise.

4. So far as you consider from the text _____ is the most important of the three sections of an architect's professional performance.

   A. schematic design   B. preliminary design
   C. working drawing   D. all above

5. _____ is the decisive factor of the possibility to sign the contract between the client and the contractor.

   A. The lowest bids-sums of money the contractor can offer
   B. The most reasonable bids-sums of money
   C. The client's favor towards the client
   D. The private relationship between the architect and the contractor

Vocabulary

I. Match the words in Column A with the corresponding definitions or descriptions in Column B.

A	B
1. accelerating	a. overseeing
2. caution	b. sketch
3. schematic	c. increasing the speed of
4. visualize	d. carefuiness
5. supervision	e. bring as a picture before mind
6. remodel	f. matter which one is authorized to do for another
7. duplicate	g. alter
8. lobby	h. entrance-hall
9. commission	i. thing that is exactly like another

II. Complete the following sentences with the words or expressions listed below, changing the form where necessary.

make one's bid	in accordance with
visualize	caution
accelerating	clear up
commission	hold true for
supervision	

1. It would be foolhardy to pretend that any description of the practice of architecture could _____ any time and any place.
2. The work executed by the contractor and his working men in the construction must be _____ the blueprints and the specifications
3. The architect presented the schematic design to the client so that he could _____ the proposed project on paper in advance.
4. We live in a period of _____ development in almost every area of human activities.
5. The lawyer decided to take the defendant's _____ to plead for him in court.
6. Before having the opportunity to construct the high-rise building, the housing developer has to _____ on the contract documents.
7. In the course of drawing a working drawing, the architect must take a great _____ in every parts and details.

Reading Material A

The Practice of Architecture (Ⅱ)

At certain points during the construction process, such as the completion of the foundations, the framing, the roof, and so on, the architect issues to contractor certificates of payment, representing that portion of the work that has been finished and found acceptable by the architect.① These certificates are actually checks, payable from funds previously deposited under bond by the client.② However, sometimes the client has no control over this money. It is the architect who draws against it.③ Of course, the responsibility for doing so correctly falls upon him; he must, for instance, verify that the contractor has paid all his own bills to date. Otherwise always the hazard that (perhaps months later) a plumbing or other subcontractor will show up, claim that he was not paid for his work, and slap a lien on building.④

Besides the quality and accuracy of the work, the contractor is also obligated to finish the building by a stated date, for if it is not, the client might be in the awkward position of having moved out, or having been moved out, of his previous premises, and forced into unexpected expenses.⑤ In the case of a factory or rental building, he will also be losing income he expected during the time lost. Therefore, the contract sometimes contains a clause providing for damages to be paid by the contractor for each day he is late-unless the delay has been caused by acts of God, such as floods, fires, or strikes. Often this potential penalty is balanced by the promise of a bonus for each day the job is finished before the contracted date.⑥

When the job is finished, and everyone else has been paid, the architect receives the final 10 to 20 percent of his fee and says good-bye to the client, though he retains a kind of godfatherly interest in building and, by law, must consider himself on call to take care of any complications or problems of an architectural nature that may arise in the future.⑦ And, against these risks, he carries insurance.

It becomes clear that there is a sharp correlation between an architect's income and the amount of time and effort he can afford to give any particular commission. The temptation becomes strong, when one has spent too much time on an especially interesting or engrossing problem, to skimp on an ordinary, run-of-the-mill project similar to those one has done many times before.⑧ Why strain a creative ligament to dream up a new solution for something for which a perfectly good one already exists in your files?⑨ This perhaps accounts for the undeniable fact that many architects repeat themselves over and over, until one can spot a design by so-and-so in a one-second glance. This may not be a bad thing, however, for it may well be that this very recognizability is what gives the architect's work its unique character, the character for which his clients have come to him. On the other hand, it is conceivable that potentially brilliant and original designs may fail to being simply because the architect involved has been unwilling, or unable, to come into give them the necessary time and thought.

It becomes clear, therefore, that the architect's involvement with his society is so complete that even his talent, or rather the use of his talent, is socially limited, in this case operating through the powerful forces of economics. To the other pressures acting upon the architect, and determining what and how he designs, we must add the simple, but all-embracing, question of making a living. It is not easy to be inspired when the rent has to be paid, or to cling to one's ideals when the phone may be shut off.

Notes

①…the architect issues to the contractor certificates of payment,…

……建筑师向承包商出示付帐单据……

②Under bond：按照契约。

③正是建筑师本人对资金有控制权。

④要不然总会出现意料不到的麻烦（也许数月后），即管道工程的人或者其它的包工头会站出来声称他们没有得到工作报酬，突然宣布对建筑的扣押权。

⑤…the client might be in the awkward position of having moved out, or having been moved out, of his previous premises, and forced into unexpended expenses.

……委托人会陷入因为已搬迁出或被人赶出原来房舍，从而被迫支付意料不到的开支。

⑥这种潜在的罚款常常是通过许诺工程每提前一天给多少奖金来协调。

⑦on call：随叫随到。

⑧run-of-the-mill: 未经检验的。
⑨为什么要拉紧一个人为的系带去凭空想出解决某个事情的办法呢？因为在你的卷宗里已经存在着十全十美的办法。

Reading Material B

The Futural Practice of Architecture

We are living in a period when change is so rapid that the future becomes the past with barely a nod to the present. Consequently, it is reasonable to try to see what transformations in architectural practice are likely to take place in the times ahead. Some of them are, in fact, already happening; others we can merely speculate upon, but though we may miss the mark in specific detail we may feel fairly confident that something along the lines of what follows will take place.①

First, a disappearance (to a large degree) of individual practice. More and more architects are allying themselves with groups of specialists — designer, engineers, specification writers, landscape architects, planners, and so forth. This trend is so evident, and so eminently necessary that one can hardly expect any kudos as a prophet for foreseeing it. The exigencies and complexities of a sophisticated building technology make it impossible to operate otherwise.

What this means in terms of the architect's role in society is two-fold.② On the one hand his creativity will suffer an inevitable loss of individuality, since everything he designs will be in one way or another subject to the influence and acceptances of his associates. On the other hand, close association with other specialists and the immediate availability of their counsel can make it possible for him to conceive and execute projects more daring than he would feel confident about if he were working on his own.

Second, a revision of the service-fee set up.③ This, also, is already taking place. A huge housing project, for instance, such as New York's co-op City, does not begin with sketches, the way projects did in the past. It begins with urban studies, financial arrangements, and negotiations with municipal, state, and federal agencies. This involves the service of, and fees to, a whole regiment of experts, including urbanologists, lawyers, ecologists bankers, and housing consultants, making the old 15 percent for sketches arrangement with today's (or is it yesterday's?) architect seem like a quaint Victorian custom. The working drawings, the specifications, and even the supervision will be spread out among so many specialists, some in the architectural firm and others outside its as associates, that the rest of the fee structure becomes equally obsolete. Most likely, the architect will not receive any fee for a particular commission, but instead will work for his own firm, on salary, and share in the total annual profits, if any.

What this means, in turn, is that the architect's involvement with his client, and his dependence upon him as a sort of employer, will diminish, since his primary employer is his firm.④ This, again, has a two-fold social consequence. For one thing, the architect will become less sensitive to the individual needs and tastes of his clients, thus presenting the hazard of an increasing impersonality in architectural expression. But since, in much very large work, there is no individual client — rather, a corporation, committee, or agency — the loss is more verbal than real. Against this one might expect, speaking optimistically, that the architect, being freer from client pressures, will be more concerned with the effect of his work on people in general and the community at large. In other words, as the architect becomes less client-oriented he has at least the opportunity to become more socially-minded. Which leads us to our final speculation.

Third, a revolution in the availability of architectural services. There are no official figures to be had, but most educated guesses estimate that some 80 percent of the building done in the U.S.A. is done with out benefit of architect. Of course a large proportion of this is work that neither requires an architect nor would attract one-garages, extensions of warehouses, shop alterations, and the like. But there remains an immense amount of building for which no architect is used for one of two reasons: either the job is so small that no architect can afford to do it for the small fee involved, or-and this is most frequent — the potential client has the widely prevalent idea that to have an architect is something of a luxury. He costs money. All he does is frill up a building a bit, and that costs money, too. Better have Joe, your good old carpenter-contractor friend, run it up for you, and leave the fancy stuff to the toffs. The fact that in most cases the architect actually saves money for his client is hard to believe, however often stated. A $50 000 house, for instance, even with the architect's $5 000 fee added, is usually a bigger and better house than could be built for $60 000, without an architect.

Notes

①事实上有些已经在发生着；另外一些我们只能去推测。但是，尽管我们可能错过某个特殊而又细小的标记，但我们感到十分有信心沿着所遵循的方向一定会出现某种事物。
②这按照建筑师在社会上的作用的措辞，含义是双重的。
③第二，提出修改服务费。
　set up：提出
④这又意味着建筑师与作为雇主的委托人的关系、以及对他的依赖将会削减，因为他的首位雇主就是他的公司。

Appendix I   Glossary

ablaze　*a.*　闪耀	08	aurally　*ad.*　听觉上,听力方面	15
aboriginal　*a.*　土著的,土著居民	03	axial *　*a.*　轴的,轴向的	15
acanthus　*n.*　茛苕叶形装饰	13	backdrop　*n.*　(舞台后部的)背景,	
acanthus leaves　叶板	13	彩画幕布	15
accelerating *　*a.*　加速的	16	bakery　*n.*　面包烘房,面包店	06
accent　*a.*　重点,强调	07	balcony　*n.*　阳台	07
accessibility *　*n.*　可达性,可接近性	02	balustrade　*n.*　栏杆,扶手	01
accommodate　*vt.*　使适应,容纳	12	banner　*n.*　旗帜	03
acoustics *　*n.*　(礼堂、剧院等的)		beauty shop　*n.*　美容店	06
音响装置;音响效果	08	bizarre　*a.*　希奇古怪的;异乎寻常的	
acute *　*a.*　尖锐的,敏锐的	08	blithering　*a.*　胡说八道的	03
adaptability　*n.*　适应(用)性,灵活性	14	blueprint　*a.*　蓝图	16
address oneself to　致力于,着手	14	booth　*n.*　小室(房),小亭	08
adverse　*a.*　相反的,逆的,不利的	11	boulevard　*n.*　宽阔的大路,林荫大道	15
aesthetic　*a.*　美学的,审美的	01	bowling alley　*n.*　保龄球场	06
affordable　*a.*　买得起的	14	bracket　*n.*　等级;托架(建)	02
agitation *　*n.*　激动不安,焦虑	15	bring forth　产生	10
aisle　*n.*　走廊,侧廊	01	budget　*n.*　预算	16
alcove　*n.*　耳房,凹室	07	building codes　建筑(施工)规范	02
align *　*v.*　排成一条直线;使一致	09	building complex　群体建筑	07
allocation　*n.*　部署,分配	14	building-to-be　未来(要施工)的建筑物	16
allow for　考虑到;估计	03	by virtue of　凭借,依靠;由于	02
alteration　*n.*　改动;变动	16	cafeteria　*n.*　自助食堂	06
amber　*n.*　琥珀,琥珀色	08	candy　*n.*　(美)糖果	06
ambiance　*n.*　气氛,环境	08	cantilever　*v.*　悬臂梁,突梁	01
amortization　*n.*　分期偿还(债务)	04	canvas　*n.*　背景,画布	15
appealing　*a.*　引人入胜的,动人的	06	capriciously　*ad.*　变化莫测的	13
apse　*n.*　多边形(或半圆形)凹室;		car-pool　*n.*　车辆合用组织	12
耳(室)房	01	caricature　*n.*　漫画,讽刺画	13
aspiration　*n.*　愿望,志向	04	cascade *　*n.*& *v.*　迭落,梯流	07
assumption *　*n.*　前提;假设	09	cast shadow　投影	08
assumption *　*n.*　假定,设想	07	catastrophic　*a.*　大灾难的;大祸的	11
attendant　*a.*　伴随的	12	categorization　*n.*　分类,分列入目录中	05
auditorium　*n.*　音乐厅,礼堂	08	catenary　*n.*　悬垂线,悬曲线	07

词	词性	释义	页
cathedral	n.	大教堂，主教堂	01
caution	n.	小心，谨慎	16
chapel	n.	小礼拜堂	01
circulation *	n.	交通线路	05
cityscape	n.	城市景观	08
clarity *	n.	清晰度，明确性	15
clear up		解除（疑虑）等	16
clearance	n.	（建）净空，间隙	12
clerestory *	n.	天窗，高侧窗	15
clerical	a.	办事员的，办公室工作的	12
client	n.	委托人；客户	04
clincher	n.	定论；定性的人（物）	04
closet	n.	壁橱；衣橱	03
cluster *	n.	群，组	09
colloquially	ad.	用通俗口语地	08
colonnade	n.	柱廊，柱列	01
colonnaded	a.	设有柱廊的	13
comcpression *	n.	压力；压缩	01
commission	n.	委托（代理）事项	16
commonplace *	a.	平凡的；陈腐的	10
communal	a.	公共（用）的；社区的	07
compact	n.	小型汽车；压制品	
	a.	紧密的，结实的	12
compatibility *	n.	互换性，一致性	05
compensate	v.	补偿；赔偿	04
conceptual *	a.	概念的；理性的	10
conceptually	ad.	概念上	16
condominium	n.	共管式；（公寓中）个人拥有的一套房间	02
cone	n.	圆锥，锥体	08
configuration	n.	外形；构造	09
conform to		与……相符合（一致）	07
confusion	n.	混乱	02
consequent	a.	作为结果的；随之发生的	11
conservative	a.	保守的，守旧的	13
conserve	vt.	保存，保养	10
consistent	a.	与 with 连用，意为和……一致（协调）	07
constituent	a.	构成的；组成的	11
constrain	vt.	强使；强制	11
constraint	n.	约束，制约	14
consultation	n.	商量，磋商	16
contextual	a.	上下文的	15
contractor	n.	承包商	16
conviction	n.	深信；确信	03
corporate	a.	共同的，全体的	12
corporate	a.	法人的；社团的；公同的	04
correlate	v.	相互关联	09
correspondence	n.	符合，一致；相应	01
cosmetic	n.	化装品	08
cost-plus	a.	在实际成本之外加以一定比例费用的	16
counterpart	n.	相对物；一对中之一	06
counterpart	n.	对应物，对方	14
crave	v.	渴望，需要	01
criterion	n.	标准；尺度	11
customary	a.	（合乎）习惯的，惯例的	02
daring	a.	大胆的	10
deck	n.	楼层面；盖板	12
default	vi.	拖欠，不履行	02
defensible	a.	能防御的	09
deformation	n.	变形	11
demystification	n.	使非神密化	15
deposit slip	n.	存款单	08
deprive (of)		剥夺，使丧失	10
design-line	n.	设计行业	10
deterioration	n.	损坏，恶化	12
deterioration	n.	变化，变质	14
deterministic *	a.	确定的；决定的	11
dictate	v.	规定；限定	01
dictate	v.	规定，要求	12
dignify	vt.	使显得有价值，使增光	15
dimness	n.	昏暗	08
disco	n.	迪士科舞厅	06
disorientation	n.	迷失方向	15
distinctive	a.	有特色的；与众不同的	11
domain *	n.	范围，领域	05

169

domical	a.	园屋顶的,穹顶的	07
doorway	n.	入口;门口	03
drainage	n.	排水;排水系统,排水管	12
drastically	ad.	猛烈地,激烈地	10
draw upon (on)		动(利、引)用;吸收	09
ducal	a.	公爵的	03
duplicate	n.	复制品	16
durability	n.	耐久性	11
dwelling	n.	住处,寓所	02
eave	n.	屋檐	07
ecclesiastical	a.	基督教会的	11
edifice	n.	大厦,大建筑物;体系	01
elegance	n.	雅致,优美	13
element	n.(pl.)	风雨	02
emblem	n.	标志,象征	13
enclosure*	n.	围墙(栏);封围	01
enlighten	v.	启迪;开导	09
entity	n.	实体;统一体	07
entrain	vt.	使(空气)以气泡状存在于混凝土中	12
epitome	n.	梗概;缩影	10
essence*	n.	本质;精华	13
establishment	n.	企业,机关	06
ethical	a.	道德的,伦理的	10
exacerbate	vt.	使(病,痛)加剧,激怒	15
excetionally*	ad.	例外地,特殊地	11
exclusively*	ad.	专有地;独占地	03
execute	v.	履行,执行	16
existing	a.	现存的,存在的	05
facade	n.	(房屋的)正面,立面	05
facilitate	vt.	便于,使容易(便利)	14
feasible	a.	可行的;可用的	11
feasible	a.	可行的,可实行的	12
fertile	a.	丰富的	04
fiank	v.	位于……侧面的(两侧的)	13
fibrous*	a.	含纤维的,纤维状的	01
fictional	a.	虚构的	04
flood light	n.	泛光灯,聚光灯	08
florist	n.	花商	06
foolhardy	a.	莽撞的,蛮干的	16
foot-candle	n.	英尺烛光	08
format	n.	格式;尺寸;形式	11
forthcoming	a.	即将到来的,即将出现的	10
fountain	n.	喷泉,喷水池	06
foyer	n.	[法](剧场、旅馆等处的)门厅,休息处	02
fragrance	n.	芬芳,香味	15
fraternity	n.	一群同职业的人(同行)	04
frisk	vt.	遍身搜查	03
frontage	n.	临街面	09
functionalist	n.	建筑实用(功能)主义者	13
gable	n.	山(形)墙,三角墙	07
gateway	n.	入口;门口	03
gear	v.	使配合;传动	12
genesis	n.	激增,发生	06
gild	v.	镀金于;涂或漆成金色	13
glare	n.	眩光,刺目的强光	
	v.	发强烈的光,发眩光	08
Gothic	n.	哥特式建筑的	01
grid*	n.	柱网;格栅	10
gridiron	n.	梁格结构,格状结构	01
gross	a.	总的,全部的	04
gross income		毛收入	04
guideline*	n.	指导路线,导向图	05
habitat	n.	住(场)所,栖息地	14
hallway	n.	门厅,过道	02
handicapped	a.	残废的,身体有缺陷的	12
headlight	n.	(汽车等的)前灯;桅灯	08
hierarchy*	n.	层次,体系	15
highlight*	v.	以强烈光线照射;使……突出(显著)	15
hilly	a.	有斜坡的,丘陵的	09
hinge	n.	折叶	03
hip	n.	屋脊,斜(屋)脊	
	v.	给屋顶造屋脊	07
hold true (for)		适用,有效	16

170

horrific	a. 极其可怕的		15
housing	n. 住房;住房建筑		02
humane	v. 人道的,仁慈的		09
humanism	n. 人情,人性		10
humble	a. 地位低下的;谦卑的		03
identifiable	a. 可识别的,可区别的		01
identification *	n. 确定,识别		05
identity	n. 个性,特性		05
illiterate	a. 文盲的,无知的		03
illumination *	n. 照明,照(明)度		08
image	n. 意象		05
immeasurably	ad. 无法计量地;无边无际地		08
imperceptibly	ad. 觉察不到地		01
impetus *	n. (原)动力;促进		14
implicit	a. 绝对的;固有的		11
impulse *	n. 刺激;脉冲		06
in consultation with	与……磋商		16
inaccessible	a. 不能接近的,不能达到的		09
incinerator	n. 垃圾焚烧炉		02
incorporate *	vt. 使实体化,使具体化;体现,使合并		12
incremental *	a. 增长的,增值的		09
incur	v. 蒙受;招致		04
indeterminate *	a. 模糊的;不确定的		03
influx	n. 流入,川流不息		09
infrastructure	n. 下部(基础)结构		14
ingenuity	n. 创造性;巧妙		09
inherent *	a. 内在的,固有的		01
initially	ad. 最初地;开始地		11
innovative	a. 革新的,富有创造精神的		14
innumerable	a. 无数的		03
incidentally	ad. 顺便提一句;附带的		16
instability	n. 不稳定性		11
institution	n. (慈善,守教性质的)公共机构,协会,学校		15
institutional	a. 社会习性的,公共机构的		13
intangible	a. 触摸不到的;无形的		03
integrate	vt. 使结合		12
integration *	n. 综合,整体;集成;积分		11
intensify *	v. 使更剧烈,加强		09
integral *	a. 完整的,整个的		13
interpretive	a. 解释的;阐明的		03
interrelate *	v. 相互联系		05
interventionist *	a. 干涉主义的		15
investor	n. 投资者(人)		04
irregular	a. 不整齐的,不规则的		07
jeopardize	v. 危害		14
join the ranks of	加入……的行列		04
keystone	n. 关键;拱顶(心)石		06
lamp-post	n. 路灯柱(杆)		05
lance	n. 长矛;旗杆矛		03
landform	n. 地形,地貌		09
landmark	n. 地标;界标;地物		05
lateral *	a. 侧面的;横向的		11
laundromat	n. 自动洗衣店(间)		02
layman	n. 门外汉,外行		07
leasable	a. 可租借的		06
legitimately	ad. 合法地;正统地		13
legitimately	ad. 合理地,合理地		08
lengthwise	ad. 沿长的方向,纵长地		07
lobby	n. (剧院、旅馆的)门廊;门厅		16
locality	n. 地方;所在地		02
loft	n. 阁楼,顶楼		07
look-like	n. 外观相似		10
lump	v. 把……归并		04
lump-sum	(金额)一次总付的		16
lure	vt. & n. 诱惑,吸引		06
make one's bid	投标,出价		16
mall	n. 林荫道		05
manipulate *	v. 熟练地使用,利用		15
mascara	n. 染眉毛(或睫毛)油		08
mansion	n. 宅第;大厦		03
mass	vt. 集中,聚集		05

171

英文	词性	中文	页
mass-produced	a.	批量生产的	02
medieval	a.	中世纪的,中古时代的	09
merchandise	v.	[美]经商,推销	06
mesh	v.	紧密结合;啮合	
	n.	网孔;网装结构	12
metropolitan	a.	都市的,大城市的	02
microclimate	n.	小气候	05
microlevel	n.	微级	05
minimally	ad.	最低限度地;最小地	11
mobility	n.	运动性;变动性	11
moderate	a.	中等的,适度的	14
module *	n.	模度(数,量);模件	01
monetary	a.	钱的;金融的	04
monolith	n.	(柱状或碑状的)独块巨石,独石柱	10
monotony	n.	单调,千篇一律	05
mortgage	n.	抵押,保证	04
mortgage	n.	抵押借款	02
motto	n.	箴言,座右铭	14
multi-hued	a.	有多种颜色的	15
multicoporate	a.	多元的,多单位的	12
nave	n.	(教堂的)正厅;(火车站等建筑的)中间广场	01
neighborhood	n.	住宅小区;街坊	02
node	n.	交叉点,中心	15
nomenclature	n.	名称,术语	05
nondescript	a.	(因无特征而)难以归类的,难以形容的	10
nuance	n.	(意义、感情、颜色、音调等)细微差别	03
obligation	n.	职责;义务	04
obtrusive	a.	强入的;强迫别人接受的	11
occupant	n.	居住着;占用者	10
octagon	n.	八边形	07
of necessity		不可避免地,必然地	12
off the mark		不合格;达不到要求	04
convex *	a.	凸的,凸面的	07
onward	a. &ad.	向前(的);在前面(的)	13
organically	ad.	有机地,有组织地	07
orient *	vt.	调整,定……的位	05
orientation *	n.	方向,方位	05
ornament	n.	装饰(物)	01
overdue	a.	期待已久的,早就成熟的	10
oversee	v.	监督,监查	16
paradigm	n.	范例,示例	15
patio	n.	庭院,天井	09
pediment	n.	山花(墙)	13
percentagewise	n.	百分比;百分数	16
perceptible	a.	可领悟的,可理解的	15
perimeter	n.	周边(长、围)	06
peripheral *	a.	周边的	06
perspective	a.	透视(画、法)的	
	n.	正确观察事物相互关	09
persuasion	n.	信念;集团	13
persuasive	a.	劝诱的,有说服力的	08
pictorial	a.	绘画的,用图片表示的	16
pillar	n.	支柱	13
pinpoint	vt.	提出,确认	05
pitch	n.	斜度	
	v.	(使)向下倾斜	07
planner	n.	设计者,规划者	05
plaza	n.	(城市中的)广场	03
plot	n.	小块地皮;基址	02
positive	a.	实际(在)的;肯定的	07
prattle	n.	空谈,废话	13
preconception	n.	预想,先入之见	09
predominant	a.	主要的;占优势的	11
prefabrication	n.	预制	14
premature *	a.	过早的,不成熟的	14
premise	n.	前提	
	v.	提出……为前提	12
presage	vt.	预示,预言	10
prescribe	n.	指令;规定	11
preservation	n.	保存,维护	05
prestige	n.	威望;声望	11
presumably	ad.	大概;估计可能	04
principal	n.	本金;资本	04

probability *n.* 可能性；概率		11
probabilistic approach 概率法		11
proceed *v.* 继续进行		16
programmatic *a.* 纲领性的,计划性的		15
prohibit *v.* 禁止,阻止,妨碍		12
project * *v.* 伸(突)出；设计		01
proliferation *n.* 激增,扩散		06
promoter *n.* 发起人；创办者		04
proposition *n.* 建议,命题		12
prototype *n.* 典型,样品,原型		14
proving-ground *n.* 检验场,试验场		14
provoke *vt.* 印起,诱发		15
proximity *n.* 接近度,邻近		12
proximity * *n.* 接(临)近		06
psychedelic *a.* 颜色鲜艳的；引起幻觉的		13
pursue *vt.* 追随；进行		14
pursuit *n.* 研究,从事		14
put down 认为，估计		03
quarters *n.*(*pl.*) 住处,住宅		02
quirk *n.* (奇怪的)行为；妙语		04
radically * *ad.* 根本地,基本地		10
random *a.* 任意的；偶然的		11
readily *ad.* 容易地,不费力		01
receptive *a.* 有能力的；感受的		03
receptor *n.* 感(接)受器		08
recreational *a.* 休养的,娱乐的		06
rectangle * *n.* 长方形,矩形		01
rectangular * *a.* 长方形的		07
rectilinear *a.* 直线的,由直线围起的		09
recycle *vt.* (使)再循环		10
redundant *a.* 多余的；累赘的		13
refine *vt.* 精选；加工		09
refined *a.* 过于讲究的,精细的		03
rehabilitation *n.* 重(改)建,更新		14
relinquish *v.* 放弃,停止		16
remainder *n.* 剩余部分		04
remodel *v.* 改造,改型		16
removable * *a.* 可拆装的；可移动的		13
renewal *n.* 更新,重建		14
renovation *n.* 整修,革新		10
rent roll 租金滚动		04
rental *n.* 租金；租赁 *a.* 出租的,租用的		04
reserve *n.* 储备；保存		11
retail *n.* 零售,零卖		10
retina *n.* 视网膜		08
revitalize *vt.* 使新生,使有新的活力		14
revolutionize *vt.* 彻底改革,使革命化		10
ridge *n.* 屋脊 *v.* 装屋脊		07
ritualistic *a.* 仪式的		13
row houses 排式平房		02
runoff *n.* (雨水、融雪等的)径流,流量		12
salvageable *a.* 可救的,可抢救的		14
sanctuary *n.* 圣所,圣堂		15
sanitary *a.* 卫生的		02
sanitation *n.* 卫生设备		02
schematic * *n.* 简图,略图		16
scrap * *v.* 废弃,作废		16
sculpture *n.* 雕塑		06
segment *n.* 部分；扇形体		14
self-buttress *n.* 自扶墙；拱墙		07
semidetached *a.* (房屋)一侧与邻屋相连的,半独立的		02
sensation *n.* 感觉；轰动		10
sentimental *a.* 感情的,情绪的		13
serviceability *n.* 操作性能；适用性		11
setup *n.* 预算；预备		04
shaft * *n.* 箭杆；柱身,塔尖		13
sheaves *n.* 捆		13
shed roof 单坡屋顶		07
shelter *n.* 住所；屏蔽		02
showcase *n.* 橱窗,陈列窗		14
showmanship *n.* 招揽生意；吸引公众注意的技巧		08
shrubbery *n.* 灌木丛(林)		06

词条	词性	释义	页
sidewalk	n.	人行道	06
signage	n.	识标,位标	05
simplification	n.	简化	04
simultaneously	ad.	同时地;一齐地	09
single-family	a.	独户的	
	n.	独户	02
skeleton	n.	构架;草图;轮廓	01
skyline	n.	(大厦等)空中轮廓	05
slab	n.	混凝土楼板;平板	12
slip	n.	纸条,板条	08
sloppy	a.	不整齐的,不系统的	07
slot	n.	狭孔;缝	03
solariums	n.	日光浴室	15
sole	a.	单独的	02
sophistication *	n.	完善化,复杂化	09
spaciousness	n.	宽敞,广阔	05
span *	v.	跨过;架设	01
		跨度	
spatial *	a.	空间的	05
spawn	v.	大量生产;酿成	09
spine	n.	地面隆起地等	15
spire	n.	塔尖;尖顶	03
spring from		升起;由……产生	07
squint	v.	斜着眼看,眯眼看	08
stand-alone	a.	独立的	12
standpoint	n.	观点,立场	05
standstill *	n.	停止,停滞不前	10
staple	n.	常用品,主要商品	06
stark	a.	僵硬的,刻板的	10
stature	n.	重要性	15
stiffness *	n.	刚度;硬度	11
stride	n.	大步,阔步	14
striking	a.	显著的;惊人的	10
sturdy	a.	结实的,坚固的	01
stylistic	a.	风格上的	13
subconsciously	ad.	下(潜)意识地	01
subdue	v.	征服	09
submit	v.	提出	16
subsequently	ad.	随后地;后来地	11
substantial	a.	相当大的,显著的	16
suburbia	n.	(总称)都市的郊区,	
		郊区居民	06
superfluous	a.	多余的,不必要的	13
supervision *	n.	监督,管理	16
sustain	v.	遭受,蒙受	09
take on		呈现(新面貌);具有(特性);	
		承担	03
take up		消除;吸收	07
tedious	a.	冗长乏味的,使人厌烦的	16
tenant	n.	房客,住户	02
tenement-house		经济公寓;租用房屋	02
tensile *	a.	张力的,拉的	01
terminal	n.	终点(站),终端	08
terrace	n.	台地,露台	02
texture *	n.	纹理,结构	08
thereby	ad.	因此;从而	11
threshold *	n.	开端;门槛	10
time scale		时间表	04
to accept responsibility for		对……承受(担)责任	02
to hold title to something		拥有……的权利	02
tolerably	ad.	过得去地,还算不错地	05
topographical	a.	地性的	11
topography	n.	地形,地势	09
tranquility	n.	安静,宁静	15
transept	n.	(教堂的)袖廊,翼部	01
transient	n.	暂时居住的人,过客	
	a.	短暂的,过路的	12
transit	n.	公共交通系统,运输	12
tribesman	n.	部落的一员;同宗族的人	03
tribute	n.	称赞,颂词	13
triumphal arch		凯旋门	03
turnover	n.	更换率;周转	04
two-way	n.	双向交通,相向的交通	12
tyranny	n.	暴虐,残暴的行为	15
upgrade	v.	改良,提高(等级)	14
upper price brackets		高级(等)	02

upside down	颠倒,倒转		07
urbanization	*n.*	城(都)市化	09
urgency	*n.*	迫切	14
vacancy	*n.*	空房间;空处	04
valid	*a.*	正确的;有根据的	10
validity *	*n.*	有效性;真实性	13
vault	*n.*	穹顶,拱顶	07
versatile *	*a.*	多方面的,多才多艺的	08
viability	*n.*	耐久性,生存性	14
viable *	*a.*	可行的;能生存的	10
violate	*vt.*	侵犯;扰乱	03
visionary	*a.*	想象的;好幻想的	10
visualize *	*v.*	使可看见;使具体化	16
void *	*n.*	空间(位),虚(空)体	

	a.	空的,无人使用的;虚的	01
wage earners	*n.*	工薪者(层)	02
walk-up	*a.*	无电梯的,直接走上去的	09
warrior	*n.*	武士;勇士	03
watt *	*n.*	瓦(电功率单位)	08
waver	*vi.*	摆动,动摇	15
whereas *	*conj.*	而;却	09
windswept	*a.*	挡风的	05
wing	*n.*	厢房,侧厅,配楼	07
with respect to...	关于……		12
withstand *	*v.*	经受得住;抵抗	01
wonderland	*n.*	奇境	08
zoning	*n.*	分区制,区域规划	02

Appendix Ⅱ   Translation for Reference

第1单元

建 筑 学

　　建筑学是建造的艺术。实质上整个建筑学都与供人使用的围合空间有关。建筑物内部一些空间的大小和形状是由那些将要容纳在该建筑物（如从工厂的装配线到住宅中的起居室）里的确切活动所规定。这些空间的排列还应有合理的关系。另外，人在建筑物中的走动需要有走廊、楼梯或电梯，其尺寸受预期交通负荷的支配。建筑方案是建筑师首先要考虑的事，它把对建筑物的各种要求安排成体现建筑意图的空间组合。好的方案可以使来访者在建筑中找到其目的地并留下印象，这种印象也许是下意识地通过把大的建筑体系中一些单元明显地联系起来而造成的。相反，坏的方案所产生的结果是不方便、浪费和视觉上的混乱。

　　此外，一座建筑的结构必须建造良好；它必须具有永久性。这种永久性既是设计意图要求的，也是材料的选择所允许的。建筑材料（石、砖、木材、钢材或玻璃）部分地决定着建筑物的形式，并被这些形式所表现。石头几乎可以无限地承受压力。在实验室中能把石头压碎，但在实际使用中它的耐压程度几乎是无限的。然而它的抗拉性却是十分脆弱的。任何横跨空间的梁都会出现在支点间下弯的趋势，从而使梁的下半部处于拉应力状态。基于石头抗拉力差的缘故，这种材料的梁须相对短，且支点多。还有，石柱必须粗而短，其高度很少超过宽度的十倍。在石建筑中，窗、门以及支柱间的空间，其高度不得不超过宽度，从而形成了狭长矩形的石建筑美。

　　木材是一种含纤维的材料，既可承受压应力，又可承受拉应力。木梁比起石梁要相应长些；木柱则比较细，但间距宽。由于木材的天然性能而形成宽度大于高度的扁而宽的矩形建筑，正如在日本建筑中所看到的那样。钢也具有等于或大于其抗压强度的抗拉强度。任何观察过正在施工中的钢结构建筑物的人，必定注意到由每块地面上伸出的细长而间隔很宽的柱子和长梁形成的横向长方形网格结构。木材和钢材的性能适用于框架（一种支撑楼面和楼顶的构架），当然还需其他的铺面材料。木材和钢材还可制成悬臂梁，伸出最后的支点以外。

　　最后，建筑不仅要满足强度和空间的实际要求，它还必须满足人类的精神需要。建筑物的构成部分应当形成美的统一体。这样，一个结构的侧部和尾部就应和前部体现出充分的一致，从而使它们在整体中成为互相关联的部分。主要的室内部分也必须在某种程度上表现在外部的设计方案上。例如，哥特式大教堂的正厅，侧廊，袖廊，耳室和四周的小礼拜堂都可从外部看见。于是，来访者对他在内部将要看到的一切都能下意识地做好精神上的准备。

　　建筑要求良好的比例，即令人感到惬意的虚与实、高与宽、长与广的关系。人们作了种种尝试通过数学公式（如黄金分割）阐明这种良好的比例关系。然而，虽然在整个设计中通过重复某种模数（如以一个柱子半径为模数）已获良好的结果，但所有这些努力尚未被普遍认可。这种重复有助于产生人类心理以似乎渴望的可视的序列。

建筑物还须具有建筑师们所说的"尺度"。也就是说它必须在视觉上传达其真正的尺寸。诸如长凳、台阶、栏杆等构件，尽管它们的尺寸可能稍有变化，但按实际用途还是与人类的正常尺度相关的。因而它们就不知不觉地成为判断整个大建筑物规模的计量单位。由于这些部分比起整个建筑物小得多，因此就需要有中等尺寸的其它构件。楼梯和栏杆提示着门道的大小；门道又提示着柱廊的大小；柱廊最后又提示着整个结构物的大小。凡尔赛的小特里安农宫殿就是一个符合尺度要求的完美例子。罗马的圣·彼得大教堂由于没有小构件，因而它的宏大很难被人们意识到。

装饰虽然在某些现代建筑中被拒绝采纳，但在过去却被使用，或是由于其内在的美，或是为了强调建筑物某一部分的重要性。装饰物可用来表达建筑物的特征，即成为其用途的视觉表现形式。因此，银行看起来就应当像银行，而教堂则应该立刻被认出是教堂。最理想的是任何建筑物都应当各得其所，和相邻建筑物以及当地的地理情况保持某种关系。

第 2 单元

住　房

住宅是人类生活的场所。它的基本作用是给人类提供遮挡风雨的栖身之处。但今天人们对住宅的要求远过于此。一个家庭在搬入一新区时，总想了解买到的房子是否达到安全、卫生及舒适的标准，他们还要弄清这套住房离教堂、学校、商店、图书馆、影剧院及社区中心有多远。

本世纪 60 年代中期，在住房建筑中最重要的是有足够的室内、外空间，大多数家庭喜欢占地约半英亩的独户住宅，这样就会有业余活动的空间。许多家庭住在尽可能远离大城市的中心区，即使家里上班的人因此要走较远的路程。约有十分之四的家庭喜欢住在乡村住宅，胜过住在郊区住宅，这主要是因为他们要远离噪音、拥挤和混乱状况，方便的公共交通已不再是住房问题的决定因素，因为大多数人都是自己驾车上班。人们主要对房子的布局、大小及卧室的多少感兴趣。

乡村和郊区的多数居民都住独户住宅。职业土地开发者建造了包括许多独户住宅的开发区。纽约莱维顿就是一个批量建造的住宅开发区，它可容纳 60 000 多人住。由于是批量修建，开发区的住房形式单一，非常相似。基于同样原因，这些住宅通常比单独修建的住宅便宜。

由于人口稠密地区地皮昂贵，所以连壁住房，即两户式住房随处可见。在连壁住宅中，两家共用一堵墙，建造和采暖要比独户住宅便宜，但是居住者感到缺乏私密性。两侧由隔墙连接的、可住许多独户的联排式房屋造价更低。

市内地皮十分昂贵，除了造价昂贵的高级住宅外，一般不用来修建小型住宅。一种更为有效地利用土地的建筑形式是在本来只能容纳几家独户住宅的地段上修建多单元高层住宅楼，也就是公寓楼。这种公寓住宅楼有的只有几层，不带电梯；有的20多层带有几部电梯。有些公寓住宅还给居民提供台地或庭院，他们可以在此种植花草，也可以就餐。许多公寓住宅设有自动洗衣间、停车库、花厅。大型公寓开发区可包括几个街区，设有公园、体育场、商店和公共活动中心。

　　现代公寓住房制度中有两种形式，一是合作式；一是个人拥有式。在合作式住宅中，所有住户组成一个会社。每个住户先从会社购买一个股份，并支付自己的那份楼房保养费、服务费和修理费。这样，他便在公寓中拥有一套住房的权力。万一某一住户不能按期支付房税或抵押借款，会社便要负责支付。个人拥有式住房的不同在于每个住户实际上拥有他所居住的公寓的所有权，并负责住房的一切财务问题。当然他也需付一份住宅楼的公共设施如电梯、门厅、垃圾焚烧炉等的保养费。

　　如果住房合乎当地风俗习惯和地方建房条例，那么它就被认为在质量上合乎标准。地方规划法为建筑基地可接受的规模确立了标准，并决定这个基地是适合居住、商用还是工业用途。建筑规范要求新的住宅规划预先提交给地方政府以获取准建证。住房规范（如城市公寓法）要求住房应该安全、卫生，并维修良好。

　　好的住宅意味着它既是一个合适的栖身之处，又位于令人满意的社区。住宅小区应是最大限度地安静、私密、干净和安全。住宅区应当有与之配套服务的医院、学校以及治安、消防、卫生设备和商场。公园和社交中心把许多住户结合成一个社区。这些条件创造了良好的标准住房。然而，全世界有一半以上的人的住房情况达不到这些标准。

第3单元

建 筑 语 言（一）

　　当我们说某个建筑物表现了这个或那个的时候，就明确认定该建筑物除了其本身的使用功能外，还是一种交际媒介。就象我们希望印在这张纸上的文字传达某种意义一样，建筑物也可表达某种意思。当然，那些需要表达意思的人（这里指的是建筑师）以及那些想要"看懂"这种意思的人必需具备使用这种语言的某些常识。这对于在同一种社会环境中成长起来的人来说并不难，他们就象学说话一样，可以毫不费力地获得这方面的知识。一个来自另一种文化背景的人，比方说一位南太平洋的土著部落人，也许会觉得理解我们的建筑就象理解我们的语言、风俗习惯和道德标准一样难。他也许看不出教堂与邮局有什么区别，其实他本来就不知道教堂是什么，更不用说邮局了。但是如果是在你自己的文化环境中，你在这种环境中成长，也许对其形成还尽过一份力，你不仅理解建筑物的基本含义，比如："我是教堂，""我是加油站，"你还能看出更深一层的意思和细微的差别，比如："我这所房子很讲究，请进，但别忘了擦脚，"或者，"我这里是宫殿，摘掉帽子，准备接受检查。"

　　由此看来，建筑师（通过其建筑物表达思想的人）必须做到：1. 非常明确要表达的内容，免得露出一付胡说八道的傻相；2. 要很好掌握这种语言，这样那些想要理解他的人——他的读者（如果你愿意这样称呼的话）——就不会把他当作一个糊涂的文盲了。

　　我们知道，语言是由符号——词、句、手势、姿势等，即任何可以结合在一起进行交际的东西构成的。在建筑中，这些符号就是墙、屋顶、门、窗户、阶梯和尖顶等，它们是构成建筑物的要素。每个建筑物都可以有无穷的设计方法，组成无数的形式。因此，建筑物的最终含义是模糊不定的，就象诗歌和音乐一样，其含义取决于作者的创造力和表现力以及应答者的理解力和感受力。因为，参与交际的双方所涉及的人有着巨大的差别，——不同的经历、不同的成见、不同的信念以及不同的敏感性。因此，同一件建筑作品，不同的人有不同的看法，而且由于偶然的原因还会引起激烈的争论，这就不足为奇了。

　　让我们来看看门这个极为渺小而又显然很简单的建筑"词汇"。什么是门？门实际上是开在墙上的缺口，也就是说先有墙后有门。修墙是为了进行分隔，把有些人留在墙内，把另外些人挡在墙外，同时它也隔风、挡雨、防寒、御狼。然而，有时特殊的人或物需要通过，因此要在墙上开个缺口，不用时可以关上，这就是门。门的尺寸和形状取决于进出的人或物的需要。

　　从门的尺寸和形状，你能"看懂"其用途。比如，为一个人进出而设置的门是6英尺高（很少有人超过这个高度），它可能是浴室的门、壁橱的门、工具库的门或简朴的农舍门。如果墙下方有小门，那就是为 Rover 或 Pussy 这类宠物开的门，而带有活页盖的槽形孔则是信箱的入口。把这三个因素结合起来，你就可以在墙壁上勾画出这样一画面：一座位于近郊或乡间养有宠物的简朴的住宅。我们知道，为出入车辆而设的门其宽度大于高度，尺寸小的是私人小汽车用的门，尺寸大的是公共汽车或飞机用的门。

　　大人物进入公爵宅第院落时常常骑着马，因此，门道就必须宽敞高大。如果是一队武士骑马出征，特别是他们凯旋而归时，门道就必须更宽更高，足以让长矛和旗帜通过。由于长期以来大门总是与光荣的事件联系在一起，它逐渐成了荣耀的象征，因而迟早会与其作为通过墙壁的功能分道扬镳而独具作用。因此，我们常常可以看到树立在广场中央，专用于节日庆典、纪念活动等的凯旋门。

第4单元

前 期 预 算（一）

　　有些建筑物如博物馆、图书馆、学校、教堂等，人们在建造时并不想以此来赚钱。然而对于大多数建筑物来说，主要目的就是为其所有者产生经济效益，如旅馆、办公楼、公寓、剧院等等。因此人们常常期待建筑师先为他的委托人作投资费用的项目分析，这个分析被称之为前期预算。它包括对地价、工程费、抵押贷款、利息、维修、收入以及盈利等多方面的分析。因为委托人，除了想给自己或他的公司树一座丰碑外，他还有一种不可理解的嗜好，即在年末岁终时看到他的帐本上是盈利的。毫无疑问，首先这种嗜好与他能够成为公司的第一把手有关。

预算做得比较精确的建筑师在客户中享有良好的声誉，而预算常常做得不合格的建筑师则会加入失业者的行列。这样，对建筑师的基本职责来说就是：除了表现社会特征并发展人类愿望而创造一个丰富的环境外，他必须优先考虑前期预算。

前期预算由三部分外加一个结论组成，人们熟知这个结论被称之为"按钮"，即定论，因为正是这个定论常常决定着该工程是否应该上马。

第一部分是估价陈述。它包括对地价、工程费用、建筑师、工程师的报酬、法律手续费、许可证费等的估算。然后整个费用被分为两个部分，一部分是投资者必须实际提供的现金，另一部分是需要借贷的资金，换言之抵押贷款。

第二部分包括工程竣工后的维持（即经营）费。最大一项大概是抵押贷款的利息和分期偿还款（付清抵押本金）。其次是大楼雇员工资、税金、燃料费、维修费、保险费等等。请注意，分期付清抵押贷款会逐年减少所贷本金，因而其年利息也逐年减少，当然前提是抵押借贷就是这样写的。随着时间的推移，其它一些项目费用也会上下波动。因此，第二部分的数值应根据时间发生变化。

第三部分，有时称之为租金滚动，它是对所建大楼将带来的毛收入的估算。一般采用这种的方法是假定整幢大楼按照目前该地区、这类建筑（比如说一幢公寓楼或写字楼）的租金全部租出，并减去10%的"空位房间"。空位一词加上引号是由于它是虚构的。当然，在建筑物短缺时，谈不上空位房间。但在供过于求时，首先该项工程也许就不能实施了。此外，用这项预算来弥补管理上带来的花费和更换住户过程中的租金损失是否有道理，人们还在争论。

定论是从第三部分毛收入减去第二部分维护费用而得出的，余项就是净收入，这是一个有魅力的数字。然后把它同第一部分中的实际现金投资比较，以获得一个百分数。这个百分数就是利率。它决定这项工程是否值得进行。通常投资者希望至少获得15%的回收利润，否则他将投资别的项目。要么他会要求建筑师重新修改整个计划以获得较高利润。

所有这一切初看起很难，实际上并非如此。也许使大家更清楚地了解这点最简单的办法是想象出一个例子并为它作出一个前期预算。

假定要建一个公寓大楼，它的整个费用人们建议是200万美元，对一幢现代化的高层建筑来说这是很平常的数字。根据粗略的估计，总数的五分之一，即40万美元将用于购买地皮，剩余的将用于施工以及其他费用，办理许可证等（为了简化起见我们把它合并在一起）。总费用的90%即180万美元将由贷款机构——银行、储蓄所、信用社、保险公司等，只要是金融机构均可，以抵押贷款的形式来提供借贷。大约10%的年利还要加上每年2%的分期偿还债务。这样只剩下20万美元需要发起人（你的委托人）来提供。这笔钱可以是他自己的，也可以是他岳父的或他在赌城拉斯维加斯赢来的，那都没关系。这是现款，他可投资进去。这就是第一部分。

第 5 单元

城市设计的范围

首先我们可以通过限定城市设计的范围来确定城市设计的要素。城市设计是指致力于提高环境形体质量的那部分规划程序，也就是说，是环境的形体与空间设计。然而，我们必须十分清醒地意识到，在环境设计的过程中，规划者和设计者不可能对所有的要素和组成部分进行设计，不可能在任何情况下都设计出完整的建筑物。这种完整的设计对于新建城镇和新规划的住宅区是可行的，但对现有社区难以实施。

另外，城市设计的范围可从建筑物的外部向外扩展延伸，同时，要考虑各个建筑物对彼此内部的积极和消极影响。城市设计的范围可以定义为"设计城市而不设计房屋"。因此我们说，建筑物之间的空间就是城市设计的范围。但是，我们该如何设计这些空间呢？

用旧金山城市设计规划的术语来表示，我们可以把相互联系的四组空间的意义区别开来：（1）内部格局与意象，（2）外部形态与意象，（3）交通流线与停车场，（4）环境质量。内部格局和意象描述了城市结构之间的微级空间意义，即城市结构的主要形体特征，也就是焦点、视点、地标和运动模式。外部形态和意象的重点是城市的轮廓、总体意象和个性。交通流线及停车场是指街道与道路的特性，即：道路的养护质量、宽敞度、秩序、单一性、流线清晰性、目的地的方向性、安全性、畅通性以及停车需求和停车场位置。最后，环境质量包括九个因素：共用性、自然环境的存在、与空地间的距离、街道立面的视觉效果、景观质量、环保质量、噪音和小气候。

上述城市设计的范围并未确认某些具体要素（如：广场、林荫道、休息场地、树木、路灯柱等），但这是对它们进行分类的合理方法，并对某些更具体的要素的研究和确定具有指导作用，而这些要素正是社区所独有的，或是致关重要的。由于每个社区都有不同的形体特点，因而社区之间、市区之间以及城市之间的具体要素的范围变化很大。

过去，多数规划者和设计者注重的是前两类要素——内部格局和意象以及外部形态和意象，这也许是因为这两类要素决定了城市设计的外型。然而，如果从功能和环境质量的角度去考虑这些要素，这些为人（无论是在街上行走的人还是呆在居室里的人）而创造的空间将会更加怡人。

例如，我们也许注意到一个设计很美的广场仅仅因为不见阳光或正当风口而空旷无人，而有些设计一般的广场却挤满了人。毫无疑问，这与某些因素有关（如地点、活动设施等），但是象风、噪音、阳光、景观和自然条件这类环境因素与成功的城市设计关系重大。

我们确定了城市设计的分析体制，即城市设计的范围之后，现在则想确定一下以政策、规划、指导方针和计划的形式表达这些信息的方法。对于城市设计要素的不同分析（或者根本不进行分析）在不同城市中产生了不同形式和不同范围的政策、规划、指导方针和计划。即使仔细观察不同城市的城市设计也无法使人肯定设计者是否使用了分析基准体系或者确定某个要素作为研究重点。也许是因为设计者对基准体系缺乏理解，从而导致了研究的重点集中在几个具体项目上。

但是，我们现在可以从上述城市设计的四组分析方法转到城市设计要素的第三种分类方法：
1. 土地的使用
2. 建筑形态及组合
3. 交通流线与停车场
4. 空地
5. 人行道
6. 活动设施
7. 标志
8. 保存

当然，我们所用的分类是相互联系的。用于特定市区或城市的城市设计战略必须根据所研究地区面临的问题和机会来组合或表现上述具体要素。

第6单元

购 物 中 心

购物中心是包含了若干商店和服务企业的一栋或一组建筑物，附近备有停车场，其地址常在郊区，但也可能在城区。

大型商场 购物中心很像汇集了许多小商店的大型商场。因此，它们与城市中长期拥有的商业区的购物商场很相似，不过购物中心的发展一直有竭力取代这些商场之意。购物中心与其在商业区的对应物在某些方面有所不同。首先，如果没有人们大量外出到市郊的活动，就不可能有购物中心。而且如果没有小汽车的大量激增就不可能有真正的都市郊区。因而从某种意义上讲，购物中心起源于小汽车的广泛使用，而且从来都是与小汽车相关的。实际上，早期的购物中心都有大型停车场，几乎挡住对面的商店。后来，购物中心的商店就转向里边，面向顾客走动的空间，背对汽车。在许多郊区，紧贴购物中心修建了办公楼和饭店，随着这些建筑物的出现和购物中心的扩展，形成了通常便于通往机场的新"边缘城市"。于是，购物中心就变成了新的适合步行的小型城市和就业中心。现今几乎所有的城市发展都出现在这些周边城市。随着人口的增长，购物中心就建在地铁站的交汇处和公路干线附近。

经销原则 由于购物中心基本上是些商店，所以如果想要成功，它们的设计就必须有利于商品的销售。购物中心应该像任何一家商店那样引起可能成为顾客的人们的兴趣，把他们吸引到中心里去。这样，顾客必然由于对出售的商品感兴趣而被吸引到中心里的一个个商店里。经销原则既适用于市区的商场，也适用于郊区的购物中心。但是作为一个规律，正像市区的商场常常吸引步行的人那样，后者必须吸引坐汽车来的潜在顾客。

一个购物中心包含着许多单个商店，其中任何一个商店都可出售从日常消费品（即必需品、家用设备等）到超前消费品（即奢侈品）。另外，整个购物中心的功能和一个百货商场一样，而中心里的商店的作用则和百货商场里的分部一样。因此，整个购物中心的经营是重要的，然而一旦进入中心，各个商店的经营也是重要的。顾客必须能够方便地在整个中心走动，必须被吸引进各个商店里，然后被里面的陈列所诱惑。

类　　型　购物中心主要分为两种类型，即社区购物中心和区域购物中心。社区购物中心常常只包含为数不多的商店，通常包括一个超级市场、一个药店，有时候还包括一个或者更多一些的营业分部。在城镇或郊区，它们服务的销售区域有限。而区域购物中心服务的销售区域就大了，有时可把许多英里之外的顾客拉过来。这些中心的关键是百货商场，一个购物中心可以有一至四个、或更多的百货商场。

一个区域购物中心可包括几乎各种各样的门市部，从小型专卖商店（如花店、糖果店、或面包房）到服务行业（如理发店、美容厅、或银行），直至完备的大型百货商场。在区域购物中心通常看不到有超级市场。此外，区域购物中心还可能有娱乐设施，如迪斯科舞厅、保龄球场等。许多中心设置有进餐设施，如餐馆、自助食堂或美食厅。有些中心有门诊所、牙医诊所等其它专业机构；还有图书分馆、邮局、加油站，以及几乎所有能够想象出的商业活动。

平面总图　购物中心的平面总图主要有两种形式：线型开发区和组群型开发区。在线型中，商店沿着人行道排列，汽车常常就停驻在街道、公路的对面。在组群型中，包括商店在内的各种要素围绕中央的行人区排列，车辆停在建筑群外围。组群型开发区通常叫做"商业街"，在门市部之间的中央地带有开放式空间或封闭式林荫道。现今大部分购物中心都是一层或两层营业，有些购物中心的营业空间则在两层以上。有时，已有的中心扩建楼层或增建新的商店。

设计带有林荫道的购物中心的重要原则之一就是林荫道本身的设计。它须搞成能吸引人的步行区，两旁是引人入胜的商店，它们的门面朝里，对着林荫道。许多林荫道边有宜人的休息场所，有灌木丛、花卉和树木、雕塑、喷水池，甚至精致的休闲娱乐设施。

购物中心设计的另一个重要方面是提供效率高的停车设施以及进入中心方便的通路。停车场可设置在外边的地面上、屋顶上、或车库里。对于购物中心来说，停车要求的空间相当大，从市区购物中心的每1000平方英尺的租赁商店面积提供约2.5辆的空间到郊区购物中心每1000平方英尺停放6辆以上的空间。

因为可能包括许多类型的商店和其他设施，还因为提供建筑物、提供汽车交通和停车、以及行人交通这一切的错综复杂性，购物中心已经变成了一种包罗万象的建筑类型。这类建筑考验着建筑师们的设计能力，他们必须用某种方法把这些难题一个个归拢在一块，以便使购物中心的整体功能和各个部分的功能一样合理。并非所有的商业中心都是成功的，这常常要归咎于难于进入中心，以及停车场有限。

第 7 单元

屋顶的设计

哪种屋顶设计与你的建筑物的特征存在着有机的联系呢?

我们知道一座完整的建筑物的大多数空间的墙壁大致都是直的(尽管不必笔直),因为只有那样,墙壁两侧的空间才是实在的,否则就会出现凸面。

我们知道一个建筑物里的大多数转角基本上都是直角(当然也不能那么确切),这就是说,一般的变化范围在 80°～100°。

我们知道,通常屋顶设计可能会包含多种形状,如半圆形、八边形等等。但就其主体部分而言,屋顶大体上是由不太规整的长方形组成的。

我们还知道,只要有可能,应把一座建筑物的所有侧翼都罩在同一屋顶下,建筑物的屋顶应建成平顶、坡顶或拱顶相混合的屋顶,重点是那些不平的屋顶。

决定屋顶设计的问题是,假如已给定任何一种上述设计方案,我们怎样才能使迭落式屋顶、遮蔽型屋顶以及屋顶花园协调一致的布局与该方案相吻合?

在详细说明屋顶的设计步骤之前,我们要强调可以提供设计步骤基础的五种设想。

1. "坡式"屋顶既可以是倾斜的,也可是斜曲线拱顶式的,或者是筒拱。在这三种情况下,通常的设计步骤是相同的(就曲线拱顶而言,坡度定义为高度与宽度之比)。

2. 假设建筑物的所有屋顶都不是平顶,且坡度大致相同。就一定的气候和屋顶的结构而言,通常保持同一个坡度为最佳,这可以大大简化施工。

3. 由于所有屋顶的坡度相同,所以覆盖的跨度或房间宽度最大的屋顶将为最高峰;而宽度较小的跨度或房间的屋顶则比较低。这和主建筑物、迭落式屋顶以及天花板高度变化都是一致的。

4. 凡是建筑物的形状有利于围合成一个室外空间或院落的地方,都需要有一个平直的屋檐线,以便形成"房间"似的空间。而不规则的屋檐线,再加上山墙端部,通常会破坏小院落的空间。因而,处在这种位置上的屋顶必须起脊,使屋檐线保持水平方向。

5. 在所有其他位置上,则可把建筑物和翼侧的端部作为山墙端部。

现在我们以一个外行所设计的房屋为例来讨论设计建筑物屋顶的一些规则。该建筑物的平面图如下所示。它是一所单层房,不带屋顶花园和阳台。

我们首先确认出由一组房间组成的最大的长方形,给其盖上一个最高的屋顶,屋脊线沿长方向延伸。

接着,我们以同样的方式确定出几组较小的房间,也盖上屋顶,直到所有主要空间都盖上屋顶为止。随后我们给剩余的小房间、耳房和厚墙盖上向外倾斜的单坡屋顶。这些单坡屋顶应当从主屋顶的基部伸出,使其免受侧推力的影响,外墙应尽可能低些。

最后,我们来确定一下室外空间,在其周围的屋顶上设置斜屋脊,以使在这些空间周围保留一个比较连续的屋檐线。

我们现在讨论稍微复杂的例子——一栋两层建筑物。

我们首先从顶层开始。在整个主卧室和浴室上加上最高屋顶,其屋脊沿纵向延伸。

现在我们再来看底层。给儿童用的侧翼盖上平屋顶，以便给主卧室营造一个屋顶花园。较大的起居室则要安排坡屋顶，屋檐也是纵向延伸。

然后我们再将主卧室上的屋顶下延到阁楼上。

最后，我们将起居室的屋脊线平缓地过渡到阁楼屋顶的侧部。至此就算完成了屋顶的设计了。

当你设计屋顶时，记住在"屋顶的迭落"一文中所概述的结构原理是非常有用的。当你做完这一切时，屋顶总的布局应成自撑式迭落形，在这种布局中每个低一层的屋顶都可消除上层屋顶产生的横向推力。于是整个屋顶截面就大致呈现出倒悬曲线的趋势。

因此，我们可以把设计屋顶的步骤归结为四点：

1. 屋顶的布局应使每个不同的屋顶与建筑物或群体建筑里的相应社会群体相符合。
2. 把那些高度最高、跨度最大的大屋顶建在最大、最重要、最具有公用性质的空间上。
3. 较小屋顶要与最高、最大的屋顶分开建造。
4. 所有最小的屋顶则要与上述较小的屋顶分开，以半拱或单坡的形式建在耳房和厚墙上。

第 8 单元

建 筑 照 明

人们看周围的事物时需要光，但有时候，更多的真实却是在黑暗中发现。

因为照明把建筑物的形态展示给人们，因而，它对建筑物可直接产生影响。它让你感受到建筑物的规模、高度、体积、质地、色彩以及装饰。一句话，照明是建筑物与外界交流的一种物理介质。至于交流些什么则是另一回事，人们已经对这个问题有了一定深度的论述。我们现在关心的是照明的过程。

照度 光太强时，你会迷起眼睛伸手去拿太阳镜；光太弱时，你因用眼过度而感到头痛。显然任何情况下适当的照度自然地要根据照明需要而变化。如果你在超级市场寻找某种牌子的鱼酱，你的确需要很强的照明以便看清商品上的标签。但是，如果你安排一次浪漫的晚餐，而且有可能在饭后向对方求婚时，则极可能需要由柔和的烛光所产生的某种有说服力的朦胧气氛。在剧院里你需要两种光的结合：观众席上只需足以找到座位的照明即可，而舞台上则需要强度照明以便看清表演（除了在"心情"场景中，导演只想让观众看到一点精心设置的微小动作以外）。

照度以英尺烛光为衡量单位，一英尺烛光即一支蜡烛向四周一英尺范围内的平面上所发光的强度。更通俗些说，经常计量的是光源而非光量，因此，所用电量具体为瓦，比如：肉食柜台上 600W、菜食柜台上 200W、化妆品柜台上 40W。

照明的分布 分布于整个房间、大厅、画廊、候机室或别的什么地方的亮度叫作总体照明。总体照明需要足够的亮度，使你到处行动都感到舒适：在饭馆里找餐桌，在商店里找柜台，在终点站找售票亭等等。对于诸如看菜单、填存款单、涂睫毛油这类特殊的照明，则需要集中于某一处的较强的亮度，这种照明叫作局部照明。

对于光来说完全和声音一样，反射面起着重要作用。白色、平滑、光泽的天花板将大大增加总体照明的效果。而色调较暗或者纹理粗糙（投下许多细微的阴影）的反射面能使局部照明不至于扩散过远，即使其直接照度很强。

眩光　眩光笼统地指亮度过分明亮，如照在雪地上的阳光，或类似的光。另外，眼睛视网膜里有两种感光的神经末梢。一种用来对付强烈的光和颜色，另一种用于对付暗光。当其中一组工作时，另一组关闭，不起作用。这就是为什么当你从阳光灿烂的室外走进影剧院，暂时不能看见走道、座位或其他人的原因。因为负责"强光"的一组神经感到亮度不够而负责"暗光"的一组神经还需要一会时间才能开始工作。同样地，当你走出剧院（假设仍是白昼），则街道好像过于明亮，照得你睁不开眼睛。

这里，值得重申的重要一点是，在一个时间里，只有一组感光器官工作。当你试图让两组光感器官同时工作时，你会有一种剧烈的不舒服感，这种感觉就叫作刺眼。黑暗房间里一盏没有罩子的灯泡刺眼。黑盒子里一根蜡烛刺眼。夜晚开车，迎面开来的车的前灯刺眼。总而言之，任何一种明、暗反差大得足以同时刺激视网膜两组感受器官时，所感受的都是眩光。

照明气氛　我们又一次发现与声学雷同。有些环境似乎特别需要适当的照明，如果没有，会让人很难受。你能否想象一下某个教堂里闪烁着拍电影的聚光灯的情景，或者某个博物馆里顶灯照在观众头上而不是照在展出的书画上的情景。如果你来自加利福尼亚，或去过那里，你可能见到那儿的花园里，每丛灌木本身都有着彩灯：兰色的、琥珀色的、黄色的，而鲜绿色的灯则高挂在树枝上。

此外，真正招徕生意的窍门往往显示在建筑照明设计上，尤其表现在夜晚建筑物外部泛光照明的应用上。外墙泛光灯的应用方兴未艾，它明显地改变了城市景观。同时，建筑师越来越认识到：建筑物的造型，特别是墙壁大面积使用玻璃的建筑物，在很大程度上取决于内部的照明。例如，冬季黄昏时刻，当办公楼灯火辉煌时，曼哈顿中心区看上去简直是一片闪烁着珠光宝气的仙境。在建筑照明上不能采用多种手法的建筑师严重地限制了其作品可能产生的效果，而那些能灵敏地采用多种手法的建筑师则懂得给自己的创作增添不可估量的情趣。

第9单元

住宅群的演变

住宅群环境是人类住宅区的最基本、最持久的形式。简单地描述，它是连成一起的住房，各单元可共用隔墙、地板以及天花板。更重要的是，它们还可分享室外公用空间以及公共设施。从历史上来看，住宅群的外观和规模只受到材料来源和当时社会建造技巧的制约。

传统上，村舍的规模和结构不仅表现了自然环境，而且也反映了社会环境。一种文化其居住形式经过几千年后，已经优化了，而住宅群的布局也变得高度结构化。这当然并不意味着房屋形式变得刻板，而是每种文化都根据自己的价值观形成秩序。

规划新的住宅群环境需要对它们的历史持有透视的观点。经过研究住宅群环境长期的演变，显示出它们在很多稳定的文化中都得到了蓬勃发展。因此，通过研究这些文化背景下的住宅环境，我们非常容易理解住宅群的规划原则。

住宅群基本上是一种城市住宅形式，它能适应很多不同的社区规模。通过引用最优秀的传统，就可能在通常的郊区和市区住房环境之间起到很有启发的协调作用。

在原始文化中，村庄的范围常常是由单个住户组织成可以围合成能防御的社区空间来确定。每个住房单元的主要入口都面对着社区的公共空间。在一些文化中，各单元连在一起，实际上形成所需要的围合空间，在另外一些文化中，它们却排成一条线（并未全部连结起来）来划定社区空间，但未必真正围合。由于局限于可利用的资源和技术水平，这些单元只有一两层。

渐渐地，随着人口的增长，村庄变成了城镇。尽管村庄的很多特点都保留下来，但是房屋与主要公共场所却更疏远了。入口不再面对作为城镇中心的主要公共空间，而是面对着通向城镇中心的道路或街道这样的社区次要空间。房屋不再是构成村庄的围墙，而是房门开向庭院，或除了一面之外周围与邻居毗邻。另外，改进了的技术可以使多层住宅修建到四、五层高。

由于遍及世界的城市化导致了人口的更大规模的集中，城市的独户式住宅群达到了尽善尽美的程度。在欧洲中世纪的城市中，由于特别狭窄的临街面和四、五层的高度使住宅群变得更加紧凑。这种基本模式是当代欧洲城市住房的起源。

随着城市开始规划，非正规的发展模式让位于更正规的、更大规模的城市整体结构的规划。在不再考虑地形的情况下城市街道按规则的几何形布局，其中以直线方格最为常见。这样形成的城市"街区"就成为标准。而曾经是随意发展变化的原动力的那种住宅群形式则被削弱并屈服于街区这一标准。

随着工业革命的开始以及农村人口大量涌入城市，这种正规的建筑群与改进后的技术在开发更高的居民住宅中结合起来，很多由套房组成的无电梯公寓高度达六到八层。随着这一趋势的发展，住宅群环境的基本价值观便被搁置一边，城市生活方式的很多优点都被经济公寓的生活冲淡了。当代公寓环境（带电梯的公寓）是工业革命的继子。

住宅向高层发展总是与市中心附近土地的大量需求及某一特定文化的土地管理业务相关联。尽管有非常明显的证据表明高层住宅会产生并遇到大量的社会问题，但这种住宅却在继续建造。对其作出改进的努力似乎更激化了这一问题。那么也许这种问题的基本假设就是高层住宅是一种很具有人情味的环境。有趣的是，一些古代文明建造了许多规模大的居住环境，它们比起同时代的其他住宅环境更富于人情味。或许由于我们的祖先想象不出高大的垂直结构的技术手段，于是，便不去理会与高层住宅相关的社会问题。

由于文化传统、气候、地形、材料和技术等诸多原因，一些文明建造了天井式住宅群和台地式住宅群组合建筑作为其基本住宅形式，而且大多数文明社会仍继续建造着这种形式。在全世界干热地区，天井式住宅群仍然是基本的形式。至于台地式住宅形式在世界各地的山坡地区自然得到发展。由于很多早期的文明为了防卫而选择在难以接近的地方建筑房屋，因而至今仍留有许多这样的古建筑。建在坡地上的台地建筑在世界各地山区仍占主导地位，但它的许多优点正在使它成为世界上其它地区具有吸引力的住宅的可选形式。

第10单元

高层建筑展望

　　70年代高层建筑的发展预示着80年代和90年代的新发展。区域规划对高层建筑物的密度和对自然采光设计可能引起道德问题将产生影响。能源方面的局限性将继续成为建筑设计面临的独特的挑战。新老建筑的结合将会给我们的城市带回人情味。要设计建造出经济实用，以人为中心的建筑物，是业主和概念设计师在80年代将会面临挑战。

　　1980年由斯柯摩尔，奥英斯和米瑞尔（SOM）设计的莱弗公寓获得了美国建筑师协会授予的25年奖"以确认具有深远意义的优秀建筑设计"。这项奖每年授予一座房龄在25～35年之间的建筑物。用刘易斯·芒福德的话来说，莱弗公寓是"第一座集现代材料，现代施工，现代功能与现代设计方案为一体的办公楼"。在当时，这样大胆的构思只有像设计师戈登·邦沙福特和业主、莱弗兄弟公司当时的总裁查尔斯·卢克曼那样富于幻想的人才能创造出来。而且，这项工程包含了几个"第一"：（1）是第一座全封闭的玻璃大厦，（2）是SOM三人合作设计的第一栋办公楼，（3）是公园大街第一座一层楼不设零售商场的办公楼。今天，经过众多外观相似而柱网变化的设计，我们已难以对建筑物进行归类，这也许是高层建筑设计的缩影。除了最近竣工的几栋楼房的低层似乎比较怡人外，在我们的许多城市中，多数高层建筑物看上去就象图表上标注的柱标，好似一块块单调而又拙笨的巨石。难道这就是高层建筑设计行业的终点吗？也许不是。有迹象表明其发展是非常令人鼓舞的。建筑师和业主最近已开始公开讨论设计问题。也许我们正处在一个新时代的开端，八十年代也许会产生一些象邦沙福特和卢克曼那样的幻想家。要是如此，他们会面临什么样的限制或挑战呢？

　　区域规划　很显然，城市可以限制高层建筑的密度，也就是减少每平方英里高层建筑的数量。1980年"堵塞网"这个术语第一次在纽约市公开使用。它的出现在公众心中引起恐慌。这个词指的是城市中四面八方的街区同时出现的交通停滞不动的现象，堵塞甚至一直延伸到隧道里和高架桥上。奇怪的是，这种事情竟然发生在纽约燃料短缺、油价高涨的年份。很显然，要想避免类似情况的出现，就必须大幅度地降低人口、活动场所以及车辆的密度，区域规划也许是唯一长久的解决方法。

　　城市居民由于受到高层建筑的遮挡而见不到阳光，因此，阳光规划将越来越受欢迎。无论高层建筑设计得如何节能，它同时有可能剥夺居住者或邻居享受阳光的权力。80年代，享受阳光的权力会成为一个十分有趣的道德问题，这个问题会彻底改变城市的建筑布局。混合用途的分区规划在70年代还只是一种经济上可行的抉择，在80年代将会得到普及，特别是将混合功能分区规划与阳光分区规划相结合，让所有的住户都享受到阳光。

整修改造 伊莫利·罗斯和桑斯两人合作设计的纽约王宫酒店是对麦迪逊大街上翻修后的古建筑维拉德公寓的补充和增色。这是一个如何对待可抢救的古建筑精品的突出实例。对大小建筑物的重复利用将成为在80年代使人情味和温馨回到建筑物的途径。无论出于什么原因，如果我们必须继续使用玻璃和铝材进行那种呆板的方格式设计的话，我们会发现新老建筑的结合将成为未来富有人情味设计的大趋势。

概念设计 有些建筑杂志认为位于旧金山的美洲银行办公大楼对于该城市来说规模过大，位于波士顿的约翰·汉考克中心不仅与该城市的规模不成比例，而且与其特点不符。对于世界各地主要高层建筑物的类似评论还有不少。这类评论提出了有关设计程序、谁是重点项目设计的决策者、以及八十年代的建筑设计应由谁来决策等基本问题。

未来的幻想家，即建筑师和业主会回到更富人情味的设计吗？在今后的几年里社会学家和心理学家会发挥他们的重要作用使这些幻想家相信一种截然不同的、合乎人体尺度的新型建筑设计早该付诸实施吗？如果这些问题的提出有其合理性的话，那么六七十年代被我们视为"最杰出的"建筑设计师到了八九十年代就变成最差的吗？他们在大学"建筑史"这门课程中应该了解到"建筑常常反映了文明社会的成功与失败，"他们会学到这有益的一课并对此作出反应吗？只有时间才会做出回答。

第11单元

高 层 建 筑

自人类文明一开始，人类对高塔高楼就很着迷，这些高楼的建造本是为了防卫，但最终被用于宗教目的。现代高层建筑始于19世纪80年代，其发展主要是为了满足商业和居住的需要。

高层商业建筑首先是为了适应商业活动必需尽可能集中、靠近市中心的需要，因而对现有土地造成极大的压力的情况。其次，由于其醒目的标志性，高层商业建筑物常常作为公司声誉的象征被矗立在市中心。此外，商务和旅游团体由于其日益增长的流动性，加剧了需要更多的位于市中心的旅馆饭店。

城市人口的迅速增长和随之而来对有限空间造成的压力在很大程度上影响了城市住宅的发展。高额的土地费用、避免市区无限向外扩张的愿望以及保护重要的农业生产的需要，所有这些因素都促使住宅建筑向高层发展。在有些城市，比如香港和里约热内卢，由于地形的限制，高层建筑成为满足住宅需求的唯一可行的解决办法。

高层建筑主要是为了满足居住、商用或者在某些情况下商住两用的需要而设计的。因此，主要的设计要求是为建筑物提供合适的室内布局。同时，满足客户对建筑物外部的审美要求也是建筑师的基本职责。因此，主要的设计标准是建筑标准，工程师就是在这些标准范围内安排结构的。只有在特殊的高层建筑物中，结构需要才会成为主要的考虑因素。

基本布局将包括在结构网内，结构网对建筑物功能要求的妨碍应尽量小。同时，建筑结构必须与各项服务系统相结合，如供热、通风、空调、供水、垃圾处理、供电及垂直运输。这类设施面广而复杂，构成了高层建筑造价的主要部分。

功能设计一旦确定，工程师必须设计出结构系统，尽可能高效、经济地满足已确定的设计标准，同时还需与建筑设计相适应。关键的结构标准是预留足够的抗破坏强度，足够的横向刚度和建筑物在使用寿命内满足功能要求。

高层建筑结构的根本性变化出现在第二次世界大战后的建设时期。在这段时期内，设计原理也发生了重大变化，规范形式已从原来的工作应力或极限强度为判据发展到现代更易被广泛接受的基于概率的方法。这种用于结构性能和负荷状态的概率法导致了如今被广泛采用的极限状态设计理论。这种方法的目的是要确保把所有的结构及其构件设计成能可靠地经受住施工和使用中可能出现的最不利荷载和变形，能在其使用寿命内有足够的耐久性。

当整个结构或部分结构达到了各种极限状态之一，不再能满足规定的极限设计条件时，就会被视为已遭破坏。以下两种基本类型的极限状态必须予以考虑（1）与会造成破坏的负荷相关的最终极限状态，包括丧失稳定性。因为与倒塌相关的事件将是灾难性的，会危及人的生命，造成重大经济损失。因此破坏的概率必须降到很低；（2）正常使用极限状态，它们涉及到决定建筑物使用寿命的标准。由于正常使用极限状态的破坏不会导致灾难性的后果，这种极限状态的出现可以允许到较高概率。正常使用极限状态注重的是建筑物是否适合通常的使用要求而不是其安全性，因而处于次要地位。

任意作用的不利组合就会达到某一特定极限状态。单独的安全系数被用于不同的状态，这些状况反映了结构和负载存在的特定情况的概率。设计计算的固有的目的是要确保把任何一种极限状态的发生概率控制在该结构所能允许的数值之下。

第12单元

停 车 场

目前和将来停车场的工程设计，必须考虑与开发高层建筑的多样化设计相结合。从最初构思到最终定案，工程的每一个阶段都应相互紧密配合。

任何一个建筑物，准备留出一块空地作为停车场时，其设计须体现一些规则。前提是在这种特定情况下，停车场是必要的，建造它也是经济可行的。

停车场可能是高层办公楼、住宅楼或者综合性商业楼的一部分，也可能是一个独立的部分。因此，每个停车场都须具备若干条件和一个独特的环境，都需要经过方方面面的分析来确定它是否适应眼前的需要，及其机动性是否足以适应将来的变化。

例如，办公楼上班的时间，通常是星期一至星期五的上午九点到下午五点。停车场需要多大的空间应根据办公楼的利用情况来确定。也就是说，如果办公楼用户多元化，那就意味着肯定有很多管理人员要驱车上班；相反，若办公楼用户单一化，则会有大量的职员，如果方便，他们通常采用公共交通工具，甚至在可能时，加入车辆合用组织。此外，办公楼用户通常停车一整天，几乎不开出开进。然而那些附设商店、餐馆和剧院（无论在大楼内还是临近周围）则要求短时停车，同时附有倒车空间。

另一方面，高层住宅楼停车场的规格取决于住户的年龄及人员成份。停车场设施或者是要适应不断进进出出的活动，不断给临时停车者提供停车空间，或者主要为很少进出活动的退休住户使用，而对暂时停车者预留很少可利用的停车空间。

购物中心通常使用停车场的时间短，普通顾客一次停车两个半小时，空间周转率应该很大。但是，根据停车场距交通要道的远近，假如停车场对来往过客停车很方便，其周转率可能非常低。遇到这种情况，就要建立防护设施以限制滥用停车场；通过使停车场的开放时间与顾客购物时间相吻合（上午10点钟以前不开放），或者建立一种对顾客有利而对来往过客不具吸引力的收费规则来达到阻止其它车辆停放的目的。

独立的停车场完全取决于顾客情况。因此，必须能够事先了解邻近四周的停车需求（所需位置的数量）、停车时间的长短、车辆进出流量的高峰、运作方法及其所需要的时间等。在停车场设计中对一些实际问题的考虑同样也是十分重要的。下面我们分几部分来叙述：

标志 停车场是否对公众开放，并被识别为公共停车场？还是仅限维系该楼营运的住户使用？场内标志是否清楚简明？简单地说，司机能否找到停车位置，然后再从那里出来回到停车场的出口而不致糊涂或迷路？

柱列 柱子的排列是否为现今的车辆提供畅通的场地？车辆能否尽量少转弯地通过停车场？是否有足够的间隙以允许相向行车？如果需要单向车道（在周转率高的停车场必然是那样），柱子的排列是否得当从而死角不多？

此外，我们目前正处在车辆规模变化的过渡时期。据估计，到1985年，路面上的车辆至少70%将成为小型汽车或小汽车类。必须考虑重新设计停车场，使之能接纳更小型化的汽车和数量可能增加的小汽车。

混凝土 混凝土的抗压强度不得低于4000磅/平方英寸。应该使用加气混凝土。覆盖在钢筋上面的混凝土厚度不得少于1.5英寸。如果可能的话，用于停车场楼面以及车道的钢筋应当是加上涂层的轧钢，以减少生锈的可能性和楼板损坏。

排水设备 应保障设有通往最近处下水道的可靠的场内排水系统。此外，气候条件也强加一些特殊要求。比如，多雪地带，大量冰雪会带进停车场，这些冰雪不可避免地融化并溶解了一些化学物质以及盐份，将会积存在停车场的地面上，这时，通往下水道的雪水流速越快，雪水渗入混凝土地面而产生破坏作用的时间也就越短。

照明 良好的照明是安全使用停车场的基本需要。尤其是车道、进出口地段，这些地方的照明应和场外亮度相当，使眼睛的适应时间缩短到最小程度。

场内布局 为残疾司机留出位置很重要。这种位置的数量，联邦政府制定了原则，它们必须包括在停车场工程中，尤其必须包括在接受联邦政府资助的停车场项目中。这种位置应留在什么地方？是否有障碍物阻止残疾司机的活动自由？残疾人停车区应设置在最安全的地段，如有可能，应离开各种车辆来往的车道。

第13单元

装　饰

　　我们通常认为装饰物是用来加在物体外表的东西，在某种意义上甚至可以拆除。然而，实际上从远古时代以来，无论是一把长矛，一件织物，或一座建筑物，装饰就已经成为人们所设计的物体的要素和基本内容的一部分。例如，一支带有羽毛的箭，不仅用来使它直线飞行，而且是取悦于猎神，这个神狂热地迷恋于羽毛；而箭杆上被涂上颜色或刻上一些格言，如"锐眼克敌"。织物上经常带有图案和花纹，意思是"幸福的妈妈"之类的东西。至于建筑物，从最一般的到最高级的差不多均带有标志、图案或雕刻。在人们的心目中，整个建筑结构的真实性就有赖于这些标志、图案和雕刻。

　　从前带有仪式含义的建筑符号经常超越时代地保留下来。这些建筑符号成为建筑结构中的永久部分，尽管原有的含义已经在变化中的社会词汇中消失了。例如，在一些节日里，扎绑在古庙宇的柱子上的叶子，最终永久性地刻成叶板并被用在一些与那些节日毫无关系的建筑物上。出现在埃及柱子上的麦捆很快被雕刻并涂上了金色，然后被用在与任何收获丝毫无关的建筑物了。

　　但是，甚至在这些装饰原先的仪式性或宗教性含义被人们遗忘了很久之后，它们仍然在建筑结构上堂而皇之地发挥着功能，作为一种表现方式表现着该结构的特征或质量。它可表达富有、重要性、雅致或仅仅是对拥有者品味的一种称赞。无论如何，这就是关健所在——装饰继续是建筑整体的一部分，而不是放在表面上的什么"十分漂亮"的东西。

　　当然，这是一种有些理想主义的说法。不幸的是，事实上许多本应该更清楚了解这一点的人，包括一些建筑师，持这样一种态度：即认为装饰不属于建筑整体，而是一种确实多余的东西，仅可能起炫耀的作用。也许，某些态度是由于现代建筑多年来处于僵化的功能主义阶段的缘故。在这个阶段，所有的装饰开始被认为是感情用事，是传统主义的，或者更糟——是反动的。另一方面，二十世纪后半叶出现某些事物的周期性交替，我们又允许自己象我们的父母及祖辈一样，运用豪华的图案、色彩和雕刻。主要区别在于由于过去的手工工艺大部分已被机器加工所代替，装饰具备了不同的品质，即一种批量生产的感觉，这种感觉由于使用通常是合成的材料而强化了，而不是削弱了。

　　鉴于这些因素，显然，一个好的建筑师应该不仅了解装饰风格的作用，而且更重要的是要了解装饰所涉及的社会根源和社会作用。装饰是语言，是建筑语言的一部分；如果它不是漂亮的空谈，那么它必须是有含义的。对那些了解建筑的人来说，掌握装饰的一些寓意是必要的。

　　倾向性　　如果大家一致认为装饰与建筑形态是整体的，不是分离的，那么形态和装饰两者结合在一起，就可给观众造成对建筑的初步印象，告诉他这是一个什么样的地方，和他是什么关系。例如，他看见一个设有柱廊的正门，顶上加盖了一个带雕塑的山花，台阶两侧各有一尊石狮，他很快就判断出这是一所社会事业机构的建筑物——博物馆、法院、市政厅等——是一个守旧的传统的机构。

　　注意装饰的特点、风格和雕塑的主题等，所有这些必须与建筑物的基调保持协调，否则，整个建筑物就会像一副讽刺画。

相比之下，如果他看到一座现代建筑，尽管从特点上看仍是社会事业性建筑，在这座建筑中，所有的装饰物都是跟上时代的，而且有现代化的雕塑。那么他会把这座建筑认作是一所进步的大学、艺术中心，或联合国一个办事处，或者现代的某种机构。请再注意，和建筑形象一样，装饰也同样表现主题。

为了形成鲜明的对照，我们不妨想象一下好莱坞日落街上的一家迪斯科舞厅。它故意采用稀奇古怪的形式，装饰则采用那种社会上认可的、变幻莫测的飞跃式流行式样。厅内采用具有暗示性的多种媒体——电子音乐、电影、彩光灯等混合在一起。问题是，虽然冒着累赘多余的风险，但由于装饰物是建筑说明中的一部分内容，因而它与整体结构不可分开，必须前后一致地构思。

导向性 对没有装饰的素面，你的目光会一扫而过；而在那些能看到趣味（壁画，雕塑等）的地方，你则会逗留下来（至少停顿一下）。你的眼光落在何处，你的脚就会移到那里；如果你的脚不能走到那个地方，比方说天花板上的绘画，你的注意力就会投向那里。于是，建筑师可以用装饰去引导你的目光、注意力以及使用该建筑物的人们潜在的活动。例如，室外装饰可告诉你入口在何处，从而使你摆脱不太舒服的犹豫；否则你就不得不体验这种犹豫，尤其是你第一次来。

第14单元

城市低层住房开发方案的选择

一群芝加哥的建筑师、规划师以及其它方面的专业人员开始调查研究他们认为是对城市高层住房模式的一种可行的替换方案。这群人被称之谓 Urbs in Horto，其名称取意于芝加哥的箴言"花园里的城市"，它反映了城市中一部分有影响的人们的愿望，这部分人关心他们想生活在其间的环境。Urbs in Horto 为了对彼特·兰德在 1981 年 3 月提出的课题作出回答而走到一起。彼特·兰德是一位建筑师兼教育工作者，他提出规划、修建一种不同的城市居住场所，以表明新的主张并指出未来的住宅方式。芝加哥是令人印象深刻的世界上高层建筑集中的试验场和橱窗，其中许多高层建筑物在世界各地被视作建筑典范。

Urbs in Horto 选择芝加哥集中试验这种新主张的可行性：即通过具有高层建筑住户高密度的优点的低层建筑来更新住宅区。如果在芝加哥试验成功，这个规划原理就可以在全世界其它城市地区采用。

在过去的 20 年当中，尽管芝加哥的人口减少了 60 多万，但它仍然住房短缺，尤其短缺适合中等收入的家庭住房。现有住房中相当一部分或者需要大幅度的改造，或者需要彻底的更换。市区当前所需住房的不足导致了人们向郊区继续迁移和市区状况的进一步恶化。提供人们买得起的住房可选方案是一个难题，市区住宅区的重建取决于对这个难题作出反应。经济压力从不像现在这样，成为（房改的）非常强劲的动力。

由于心里有这种急切感，Urbs in Horto 开始研究寻求解决这个住房问题的可能的途径。高层技术的飞速发展使得现代高层楼房成为人们买得起而又切实可行的解决办法，不过大众追求的是多种多样的住房选择。当前几乎没有什么可行的市区住房替代方案，对其它类型高密度住房的类似研究又受到时代的限制。然而近期的研究表明有些住房形式有希望达到许多高层楼房所提供的住户密度（图14-1）。它们是 Urbs in Horto 目前致力于研究的城市住房选择方案的建筑形式。

这群专业人员的首项目标是提高对低层、高密度住房的认识——使它达到和高层住宅的艺术和技术一样的现代化程度。这就要求许多学科的专业人员进行合作，如建筑学、工程学、城规、金融、施工技术、法律、社会学、心理学以及其它相关学科。Urbs in Horto 开始调查这个解决住房问题的方法，但还有大量工作有待完成。

这群人员的为实现低层、高密度住房设计方案而奋斗的目标是多方面的，当然也包括为不太适合高层建筑的生活方式提供便利设施。设计方案如何才能更充分促进这个目标，并且面对明显的约束如何才能便于个人的表达，有必要对此进行检查。

为了适应市区住宅小区的要求，低层住房必须确实经济实效。这群人的工作最初的迹象表明，建筑结构需要的是组合在一起的二层、三层和四层的无电梯单元，适应芝加哥的网格布局（图14-2）。地板规划可能会简单些，生活空间具有灵活机动性，卧室、洗澡间等设施则比较紧凑、实用。空间分配反映了用途，即使用者的生活方式。住宅单元的组合能以节能的形式产生经济效益——这是当今尤为迫切的要求。通过规划和设计，住宅单元可利用太阳和风提供的好处，即自然照明、太阳能采暖以及过堂通风。如果要实现实质性的经济效益，还需要研究建材以及预制技术。为满足不断变化的需要，住宅单元的适应性在低层、高密度建筑物的长期经济效益中将证明是重要的因素。上面提到的住房的各个方面在许多需要研究的地区都具有代表性。

这群人的第二个主要目标是研究把这种类型的住房结合到芝加哥现有住宅小区模式的方法。从这个地区过去几十年不成功的角度来看，这是一个特别重要的目的。建造富有创新精神的、中等收入家庭住房的目标，必须和使整个住宅小区新生的目标相结合。

试图在这个阶段去鉴定芝加哥某些特定的住宅区中上述建议的住房样式能否成功地实施并经受检验还为时过早。然而，被调查的住宅区应当满足几个基本条件。它们应当是些有生命力的社区，需要新的住房，备有必不可少的基础结构和适当的服务设施，包括诸如公共交通、学校、医院、娱乐设施等。缺少这些要素的一部分或大部分的住宅区，不管住房本身有什么优点，整个项目都不会是个成功的项目。

Urbs in Horto 的第三个目标是超脱纯理论研究而去建造实用住宅区。一个实用住宅区，作为富有生命力的住房选择方案会以完整的形式表现出高密度、无电梯居住特点。剩下的问题就是为什么这种规划原理须以住宅小区的规模来研究。这种新的城市居住场所的规模必须允许它相对其它选择方案是一种具有竞争性的住房形式。这群专业人员相信，在芝加哥住宅区场址的合适面积应该是12至15个街区，但是经过进一步的调查研究，场址的面积还可发生变化。

第 15 单元

医院建筑——打破常规

医院是社会上最重要的民用建筑之一。它常常是人们出生和死亡的地方，也是一生中常常拜访的地方。因此，医院建筑既要考虑包含期待或不幸的情感因素，又要考虑治疗和技术功能的需要。不幸的是，医学功能的需要在建筑设计过程中往往压倒了一切，更为常见的是，当病人的身体接受治疗时，病人的精神方面完全被疏忽。我们在工作中试图摆脱医院建筑方案中所看到的不人道行为，以挖掘空间和设计中的最大潜力，努力帮助病人的身心尽快康复。

医院里的建筑物可以说是不断变幻的情节和动作的永久性舞台背景。医院就象剧场，是人生快乐乃至恐怖等经历的场所；它又象博物馆，应当提供尽可能宽阔的背景以供展示。医院的建筑形式和建筑材料必须考虑科学技术不断高速发展，每次发展都会引起形式和功能上的连续变化。一座医院的应变能力，尤其当新的保健设施和治疗方式确立时，必须从它的最小部门延伸到整体范围，并照顾到各部门之间的关系。同时，作为医疗和公众健康的永久性优秀场所的状况决不能动摇。

我们在工程项目中认识到，医院的概念要比医院建筑本身长远的多。这一认识使我们采用了如下建筑对策：非封闭式过道、走廊和大跨度建筑结构以及对开发地点的具体选择。另外，我们不断地重新估计当前保健政策以及医疗的正常的、计划内的需要。通过对文化、科学、政治模式的分析，能够更好地全面了解医院的真正功能。知道了各医疗部门内部和部门之间的复杂关系，会帮助我们以功能和形式上的有效方式利用空间，使医院建筑（即使是那些要求最苛刻的项目）不仅仅是"医疗技术的外包装"。

医院内建筑物的分布与联系上的清晰性和具体建筑物的灵活性同样重要。人们走进医院时，往往处于高度焦虑状态。施于病人的干预性治疗（尽管这种治疗是必要的、有益的）往往会加重病人的牺牲感或迷惑感。因此，任何时候把将要进行治疗的先后次序弄清楚是至关重要的。这种弄清楚要从医院内部结构的布局上入手。常常作为医院一部分的健康管理部门应按不同的体系设置在公众易于涉足的空间和入口处，这很重要。此外，医疗建筑的布局必须考虑医务人员的分配，稀有贵重医疗器械的分布以及病人的流动性。医院内部组织结构及其沟通要从建筑物的内部和外部同样清楚地表现出来。为此，我们在工作中使用了城市建筑设计原理，如：宽阔的林荫大道、长廊、庭院，目的是在医院内部和外部都建立起通行系统。把公用空间、私用空间按明显的轴线安置在这些通道和交叉点的两侧，为人们在常常是复杂建筑物里如何活动提供可见线索。最终我们期望，当医疗组织结构达到简化，建筑物提供易于辩别的循环通道和功能时，医院建筑就能有助于治疗过程的非神秘化。

医院里的通道以及大型空间的一些重要活动场地，往往通过使用自然光线使其处于显著位置。散落于各部门间的中庭、外廊、高侧窗、天窗、百叶窗把自然光线透入各部门的具体环境中，给它们提供一点轻松氛围。病房内，更要充分发挥变换的自然光线以及病人控制这种光线的能力。这种控制光线的能力，对于尤其是身体可能有残疾的病人来说，是维护其住院期间尊严的重要因素。

　　除了提供明显的功能性以及灵活性以外,医院应该使人强烈地感到有人关怀和服务。一个病人,就好像一座一流宾馆的客人一样,需要感到随时有医务人员关照其身体和心理上的需要。设计中应考虑增强病人与医务人员的交流,能看见医务人员并和他们交谈。在建筑物的内部广泛使用玻璃镶嵌、公用图书馆、起居室、日光浴室和其他公用、半公用场所,使病人有地方聚集、交流。另外,内部广泛使用玻璃,能使医生、护士随时察看病人及其家属的情况,避免任何隔离感。与此同时,在医院复杂的格局中,病房应被看作属于个人的安全圣地,在这里,病人自己是他(或她)生活的主宰者。在我们的设计中,装饰物被限制在最小程度。让光线的明暗、水声、花园里的芳香提供一种美的愉悦感。大量使用内外庭院、花卉、水池以及透入多种颜色的丰富的自然光线使人感到安宁。让颜色和质感构成有机的联系,供其在一个更大的系统中编织出欣欣向荣并溶为一体的旋律。这种对自然材料的充分强调,似乎补充了我们为治愈过程创造一个简朴、高雅的空间所作的努力。

第 16 单元

建筑设计的业务实践(一)

　　在人类活动如经济、工业、科学、职业、性别、艺术等各个方面正在飞速变化的时代,妄称任何描述都适用于长久而非短暂的时期,显然是不慎重的。因此,我们将要分两部分来讨论建筑实践这一问题:第一,建筑设计的业务实践目前是怎样的,或者确切地说,它是怎样发展到目前状况的;第二,它将怎样变化并且大概向什么方向变化。

　　带着这样的谨慎,我们开始讨论这个问题,先重复一下,建筑是一个服务行业,那就是说,建筑师既不买、卖地皮或大楼,也不像承包商那样通过施工来赚钱。他作为一个顾问和设计师来销售自己的业务技能。通过这项服务,他获得一些报酬,这个报酬通常是以该项建筑工程的造价为基础的。对一个私人住宅工程来讲,这笔费用可达大约10%的程度。因此,对一个造价50 000美元的工程来说,这个报酬就应该是5 000美元。如果委托人请一个"有名气"的建筑师,而这个建筑师又推掉了一些他处理不过来的委托事务,这个报酬会更多一些。若是工程改造,报酬则会更高一些,在大多数情况下可达15%。对于一些造价可达几百万的大型建筑物、公寓楼、写字楼等,报酬的百分数会低得多。因为设计一个40层高的楼不比设计一个20层的楼房花的工夫多多少。因为许多楼面设计方案是重复的。但是1亿美元的5%或6%是笔相当可观的数目。当然这样的活每年为数不多,何况建筑师也有个人所得税的问题。

　　建筑师要履行的服务职责分为三部分,或三个阶段。

　　方案设计　在与委托人商议、考察了工地、研究了预算等以后,建筑师要准备拟建的建筑物的平面图和外观图(往往是模型),以使委托人感到满意。提醒你,这些都是草图而不是蓝图。这些草图包括以绘画表现出来的树木、云彩、人物、汽车等。这样,委托人可以更容易地观察到最终的作品。如果委托人满意的话,他就会通知建筑师继续往下干。并且按照协议付给他酬金的10%~15%。在上述例子提到的5万元工程中,总报酬为5千元,如果完成了第一步,这个建筑师就得到500~750元。如果委托人不满意,他就会要求建筑师拿出更多的草图,出更多的点子。如果他们的意见不能达到一致,委托人就会另请高明。在这种情况下,第一位建筑师就会失去这份工作。但无论如何,他会得到他的10%~15%的报酬作为所完成工作的酬金。

  初步设计 这是方案设计的延伸。它在理论上包括有关未来建筑物的基本构想。草图方案通过以后,该建筑师就继续搞出大量的详细方案来,以便人人都确信各部分,如走廊、房间、门厅等都按要求那样非常协调,并且确保在预算内从功能和美观角度满足委托人的需要。在这个阶段上,对通过了的方案设计也会做出一些修改。实际上,这主要是确保方案设计的正确性,继而确保初步设计的正确性。当这一切都完成而且大家都很高兴,那么这位建筑师就可获得总报酬的另外的20%~25%,在我们想象的例子当中,这次应得1 000~1 250元。

  施工图 这是最难、也最使人厌烦的一部分工作。建筑物的每一部分,每一层平面图,每一个细部都应该仔细地画出来,并标出尺寸,以便用这份图指导整个建筑物的修建。此外,还要附上建材、工艺等所要求的书面说明;这个说明称为"施工说明"。施工图和施工说明书合在一起被称为合同文件,根据合同文件承包商投标求包,签订并履行合同。当合同文件确定好以后,建筑师与甲方进行商议,选出几个有声誉、而且以前所施工的工程质量似乎令人满意的承包商,邀请他们阅读合同条款,提出他们保证完成符合这个设计方案的工程标价,在预定的某一天封标。到了这一天,甲方和建筑师启封,并接受其中的一个标价,但不一定是最低的,因为比方说最低者未必比较低者更为理想。要么有时会出现这种情况:所有的投标都被否定了,这项设计就会被取消或送回绘制部门重新修改。顺便提一句,这种标价被称为总付标价,因为这是承包商(乙方)所提议的投标总额。有时,例如修建博物馆及类似的建筑物,质量比钱更显重要,或当建筑工期居于首位时,在实际成本之外一定的附加费也会被甲方接受。在这种情况下,甲方除了支付承包商的全部费用外,还给他一定数额的利润(毋需说,这种合同是每个承包商都梦寐以求的)。

  在任何情况下,只要到了这一阶段,即所有的合同文件都已经签订,建筑师便可再拿到40%~50%的酬金(在我们上述50 000美元工程的例子中,这应是他酬金中的另外2 000~2 500美元)。

  监督 建筑师的第三部分工作(也许是最关键的)是监督建筑物的实际施工。在选定好的时间他去检查工作,以确保正在进行的施工严格按照合同即施工图和说明书进行。另外,他应该能随时解决承包商的任何不十分清楚的问题,并提供必要的补充详图。建筑师因这部分工作通常得到10%的酬金。

Appendix Ⅲ Key to Exercises

UNIT ONE
Reading Comprehension
Ⅰ. 1. T   2. F   3. F   4. T   5. T   6. T   7. F
Ⅱ. 1. logical relation to
   2. supports, under tension
   3. frame construction, surfacing material
   4. unity
   5. bear sufficient correspondence
   6. for its inherent beauty, to emphasize some point of importance
   7. size, height, whole structure

Vocabulary
Ⅰ. 1. enclosure   2 withstand
   3. correspondence 4. inherent
   5. identifiable
Ⅱ. 1. B   2. C   3. A   4. C   5. D
   6. B   7. A   8. D   9. D   10. C

UNIT TWO
Reading Comprehension
Ⅰ. 1. T   2. F   3. F   4. F   5. F   6. T   7. T   8. T   9. F   10. T
Ⅱ. 1. C   2. D   3. B   4. A   5. C   6. D   7. D   8. A   9. C

Vocabulary
Ⅰ. 1. house   2. elements   3. mass-produced   4. quarters   5. semidetached
   6. single-family   7. accessibity   8. by virtue of   9. rang from... to   10. holds the title to
Ⅱ. 1. B   2. A   3. C   4. D   5. B   6. A   7. D   8. C   9. D

UNIT TREE
Reading Comprehension
Ⅰ. 1. F   2. T   3. T   4. F   5. F   6. T   7. F   8. T
Ⅱ. 1. size and shape
   2. bottom, slot, mail

3. wider than, small scale

4. have been raised, had a hand in shaping

5. glorious events, take on

Vocabulary

I. 1. put down   2. innumerable, infinite   3. indeterminate   4. small wonder
   5. exclusively   6. refined   7. allow for   8. take on

II. 1. B   2. D   3. A   4. A   5. B   6. D

UNIT FOUR

Reading Comprehension

I. 1. F   2. T   3. T   4. F   5. F   6. T   7. T   8. T   9. T   10. F

II. three, conclusion, clincher (button), part three, gross, net, profit rates.

Vocabulary

I. 1. b   2. c   3. d   4. a   5. f   6. e

II. 1. setup   2. investor   3. in the black   4. clincher   5. by rule of thumb
    6. compensate... for   7. put up   8. off the mark   9. joined the ranks of
    10. is justified in

UNIT FIVE

Reading Comprehension

I. 1. T   2. F   3. F   4. T   5. F   6. F   7. T   8. T   9. T

II. 1. planning process, the physical quality of the environment, the physical and spatial, of the environment.

2. the exterior of individual buildings outward, the buildings.

3.

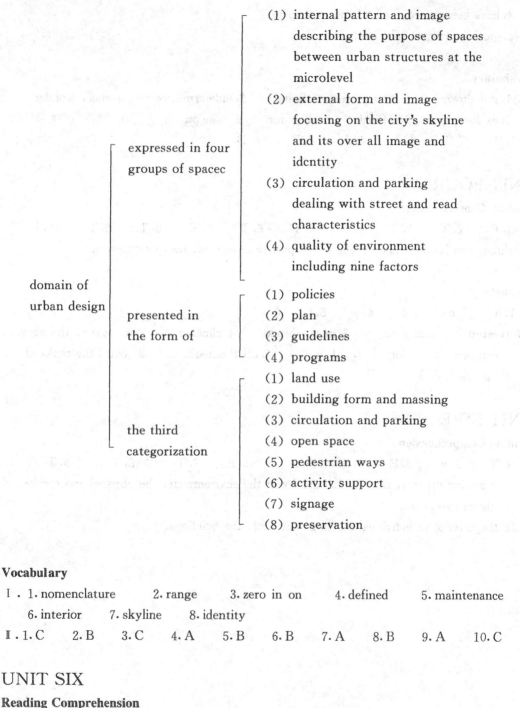

Vocabulary

I . 1. nomenclature   2. range   3. zero in on   4. defined   5. maintenance
    6. interior   7. skyline   8. identity

II . 1. C   2. B   3. C   4. A   5. B   6. B   7. A   8. B   9. A   10. C

UNIT SIX

Reading Comprehension

I . 1. F   2. T   3. T   4. F   5. T   6. F   7. T   8. T   9. T   10. F

II.

Items	Concepts
types of shoping center	1. community center 2. regional center
location	1. suburban areas 2. urban areas
types of master plan	1. row or strip developmnts 2. cluster developmnts
pinciples in designing a center with a mall	1. the design of the mall itself 2. efficient parking facilities 3. easy access into a center

III. 1. C   2. A   3. B   4. D   5. D

Vocabulary

I. 1. c   2. d   3. f   4. a   5. b   6. g   7. e
II. 1. fountains   2. beatuty shops   3. sidewalks   4. proximity   5. keystone
    6. scultures   7. establishments

UNIT SEVEN
Reading Comprehension

I. 1. F   2. T   3. F   4. T   5. T   6. F   7. T   8. T
II. shapes: rectangles,   half-circles,   octagons
    types: flat roofs,   sloping roofs,   domical roofs
    arrangements: cascades of roofs,   sheltering roofs,   roof gardens

Vocabulary

I. 1. conforms to   2. pitches   3. simplify   4. be hipped   5. relieve of
   6. lengthwise   7. catenary   8. communal
II. 1. d   2. f   3. a   4. c   5. b   6. e

UNIT EIGHT
Reading Comprehension

I. 1. (1)   2. (9)   3. (2)   4. (8)   5. (3)   6. (6, 7)   7. (4)

8. (5)

II. 1. D　　2. D　　3. C　　4. A　　5. C　　6. C　　7. A　　8. B

Vocabulary

I. 1. cityscape,　　2. booths　　3. texture　　4. dimness　　5. cast shadow　　6. ablaze

II. 1. c　　2. a　　3. b　　4. d　　5. f　　6. e

III. 1. flood light　　2. ambiance　　3. illumination　　4. glare　　5. shwmanship
　　6. persuasive

UNIT NINE

Reading Comprehension

I. 1. F　　2. T　　3. T　　4. F　　5. T　　6. F　　7. F　　8. T

II. 1. B　　2. D　　3. A　　4. A　　5. B　　6. D　　7. C　　8. C　　9. B

Vocabulary

I. 1. b　　2. a　　3. g　　4. e　　5. c　　6. f　　7. h　　8. d

II. 1. configuration　　2. adaptable to　　3. flourish, yield to　　4. adjacent
　　5. Regardless of　　6. correlated

III. 1. B　　2. C　　3. A　　4. B

UNIT TEN

Reading Comprehension

I. 1. T　　2. F　　3. T　　4. F　　5. T　　6. T　　7. F　　8. T

II. 1. glass and aluminum, human design trend
　　2. old and new, bring back human scale
　　3. described, combined with
　　4. people-oriented, repetition
　　5. conserve, solar access

Vocabulary

I. 1. function　　2. deprive... of　　3. limitation　　4. renovation, conserving
　　5. scale　　6. design-line　　7. standstill

II. 1. B　　2. C　　3. D　　4. A　　5. B

III. 1. C　　2. E　　3. F　　4. D　　5. B　　6. A　　7. H　　8. I　　9. J　　10. G

UNIT ELEVEN

Reading Comprehension

I. 1. F　　2. T　　3. T　　4. T　　5. F　　6. F　　7. T　　8. F

Ⅱ. A. 4, 2   B. 1, 3   C. 6, 9, 11   D. 5, 7, 8, 10, 12, 13

Vocabulary

Ⅰ. 1. e   2. d   3. c   4. j   5. f   6. i   7. g   8. a   9. h   10. b
Ⅱ. 1. performance   2. criteria   3. occupancy   4. lay out   5. instability
   6. accommodations
Ⅲ. 1. C   2. A   3. B   4. D   5. C

UNIT TWELVE
Reading Comprehension
Ⅰ. 1. (2)   2. (6)   3. (3)   4. (1)   5. (13)   6. (4)   7. (12)
   8. (5)   9. (7)   10. (10)   11. (8)   12. (9)
Ⅱ. 1. A   2. D   3. B   4. C   5. C   6. B

Vocabulary

Ⅰ. 1. deck   2. intergrate   3. accommodate   4. of necessity   5. incorporates
   6. with respect to
Ⅱ. 1. C   2. B   3. C   4. C   5. B   6. D   7. A   8. C

UNIT THIRTEEN
Reading Comprehension
Ⅰ. 1. T   2. F   3. T   4. F   5. T   6. T   7. T   8. F   9. T
Ⅱ. 1. D   2. B   3. C   4. A   5. B   6. C

Vocabulary

Ⅰ. 1. f   2. a   3. g   4. i   5. b   6. h   7. d   8. c   9. J   10. E
Ⅱ. 1. stylistic, social origin, ornament
   2. ornament, architectural form
   3. style, sculpture
   4. attention, movement

UNIT FOURTEEN
Reading Comprehension
Ⅰ. 1. (5)   2. (8)   3. (10)   4. (1)   5. (4)   6. (3)   7. (6)
   8. (7)   9. (9)
Ⅱ. 1. d   2. b   3. c   4. f   5. a   6. e   7. j   8. g   9. h   10. l
   11. i   12. k

Vocabulary

I. 1. D   2. A   3. B   4. C   5. C   6. A   7. D   8. B

II. 1. prototype   2. rehabilitation   3. prefabrication   4. upgrading
    5. deterioration   6. viability   7. incorporate   8. showcase

UNIT FIVETEEN

Reading Comprehension

I. 1. (6)   2. (4)   3. (2)   4. (3)   5. (5)

II. 1. B   2. C   3. C   4. A   5. B   6. C   7. C   8. A   9. B

Vocabulary

I. 1. b   2. d   3. e   4. a   5. g   6. c   7. h   8. f

II. 1. Paradigm   2. clerestories   3. backdrop   4. allowingfor   5. has provoked
    6. agitation   7. disorientation   8. place off   9. boulevrd

UNIT SIXTEEN

Reading Comprehension

I. 1. (3)   2. (4)   3. (2)   4. (7)   5. (1)   6. (6)   7. (5)

II. 1. C   2. B   3. D   4. D   5. B

Vocabulary

I. 1. c   2. d   3. b   4. e   5. a   6. g   7. i   8. h   9. f

II. 1. hold true for   2. in accordance with   3. visualize   4. accelerating
    5. commission   6. make his bid   7. caution

图书在版编目（CIP）数据

建筑类专业英语．建筑学与城市规划．第1册/王庆昌，余曼筠主编．—北京：中国建筑工业出版社，1997（2025.6重印）
高等学校试用教材
ISBN 978-7-112-03026-2

Ⅰ．建⋯　Ⅱ．①王⋯ ②余⋯　Ⅲ．①建筑学—英语—高等学校—教材②城市规划—英语—高等学校—教材　Ⅳ．H31

中国版本图书馆 CIP 数据核字（2005）第 090444 号

本书为满足高等院校建筑学与城市规划专业的专业英语教学之需要而编写。取材范围、内容深浅、项目设置，均按国家教委颁发的《大学英语专业阅读阶段教学基本要求》设定，在满足教学大纲要求的前提下，尽量选用新颖而趣味性强的内容，以开扩读者的眼界并增加对学习的兴趣，由于注释详细并有参考译文，也可供相关专业人员自学专业英语之用。

高等学校试用教材
建筑类专业英语
建筑学与城市规划
第一册

王庆昌　余曼筠　　　主编
谢工典　赵凤霞　刘雁鹏　编
霍维国　　　　　　　主审

*

中国建筑工业出版社出版、发行（北京西郊百万庄）
各地新华书店、建筑书店经销
建工社（河北）印刷有限公司印刷

*

开本：787×1092 毫米　1/16　印张：13¼　字数：322 千字
1997 年 6 月第一版　2025 年 6 月第三十二次印刷
定价：23.00 元
ISBN 978-7-112-03026-2
（20777）

版权所有　翻印必究
如有印装质量问题，可寄本社退换
（邮政编码 100037）